Archaeology of Colonisation

Critical Perspectives on Theory, Culture and Politics

Critical Perspectives on Theory, Culture and Politics is an interdisciplinary series, developed in partnership with the Centre for Critical and Cultural Theory, which is based in the School of English, Communication and Philosophy at Cardiff University, UK. The series focuses on innovative research produced at the interface between critical theory and cultural studies. In recent years much work in cultural studies has increasingly moved away from directly critical-theoretical concerns. One of the aims of this series is to foster a renewed dialogue between cultural studies and critical and cultural theory in its rich, multiple dimensions.

Series editors:

Glenn Jordan, Visiting Research Fellow, Cardiff School of Journalism, Media and Cultural Studies, Cardiff University. Former Director of Butetown History & Arts Centre.

Laurent Milesi, Reader in English, Communication and Philosophy and Chair of the Centre for Critical and Cultural Theory, Cardiff University.

Radhika Mohanram, Professor of English and Critical and Cultural Theory, Cardiff University.

Chris Müller, Department of Media, Music, Communication & Cultural Studies, Macquarie University.

Chris Weedon, Professor Emerita and Honorary Chair, Centre for Critical and Cultural Theory, Cardiff University.

Titles in the Series

Culture Control Critique: Allegories of Reading the Present, Frida Beckman

Prometheanism: Technology, Digital Culture and Human Obsolescence, Günther Anders and Christopher John Müller, translated by Christopher John Müller

Creole in the Archive: Imagery, Presence and the Location of the Caribbean Figure, Roshini Kempadoo

The Attention Economy: Labour, Time, and Power in Cognitive Capitalism, Claudio Celis

Performative Contradiction and the Romanian Revolution, Jolan Bogdan

Chinese Subjectivities and the Beijing Olympics, Gladys Pak Lei Chong

The Extreme in Contemporary Culture: States of Vulnerability, Pramod K. Nayar

Superpositions: Laruelle and the Humanities, edited by Rocco Gangle and Julius Greve

Credo Credit Crisis: Speculations on Faith and Money, edited by Laurent Milesi, Christopher John Müller and Aidan Tynan

Materialities of Sex in a Time of HIV: The Promise of Vaginal Microbicides, Annette-Carina van der Zaag

From Shared Life to Co-Resistance in Historic Palestine, Marcelo Svirsky and Ronnen Ben-Arie

Affective Connections: Towards a New Materialist Politics of Sympathy, Dorota Golańska

Homemaking: Radical Nostalgia and the Construction of a South Asian Diaspora, Anindya Raychaudhuri

Hypermodernity and Visuality, Peter R. Sedgwick

Partitions and Their Afterlives: Violence, Memories, Living, edited by Radhika Mohanram and Anindya Raychaudhuri

Back Issues: Periodicals and the Formation of Critical and Cultural Theory in Canada,
Gary Genosko, with Kristina Marcellus

Archaeology of Colonisation: From Aesthetics to Biopolitics, Carlos Rivera-Santana

*Contested Borders: Queer Politics and Cultural Translation in Contemporary Franco-
phone Writing from the Maghreb*, William J. Spurlin (forthcoming)

Archaeology of Colonisation

From Aesthetics to Biopolitics

Carlos Rivera Santana

ROWMAN &
LITTLEFIELD
INTERNATIONAL
London • New York

Published by Rowman & Littlefield International, Ltd.
6 Tinworth Street, London SE11 5AL
www.rowmaninternational.com

Rowman & Littlefield International, Ltd. is an affiliate of
Rowman & Littlefield
4501 Forbes Boulevard, Suite 200, Lanham, Maryland 20706, USA
With additional offices in Boulder, New York, Toronto (Canada), and London (UK)
www.rowman.com

British Library Cataloguing in Publication Information
A catalogue record for this book is available from the British Library

ISBN: HB 978-1-7866-0900-7

Library of Congress Cataloging-in-Publication Data Available

ISBN 978-1-78660-900-7 (cloth)
ISBN 978-1-5381-4797-9 (pbk)
ISBN 978-1-78660-901-4 (electronic)

Contents

List of Figures   ix

Acknowledgements   xi

Disclaimer   xiii

1   Introduction: Archaeology of Colonisation   1

Part 1: Origins: Colonial Aesthetics (The Caribbean)   **19**

2   Aesthetics of Ugliness   23

3   Monstrous Anthropology   39

4   *Blackness*   61

Part 2: Command (Queensland, Australia)   **89**

5   Biopolitics in Colonisation: The Inequality of Human Races   91

6   The Blanket Approach: Colonisation in Queensland, Australia   109

7   State of Exception in Australia   135

8   Conclusion: Colonisation   153

References   173

Index   179

About the Author   187

List of Figures

Fig. 1.1   Danie Mellor's *Memento mori* (2009).   2

Fig. 2.1   Hieronymus Bosch's triptych of *The*
            Temptations of St. Anthony (1505–1506).   34

Fig. 3.1   Lorenz Fries, *Auslegung der Carta Marina*
            (Estrasburgo, Johannes Grieninger, 1525).   41

Fig. 3.2   Map Kunstmann II, ca. 1505, Bayerische
            Staatsbibliothek, Múnich (Cod. Icon. 133).   44

Fig. 3.3   *Wahrhaftige History* (Hans Staden, Marburg,
            1557).   45

Fig. 3.4   *America* (Galle, Antwerp, 1590–1600).   48

Fig. 4.1   Slave trade from Africa by region (Ianni [1976]
            in *Capitalismo y Esclavitud* [Capitalism and
            Slavery]).   76

Fig. 4.2   *Los tres mulatos de Esmeralda* (1599)   79

Fig. 8.1   *Piccaninny Paradise* 2010, Danie Mellor.   161

Fig. 8.2   *America can (We) Be Born Again*, 2014,
            Diógenes Ballester.   166

Acknowledgements

I want to acknowledge the Aboriginal and Torres Strait Islander Studies unit (ATSISU) of the University of Queensland for giving me a place and sharing their knowledges to think about this topic, and the Center for Puerto Rican Studies at Hunter College, City University of New York for supporting me throughout this book project. Special thanks to Jon Willis, Cindy Shannon, Uncle Shane Coghill, Martin Nakata, Bryan Mukandi and Trisha Poole (for all the help with editing). Also, thanks to Danie Mellor and Diógenes Ballester for engaging with my work and generously letting me use their sublime artwork, and the many more people who shared their knowledge and perspectives that one way or another are reflected in this book. Whilst this book seems to be at first glance theoretical and archival in nature, a community of peoples has certainly informed it, and the engagement with all of them is at the heart of this work.

Disclaimer

DISCLAIMER ABOUT NAMING

In this book, I will be using the capitalised words 'Indigenous peoples', 'African peoples', 'Indigenous Australian', among other notions to refer to a plethora of nations in the Caribbean, Queensland, and around the world with the intention to communicate the utmost respect to its peoples, as opposed to the Western discursive devices, lower-case terms of 'indigeneity' and 'blackness' given that these notions will be understood as manufactured tools for racism. Tainú-Arawak, Yoruba, Igbo, Nahualt, Turrbul, Jagara/Jagura, Mapuche, Mutumui, Mutjati, Muragan, Muluridji, Mitjamba, Mitaka, Mingin, Mimumgkun, Mian, Mbewun, Marulta, Marrago, Maranganji, Maithakari, Mijabi, Madjandji, Lanima, Kuungkari, Kwantari, Kutjala, Kungkalenja, Kunggari, Kulumali, Kukatja, Korenggoreng, Kokowalandja, Kokokulunggur, Kikojawa, Koko-Yimidir, Kokangol, Koamu, Karingbal, Kangulu, Kambuwal, Kalkadunga, Kalali, Kaiadilt, Juru, Jungkurara, Juipera, Jirandali, Jiman, Jetimarala, Jathaikana, Jarawair, Jangga, Jambina, Jalanga, Jagalingu, Irukandjii, Ilba, Idindji, Gulngai, Goeng, Giabal, Gia, Ewamin, Djirubal, Djiru, Djakunda, Darambal, Buluwai, Bitjara, Biria, Bindal, Bigambul, Barrungguan, Barna, Barbaram, Barada, Bandjin, Bakanambia, Baiali, Badjiri, Atjinuri, Araba, Ankamuti, Ajabatha, Ajabakan, Nawagi, Ngandandara, Ngaro, Ngathokudi, Ngatjan, Ngaun, Nggmadi, Ngoborindi, Ngugi, Ngulungbara, Ngundjan, Ngurawola, Nguri, Njuwathai, Nunukul, Olkolo, Ombila, Otati, Pakadji, Pitapita, pitjara, Pontunj, Punthamara, Rakkaia, Ringaringa, Rungarungawa, Tagalag, Taior, Taribeland, Tepiti, Thereila Tjapukandji, Totj, Tulua, Undanbi, Unjadi, Wadja, Wadjabangai, Wadjaland, Wakabunga, Wakaman, Wakara, Wakawaka, Walangama, Walmbaria, Waluwara, Wanamara, Wangan, Wanjuru, Warakamai, Warungu, Warakamai, Wanjuru, Warakamai, Warungu, Wik-kalkan, Wik-Munkan, Wikampama, Wikapatja, Wika-tinda, Wikepa, Wikianji, Wikmean, Wiknantjara, Wiknatantja, Winduwinda, Wiri, Wongkadjera, Wongkumara, Wulgurukaba, Wulili, Wulpura, Yir-Yoront,[1] and many more Indigenous peoples around the world were nations that existed well before colonisation and still assert their nation status today. This is the case with Indigenous nations in Australia, Indigenous nations in the Caribbean, Indigenous nations in the Americas and Indigenous nations around the world. This book acknowledges that the use of the category of 'Indigenous' and other racialised terms are problematic because it reifies the coloniser–colonised binary and, by that, 'the binary of superior and inferior beings that justifies the logic of domination' (Chalmers, 2014, p. 28). However, in order to re-examine the operationalisation of colonisation this work is limited by the problematic language of colonisation to use, at times, the word 'Indigenous' to refer to the subject position of the end point of the operation of colonisation, and this 'naming' can be problematic because it can (re)produce colonising practices.

Racialised categories have been used as a vehicle to enable a subject position of disadvantage in colonisation (Chalmers, 2014; Grosfoguel, 2008a; Quijano, 2000). In the cultural and legal sphere, terms like 'Indigenous' or 'Aboriginal' have been 'defined' in hierarchal lower positions to function as a tool for colonising practises. In order to problematise racialised terms, Chalmers, an Indigenous Australian scholar, calls for: 'A decolonial analysis of taken-for-granted terms like "Aboriginal" [to] provide us with another option to reorient ourselves away from continuing to make the same mistakes regarding indigenous peoples' place in this nation [Australia]' (Chalmers, 2014, p. 29). Though this book attempts a decolonial critique of the mechanism of colonisation and how it is operationalised, it must be acknowledged that problematic racialised categories are used throughout this book to address the end point of colonising practises. Therefore, there is a danger of (re)producing colonising practises that this research aims to critique in the first place. While my intention is to communicate respect through using the capitalised words 'Indigenous peoples', 'African peoples', 'Indigenous Australian', and others in this book, these terms do not cease to be problematic simply by writing about my intentions.

NOTE

1. Some names were retrieved from the Australian Institute of Aboriginal and Torres Strait Islander Studies website, http://aiatsis.gov.au/.

Chapter One

Introduction

Archaeology of Colonisation

In other words, the essential thing here is to see clearly, to think clearly—that is, dangerously—and to answer clearly the innocent first question: what, fundamentally, is colonization? To agree on what it is not: neither evangelization, not a philanthropic enterprise, nor a desire to push back the frontiers of ignorance, disease, and tyranny, nor a project undertaken for the greater glory of God, not an attempt to extend the rule of law. To admit once and for all, without flinching at the consequences, that the decisive actors here are the adventurer and the pirate, the wholesale grocer and the ship owner, the gold digger and the merchant, appetite and force and behind them, the baleful projected shadow of a form of civilisation which, at a certain point in its history, finds itself obliged, for internal reasons, to extend to a world scale the competition of its antagonistic economies. (Cesaire, 1972, p. 33)

This book begins and ends with an aesthetic contemplation of Danie Mellor's thinking through his art that showcases the spectacle of Empire through manufactured stories of Blue-and-White Spode China transfer (blue and white transfer). Indigenous Australian contemporary artist Danie Mellor uses blue and white transfer, similar to blue-china dinnerware, as a contemporary art technique that addresses Cesaire's dangerous question better than words have, by transfiguring the fundamental nature of colonisation. In the piece *Memento Mori* (see book cover and figure 1.1), the spectacle of Empire takes the thanatological form of a 19th-century anatomical lecture theatre where death is explicitly represented in blue and white everywhere, focussing on the dissection of a human body. The blue and white representation in the lecture theatre is intricately designed and adorned with dissected animals and framed in a beautiful pattern of flowers and leaves. Indigenous peoples and

1

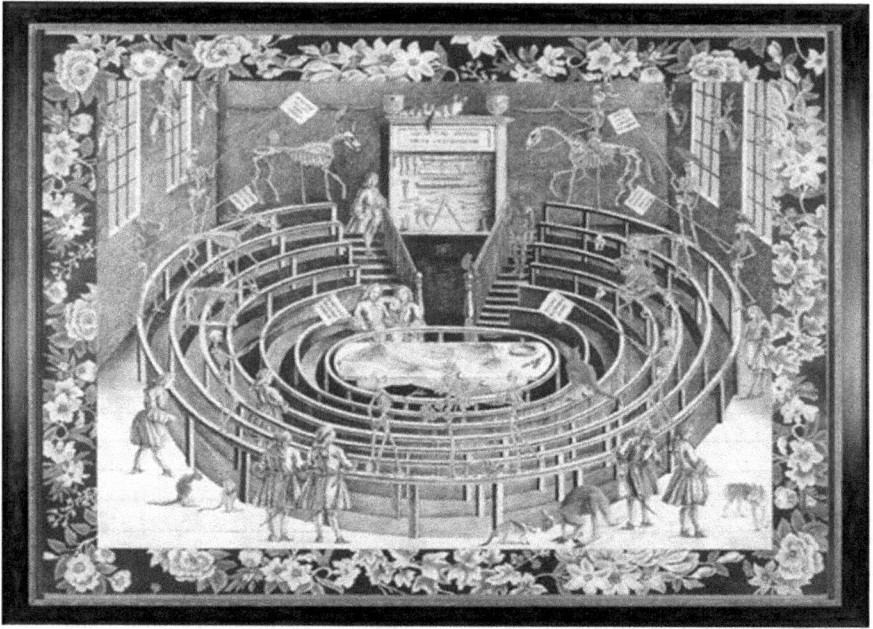

Figure 1.1.   Danie Mellor's *Memento mori* (2009). Courtesy of artist.

some Totemic beings are represented in their real colours yet surrounded by this blue and white scene. All eyes, including the viewers outside the painting, are directed to the unknown dissected being covered by a white and blue blanket. This virtual reality made of blue and white becomes a representation of the transformation of the history of Indigenous peoples, yet in the blue and white transfer painting series the subject is colonisation and not Indigeneity. The blue and white transfer conceptualist art technique transfigures back to the viewer the operation of colonisation in all its aesthetic and paradoxical glory through a parallax representation of the transformation of the landscape of history using a synthesized colour—blue. Blue draws the manufactured Western history that surrounds the colonised body and transforms its local landscapes with imported colonial narratives. Mellor states that blue features in his technique because:

> I haven't been able to find an Aboriginal language word for the colour blue. It's almost like blue was not conceptualised, it was recognised through words for sky, for instance, or water. So it's almost like the transformed landscape talks about that which was brought with Western culture—in a way talking about the symbolically manufactured, or the 'change forever'. (UQ Art Museum, 2014, p. 8)

The logics in the blue and white transfer technique are outside those of racial colours, and blackness, indigeneity, and Indigenous worldviews become the Real. The 'Real'—Indigenous Australian peoples and their Totemic Beings—are present to balance this spectacle of Empire or, better stated, of the operation of colonisation. Moreover, they are surrounded by the intricate manufacturing of another type of reality that was created in order to transform the world that is painted using the white spaces in between, which delineate what this blue transformation should look like. The paradox resides in the apparent harmony of this landscape transformation and its baleful entrapment in direct opposition to the Real, as it never *sees* reality because it is not blue. Blue rarely represents death, but Mellor's work suggests this by entrapping the Real, in a similar manner that colonisation and race, while historically manufactured, entraps peoples, having very real effects on them.

What follows is a historical-philosophical critique of colonisation that attempts to answer what colonisation is, through asking, 'How has colonisation been operationalised?' It will be argued that colonisation was constituted as a form of government, and it is operationalised *micropolitically* (locally) and *macropolitically* (globally). Colonisation's global operation originated within the frame of aesthetics (and not that of Social Darwinism) in the Caribbean, and its local operation is defined by the biopolitical function of the administration of the colonised in the specific way that the context dictated. In this book, the context of Queensland, Australia, will be used as an illustrative case study. In order to understand how colonisation has specifically operated, this book uses Foucauldian archaeology. Although this archaeology of colonisation begins from a Caribbean and Latin American political-theoretical context in conversation with an Indigenous political-theoretical perspective, Foucauldian archaeology is used as a methodological tool to unearth the fundamentally Western operationalisation of colonisation.

This archaeology of colonisation could well be an archaeology of race because the operation of colonisation begins by attempting to conceptualise peoples from a given, in this case Western, worldview. The discursive construction of race should carry at its heart a hierarchy informed by inequality where whiteness is at the top. However, one of the main arguments of this book is that the discursive construction of race reflects an aesthetic history of colonisation that locates the subject in an heterarchical subalternisation. In other words, racism starts with colonial aesthetics. Colonisation began when *indigeneity* and *blackness*—which are the founding racial conceptual tools in colonisation that were assembled in the 15th and 16th centuries—did not mean what they did in the following centuries, and even today. Through the aesthetic assemblage of race, colonisation became more than land occupation and invasion as its starting point and its end, because what is colonised is the territories of the self or the colonised in colonisation: the negative reflection of Western culture deposited in the 'other'. The colonised become entrapped in this manufactured fiction that surrounds its being in a different manner than the non-colonised, which is surrounded by a fiction that aims to biopolitically shape it in order to enhance the life conditions of the subjects that the State favour to they are made to live (Castro-Gómez, 2007; Foucault, 2011). The subject that colonisation speaks of, the undesired races, operates biopolitically differently as they are left to die (Foucault, 2011). This distinct form of subjugation of the colonised is what Franz Fanon explained in the terrains of the micropolitical, yet it coextends to the macropolitical, with the difference between the master–slave relationship and the coloniser–colonised relationship. Race and colonisation in Fanon, and in what this book attempts to illustrate, is the structure of a second fold of subjectivity that functions analogously at the individual level and at the social level.

To 'dangerously' answer the question of how colonisation operated or operates through a Foucauldian archaeology, the *arché* must be determined. According to Agamben (2009), archaeology can be defined as the search for the *arché*, which is a Greek term with two meanings: the origin and the command.[1] Agamben (2008) states that Foucauldian archaeology is the search for the beginning and the command, and their constitutive complicity, because 'the beginning not only commands the birth, but also the growing, the circulation, and the transmission . . . in one word the history, of whatever this may be, an idea, a praxis, an institution, etc.' (Agamben, 2009, p. 100). Therefore, the origin is not merely a start that disappears in what follows; on the contrary, the origin never ceases to command, to govern, and to control. This inseparable relationship between the origin and the command is the central discussion in Foucault's *The Order of Things* and *Archaeology of Knowledge* (1974) when he locates the origins of Western knowledge in their threshold of formation and their inseparability from power, with knowledge being the *commander* of the exertion of power (Agamben, 2012a; Rajchman, 2007). Using Foucault's conceptual tools, including philosophical archaeology, to critique colonisation from an Indigenous standpoint is seen frequently due to its productive capacity to problematise Western discourses, such as the philosophical anthropology discourse in Modernity. For instance, Indigenous theorists Martin Nakata (2007) and Aileenn Moreton-Robinson (2015) (their work is engaged throughout this book) use Foucauldian tools to rediscover the constitutive elements of Indigenous subjects in how they have come to be colonial objects. In a similar manner, this book engages with how the colonial conceptualisations of *indigeneity* and *blackness* operate as discursive objects.

The unearthing of colonisation finds that the origin of the Western conceptualisations for the colonised were aesthetically formed in the Western conceptualisations of *indigeneity* and *blackness*.[2] These conceptualisations were not originally formed in the 18th or 19th century as a by-product of Social Darwinism, but rather this book argues that they were first formed and conceptualised through the constitution of their imageries and what they narrated in the 15th and 16th centuries in the first colonial experiences in the Caribbean. The second part of this aesthetic process in colonisation unfolds in the Modernity period after the Enlightenment, where the discourse of philosophical anthropology turned colonial governance into a biopolitical form where the aesthetics of race functioned as markers that framed the colonised as 'undesired races' and, thus, to be left to die in the manner that the specific local history was operationalised. In this book, we will examine the case study of Queensland, Australia, where colonisation biopolitically functioned using a *Blanket Approach* mechanism and also in a state of exception form. Colonisation then operated from aesthetics to biopolitics through the formation of race to the local and global operation of a specific history of colonisation. Before we review the historical landscapes of this constitutive map of colonisation, the conceptual context in which this work makes sense is discussed.

ONE COLONISATION: MULTIPLE VIEWS

> Every colonised person—in other words, every person in whose soul an inferiority complex has been created by the death and burial of its local cultural originality—finds itself face to face with the language of the civilising nation; that is, with the culture of the mother country. (Fanon, 2008, p. 55)

What is colonisation? The answer to this question should be simple if colonisation is only defined. Colonisation is defined as 'to settle and establish control over the indigenous people in a given area'.[3] Therefore, colonisation can be understood simply through the settlement and establishment of control in Australia, Puerto Rico, Mexico, and every other colonised country. Or when colonisation refers to the non-human realm, it refers to an animal, plant or even a microorganism that establishes itself in an area: in the case of bacteria, it is an area where they have a high presence and are not making the host sick, but they can have the potential to do so (Kirkland, 2009). In colonisation studies—the multiple disciplines that address colonisation, from postcolonial studies and history, to critical Indigenous studies—we know that the question 'What is colonisation?' is not fully answered using isolated events in history or the times and places where it occurred. The task is to map how colonisation unfolded with the main actors being the colonisers and the colonised. Therefore, the question of 'What is colonisation?' is reconceptualised to 'How has colonisation occurred and worked (operated) to produce different peoples (both colonised and coloniser)?' The research surrounding colonisation is typically more interested in mapping colonisation rather than the specifics of how colonisation can be defined as an outcome of a linear logical sequence, because it can further explain rather than only describe the ongoing effects of colonisation on the subjects it continues to speak of, such as Indigenous peoples.

Even though there is a general consensus that colonisation is strongly influenced by an ongoing global process (see Anzaldúa, 1999; Bhabha, 1994; Castro-Gómez, 1996; Dussel, 1993; Fanon, 1990; Grosfoguel, 2008a; Lugones, 2016; Maldonado-Torres, 2008; Mignolo, 1995; Oliver, 2004; Pagán-Jiménez & Rodríguez-Ramos, 2008; Quijano, 2000; Said, 1978; Smith, 2000; and Spivak, 1999, among many others), its theorisation is often limited by the segregated spaces that are dictated by the 'coloniser's' agenda. Colonisation studies are usually regarded as having begun with the works of Aimé Cesaire, Fanon, and others, in the context of the global fight for self-determination. After self-determination was achieved in most countries, colonisation lost relevance and a new area of research was formed called 'postcolonial studies'. This new area of research focused on the subaltern, deconstruction, and decolonisation of the mind predominantly viewed from poststructural studies on subjectivity (Castro-Gómez, 2007). In Latin America, another term, coloniality, emerged for the continued study of colonisation: it emerged from the context of social justice, and it is closely linked with theology of liberation. Together, these new areas of research have been labelled coloniality-decoloniality studies (Grosfoguel, 2008b). These studies have focused on epistemological colonisation or 'epistemecide' (Soussa-Santos, 2017), which refers to the way that colonisation focused on the subalternisation of thought forms rather than only on the occupation of the land. In contrast, theorists from the Indigenous nations of the United States, New Zealand, Australia, South Africa, and other countries (including many Latin American nations) have declared that, for them, colonisation is not over and decolonisation must still happen (Anzaldúa, 1999; Mbembe, 2017; Moreton-Robinson, 2003; Nakata, 2007; Smith, 2000). Now, ways to critique racism and Eurocentric thought, and to decolonise knowledges, are being researched and theorised. This vast body of research, notwithstanding of the consensus that colonisation is an ongoing process, is often divided by national Western practices such as the Spanish, Portuguese, and English languages. For example, Latin American (Spanish and Portuguese-speaking) literature is often not considered in Anglo (English-speaking) countries, and vice versa. Although some theorists have started to reference each other given the useful concepts and critiques that they have developed, for example, Nakata, Nakata, Keech and Bolt (2012), Soussa-Santos (2017), and Maldonado-Torres (2008), the gaps reflect that the problem is beyond simply translating and referencing. Let us briefly examine some views in mapping colonisation from its multiple voices, especially coloniality-decoloniality, postcolonial studies, critical Indigenous studies and anti-colonial thought (acknowledging that there are many more views on colonisation).

Latin American thought, which has been influenced by the works of postcolonial thinking and theology of liberation, has found echoes in many universities, particularly in Latin American and North American universities (Castro-Gómez, 2007). Theorists, including Immanuel Wallerstein, Anibal Quijano, Nelson Maldonado-Torres, Maria Lugones, Enrique Dussel, Linda Alcoff, Walter Mignolo, and Ramon Grosfoguel, among others, draw from the coloniality-decoloniality framework to reexamine colonisation. The Latin American perspective has identified certain particularities of colonisation including that it operates simultaneously with the processes of Modernity, capitalism, and patriarchy (Dussel, 1993; Quijano, 2000). In particular, co-lonisation has been described using the triple formation of the colonisation of power, the colonisation of knowledge, and the colonisation of the being (Castro-Gómez, 1996; Dussel, 1993; Mignolo, 1997). According to some coloniality-decoloniality theorists, the colonisation of power operates through the system of social classifications that was established in the 16th century in which social privileges were established according to the symbolic and phenotypic race of the subjects (Castro-Gómez, 2007; Grosfoguel, 2012; Mignolo, 1997). These triads of symbolic indicators have their genealogical roots in the ideological processes of the Biblical story of Noah's descendants who populated the Earth after the Great Flood (Castro-Gómez, 1996; Dussel, 1993; Mignolo, 1997). The descendants of Jafet, Sem, and Cam respectively represent the socially implied hierarchy of European, Indigenous, and African peoples (Castro-Gómez, 1996; Dussel, 1993; Mignolo, 1997). The colonisation of knowledge refers to the way in which technocratic science rationality represents a determinant factor of the 'progress' of industrialisa-tion and the movement from a 'Third World' ideology to a 'First World' ideology. Castro-Gómez (1996) illustrated how after the Borbonic Reforms in Spain in the 18th century, the idea was imposed that 'to know' was to distance oneself from the world and to see it in a 'passion-free' and systemat-ic manner. This supposes a colonisation of the mind that threatens and direct-ly battles the epistemic multiplicity of the world. This notion is what is referred to as coloniality.

In contrast, postcolonial thinkers such as Spivak (1988) and Bhabha (1994) have assimilated the poststructural perspective on subjectivity. The deconstruction of the subject of Modernity demonstrated that subjectivity focuses solely on subject formation (Derrida, 1995). That is, behind the subject formation—that is, behind the social and historical constructions that subjected the self—there is nothing else. The very idea of an individual, a centred self with a psyche, a personal lived experience with emotions, was contested because, in its deconstruction (Derrida, 1995) or in its genealogy (Foucault, 2007), it was found that these notions were produced and situated in a particular time, in a particular social context, and with a particular agenda. When referring directly to subjectivity and colonisation, Spivak states 'between patriarchy and imperialism, subject constitution and object formation, the figure of the woman disappears, not into pristine nothingness but into a violent shuttling which is the displaced figuration of the "third world woman" caught between tradition and modernization' (1988, p. 102). The constitution of colonisation is affected in the constitution of subjectivity, obliterating the previous subject formation of a woman and the subject formation of cultural processes.

Closer to the Caribbean where colonisation started in the Americas, Fanon's work inaugurated colonisation studies in France (Fanon is from Martinique) as a philosophical-phenomenological object constituted by the colonised and coloniser relationship, as first portrayed in *Black Skin, White Masks* (in 1952 [2008]). This theorisation that is located in the relationship between the coloniser and the colonised implies a subjugating relationship, not only from the coloniser as a person, but also the coloniser as a representation that can be located in the coloniser-as-person and the coloniser-as-institution, and in the colonised-as-person and the colonised-as-subjectivity. In Fanon, colonisation is viewed from the subject positioning of the colonised in relation to the coloniser, in which the colonised needs the coloniser in order to constitute its subject positioning, as much as the coloniser needs the colonised in order to maintain its subjugation (Fanon, 1990, 2008). This relationship is similar to the Western Hegelian master–slave dialectic, yet with the added complexity of the second fold of colonisation that dehumanises the coloniser–colonised relationship. Fanon's work will be explored further in later chapters in this book.

The last example of this multiplicity of voices, and closer to the Australian case study that features in this book, is the work in Critical Indigenous Studies of Indigenous Australian scholars such as Aileen Moreton-Robinson and Martin Nakata, among others. Of particular interest here is the historical-theoretical work of Nakata presented in his book entitled *Disciplining the Savages, Savaging the Disciplines* (2007). His book critiques the knowledge provided to Torres Strait Islanders[4] by Westernisation; it also rigorously critiques the production of knowledge in the fields of education, language, spirituality, and other Western inscriptions. Nakata revises more than 200 years of history in order to contest the knowledge produced from the coloniser's eye. For example, when critiquing the reports on Torres Strait issues written to feed the broad field of social sciences, Nakata argues that the construction of Indigenous peoples as colonial object made it possible for the inception of a classification system that made Torres Strait Islanders, but arguably Indigenous Australian peoples in general, slip into the hierarchy of racial inequality determined by Social Darwinism (Nakata, 2007). Nakata's work, and others' work from different perspectives, unearths the Social Darwinist discourse of modern anthropology. Through problematising the 'taken for granted' knowledge that is built, by social sciences for example, for Indigenous peoples, another sense of being can be imagined.

USING FOUCAULT'S CONCEPTUAL TOOLS TO UNEARTH COLONISATION AS WESTERN PRAXIS

History is always the object of a construction in an un-constituted place. It is not constituted by homogenous time but by a full-time, time-of the now. (*14 Thesis for a Philosophy of History*, Walter Benjamin, 1934)

In the micropolitical stream of colonisation, Foucault is unable to articulate almost anything regarding identity, lived experiences, or any microphysical analytical tool because he theorises from Western and French worldview perspectives, and research in the micropolitical stream is often classified and validated using racial categories such as Indigenous, black, Latin American, African American, and so forth. Foucault also never focuses his research on colonisation or race, which is a glaring omission that will be revisited on the following pages.

In this book, Foucauldian philosophical archaeology was used not as a starting point but as a methodological tool to unearth the fundamentally Western machinery and operationalisation of colonisation. It is not surprising that Indigenous theorists, for example Professor Martin Nakata, use Foucauldian conceptual tools such as the archaeological approach to think about colonisation. Nakata, particularly, uses Foucauldian archaeology to unearth the ways in which discursive relations between the subject and the object—in his case Torres Strait Islander and *indigeneity* as colonial assemblages— become constitutive by the Other, establish differential and unequal relations (coloniser-colonised), and make Indigenous peoples be heard in a constrained way (Nakata, 2007). Nakata (2007) uses Foucauldian archaeology to measure the architecture of the apparatus of colonisation and the way an Indigenous Australian standpoint is stripped from an intelligible civilisation with more than 50,000 years of experience. Yet, for Nakata, once the design of the colonising apparatus is unveiled, an even more situated Indigenous standpoint can emerge that can contest the Western colonial assemblages politically and epistemologically (Nakata, 2007). Following Nakata's lead, this book uses Foucauldian conceptual tools to problematise colonisation as a Western product, because it has been proven to be effective in shaking the very foundations of Western institutions and practices, such as the medical, psychiatric, criminal, knowledge, and political institutions (and more) in the last five decades.

Philosophical archaeology addresses specific historical processes through the identification of their *origin* and *command*, as well as their intimate relationships, which includes the mechanisms through which the commands were delivered (Agamben, 2009). The etymological definition of archaeology signifies both origin and command. Therefore, this notion explicitly refers to the notion of history, but not a history founded in Kantian anthropocentric philosophy or philosophical anthropology. Archaeology is the history of words and objects, and their relationships. Furthermore, the words and objects are understood and perceived by their positivities (presence), and this positivity implies a topological distribution of history, power, and discourses (Deleuze, 1985). The archaeology of knowledge that Foucault engaged with in his work *The Order of Things* (which is literally translated as *On Words and Things*) is the beginning of the search for the history of knowledge in Western culture through unearthing its origins and the operation of its command. Foucauldian archaeology is not an inquiry of formal or interpretative history, nor is it a structuralist method like the history of ideas. Foucauldian archaeology is an inquiry that navigates between origin and command, and it maps the historical threshold processes of the concept, notion, or praxis in question, in order to construct a history of the positivities (presences) and their correlation with the negativities (absences) in order to identify its constituting processes.

The episteme is a central notion in philosophical archaeology. However, in *The Order of Things*, it is sometimes wrongfully framed as a worldview perspective. It can be understood in this way because Foucault describes epistemes from within rather than from without; he describes them as landscapes of knowledge formation, focusing on their features rather than their content. For example, Foucault (1973) describes the episteme of the 16th century, but then he specifically mentions that he will 'brutally generalise it in a period':

> Such, sketched in its most general aspects, is the 16th century episteme. This configuration carries with it a certain number of consequences. First and foremost, the plethoric yet absolutely poverty-stricken character of this knowledge. Plethoric because it is limitless. Resemblance never remains stable within itself; it can be fixed only if it refers back to another similitude, which then, in turn, refers to other; each resemblance, therefore, has value only from the accumulation of all other, and the whole world must be explored if even the slightest of analogies is to be justified and finally take on the appearance of certainty. (Foucault, 1973, p. 29)

Here, Foucault describes the episteme of the 16th century as he would describe a painting through highlighting what features brings the topological formations of knowledge together. Later in the text, he states:

> In fact, it is not from an insufficiency of structure and rigour that the 16th century knowledge suffers. On the contrary, we have already seen how very meticulous the configurations that define its space. It is this very rigour that

makes the relation of magic to erudition inevitable—they are not selected contents but required forms. (Foucault, 1973, p. 31)

He continues on to describe the possible forms of the epistemes not in a prescriptive or formed in manner, but in a continuing flux. This aligns with Foucault's understanding of the notion of episteme, which focuses on its capacity to produce multiple discursive and non-discursive forms (Foucault, 1973). Later, in *The Archaeology of Knowledge*, he attempts to explain what the notion of episteme entails:

> By episteme, we mean, in fact, the total set of relations and processes that unite, at a given period, the discursive practices that give rise to epistemolog-ical figures, sciences, and possibly formalized systems; the way in which, in each of these discursive formations, the transitions to epistemologization, scientificity, and formalization are situated and operate; the distribution of these thresholds, which may coincide, be subordinated to one another, or be separated by shifts in time; the lateral relations that may exist between episte-mological figures or sciences in so far as they belong to neighboring, but distinct, discursive practices. The episteme is not a form of knowledge (*con-naissance*) or type of rationality which, crossing the boundaries of the most varied sciences, manifests the sovereign unity of a subject, a spirit, or a period; it is the totality of relations and processes that can be discovered, for a given period, between the sciences when one analyses them at the level of discursive practices. (Foucault, 1974, p. 191)

When searching for a history of commandments, through a Foucauldian archaeology, Agamben (2012a) found that no philosophy scholar had written about commandments in more detail than a few lines or phrases. As men-tioned earlier, *arché* means both origin and command. This means that the archaeology of a commandment is the search for the origin and command of the commandments. This seemingly contradictory task is at the heart of language—assuming that the nature of language is polysemic (i.e., one word has the potential to have multiple meanings) and constituted by polarities. Agamben went to Aristotle to find a reference to commandments, which provided a route to understand why commandments and other similar activ-ities are not written about in philosophy and similar disciplines. In *On Inter-pretation*, Aristotle distinguishes two forms of statements: apophantic and non-apophantic statements. Apophantic statements are those that can be shown to be true or false. For example, 'I am sitting and typing on my computer': this statement is apophantic because it can be shown to be true or false. Non-apophantic statements cannot be shown to be true or false, such as when communicating a command. That is, a parent can say, 'Sit down' in its imperative form. Regardless of whether the command is obeyed or not, it remains a command; whether the statement is true or false is outside the realm of the order. Another example of a non-apophantic form is a prayer: it is not the concern of the prayer if it is or becomes true or false because a prayer states a petition based on faith. In his book, Aristotle states that philosophy is only concerned with apophantic discourse and that non-apophantic discourse is a matter for other practices such as poetry (*poesis*). Therefore, Agamben recalibrated his gaze to non-apophantic practices, which the discourse of philosophy has intentionally ignored. He turned to theology and found the first book of the Bible, Genesis, and the books of John. He found that God created the world with a command: 'Let there be light . . . Let there be a vault between the waters to separate water from water . . . Let the land produce vegetation . . .' (John 1:1–5). In the Alexandrian translation of the Bible, the specific word used was *arché*.

In sum, Foucauldian archaeology is the historical inquiry that aims to map the origin and its relationship with the command through drawing the relationships that determine the object in question. It achieves this through mapping the areas of a given concept, notion, or praxis, and through illustrating the various situations that can occur around where its productive and reproductive capacity coalesces in the historical processes determined in the landscapes of the epistemes. When addressing colonisation, however, power also becomes a central feature in which Foucault's conceptual tools become useful. While postcolonial studies and coloniality have used Foucauldian notions of power relations to an extent, when addressing politics and race in colonisation, they are typically conceptualised along the lines of a Marxist perspective.

Castro-Gómez (2007) and Grosfoguel (2008b), among others, have argued that the foundation of the coloniality theoretical view draws from a Marxist-structuralist theory of power that conceptualises topics in colonisation—such as race in a hierarchal system—differently from a Foucauldian heterarchical theory of power (Castro-Gómez, 2007). As Castro-Gomez reviews in an article in *Tabula Rasa*, coloniality is primarily viewed as a macropolitical process (such as colonisation ruling or being the 'ultimate truth') and it has hidden micropolitical processes such as the local histories of race in different countries. While postcolonial and coloniality/decoloniality research are far more diverse than what is discussed here, it can be said that coloniality and postcolonial discourse focus on the macropolitics of colonisation, where a top-down operation is conceptualised as coloniality or the international division of labour among other global notions; it ignores the micropolitics of colonisation and argues that it operates as an ideology. This was famously expressed in Spivak's article, 'Can the Subaltern Speak', where she states that poststructuralists like Foucault 'ignore the international division of labor . . . it is incapable of dealing with global capitalism: the subject-production of worker and unemployed within nation-state ideologies in its Center' (Spivak, 1988, p. 67). Spivak's main thesis is that the microphysics of power function as an ideology that hides the macrophysics of power. Other authors who have acknowledged their theoretical debt to Foucault, such as Edward Said in *Orientalism*, later distanced themselves from Foucault's work: Said argued that he did not acknowledge the macroeconomic processes that enabled Western culture to constitute itself as such (Castro-Gómez, 2007). Thus, postcolonial and coloniality/decolonialty studies privilege Marxist structuralism in understanding power, at least when addressing the problem of race and racism (Castro-Gómez, 2007).

Criticisms of Foucault's microphysics of power assume an ontological nature of power, which is characterised by it being hierarchical and not outside the simplistic top-down/unidirectional 'nature' of power relations. Others, like Castro-Gómez (2007), argue that Foucault conceptualises power relations in a non-hierarchical operation, not exclusively constituted in the microphysical levels. For Foucault, power is clearly not only globally constituted nor only locally constituted, but simultaneously produced locally/microphysically and globally/macrophysically. Thus, we must consider a non-hierarchal or heterarchical assumption of power relations in Foucault's theory.

Heterarchies are complex structures in which there is no basic order that governs one over another; all levels exert some degree of mutual influence in particular aspects and in their different historical contexts (Castro-Gómez, 2007). In heterarchical power relations, the power apparatuses never fully subjugate the object in question, unlike in hierarchies where the object in question is fully encapsulated in a determined plane. This means that the global apparatuses of capture are never absolute and, in extreme cases, can become long-standing through violence—be it physical, economic, social, or epistemic—or can remain stable in the way local levels can easily attach themselves to global planes of power. In 'Society Must Be Defended' (2005), Foucault offers two methodological precautions regarding the way he conceptualises power. First, power is not a homogenous and unidirectional phenomenon, but one that circulates in various directions and through web-like operations (capillaries); second, that power can be found in various levels or dimensions in the exercise of that power. Foucault certainly prefers to look at the lower levels of power—where power transverses the body—but he also acknowledges that other levels exist, which are able to transform and serially redeploy the exercise of power. In other words, in Foucault, the microphysics and macrophysics of power cannot be thought of as ontologically autonomous.

Some coloniality/decoloniality scholars, such as Grosfoguel and Castro-Gómez, have identified the dangers of a hierarchal theory of power in analysing the *praxis* of colonisation. Castro-Gómez (2007) argues for a heterarchical theory of power in coloniality/decoloniality studies. Grosfoguel states that colonial power cannot be thought of as ultimately residing in the relationship between capital and labour, but as an 'entangled and multiple web of

relationships far more complex than the reductionist and distinctively Eurocentric economic form of thinking' (Grosfoguel, 2009b, p. 198). This simply
means that colonial power is not only constituted by the global economic
power over the territories of the peripheries—or the 'global south'—but it is
also constituted by the local colonial apparatuses that operate at a micro-level
and also include resistance technologies and historicities. If, at a global level,
we acknowledge that these power apparatuses or discursive practices operate
like a web that can entangle themselves with other levels—such as labour
spaces, epistemic relations, sexuality, and gender, among others—this does
not mean that one is not reduced or cancelled by the other. Rather, there is
not only one coloniality of power or one type of colonial power, but there are
many and their functions vary in relation to their spaces of operation and
from which levels they are produced and reproduced (micro, meso, or macro
levels).

Thus, this book assumes a heterarchical approach to power relations
where the local *and* the global forms of power—such as the ones displayed in
colonisation—are accounted for simultaneously, even if they appear completely different from each other. That is, the local and the global will be
viewed at the same time where there is no specific order implying that one
process is more influential than the other. A focus on macrostructural spaces
can ignore the complexities of the logics of local histories, the logics of
bodies, and the logic of subjectivity; this view can be absolutist, and it can
obfuscate and invisibilise the specific histories of the micro-sphere. Similarly, a microstructural view can be myopic given that local colonial experiences do not occur in a vacuum, and this nearsightedness can help redeploy
geopolitical narratives as template forms of governments.

A key example of this myopic effect occurs in anthropological discourses,
as Nakata shows us in his book *Disciplining the Savages, Savaging the
Disciplines* (2007). After reexamining the Haddon Expedition, completed in
1898 (Haddon, Rivers, & Wilkin, 2010), Nakata concludes that this detailed
study on Torres Strait Islanders can never describe them because something
else is operating that determines their view:

> The data contained in the Cambridge team's reports (1904, 1908 & 1912) is
> impressively extensive and detailed. The product of a lengthy intellectual ges-
> tation, it was not to be published in its entirety as a general ethnography of the
> Torres Strait until 1935, decades after the studies were carried out. As noted
> earlier, this report is increasingly regarded by both Islanders and non-Islanders
> a valuable source of data on the Islander beliefs and traditions and, by defini-
> tion, of Islander people. Yet, despite the wealth of detail, these remain little
> more than random snapshots. In fact, they can never be more than this no
> matter how carefully they are reinterpreted or filtered simply because the
> viewpoint from which they were framed was, from the beginning, constrained
> both historically and intellectually. Ethnology and early anthropological theo-

ry once again informed practice in a way that not only framed the snapshot but also provided a background against Islander society itself became in reality little more than an offstage presence imagined into being by a scientific audience. (Nakata, 2007, pp. 101–102)

Certainly, the global operation of the discourse of anthropology is powerfully described here. Beyond his methodological influence in this book being archaeological, the critique of Modernity is local and transnational given the international composition of the Haddon Expedition. Torres Strait Islander peoples and Indigenous peoples in general were being imagined using a frame that was imported from abroad and their colonial experience was specific to the time period and the place; namely, it was Social Darwinism deployed by anthropological disciplines. However, how would a global reexamination of colonisation appear while still conserving a local deployment? Has it always been the case that Western culture conceptualised Indigenous peoples and other non-white 'races' along the lines of this Darwinist system of inequality? If not, then how have Indigenous peoples been conceptualised before this, from the beginnings of racial concepts in colonisation—namely the origins of the conceptualisations of *indigeneity* and *blackness*? How has colonisation operated to initiate its perspective, which can be the origin of this 'historical and intellectual constraint'? How did colonisation's conceptualisation begin in order to frame this mechanism?

Part 1 of this book focusses on the aesthetics constitution of race in colonisation—and specifically indigeneity and blackness—as key founding conceptualisations for the assemblage of colonisation. It reveals that the origins of the Western conceptualisation of indigeneity were informed by aesthetics, prior to the racial hierarchisation of indigeneity that occurred with the emergence of the discourse of anthropology and Social Darwinism. Chapter 2 locates itself within the epistemological frame of the edges of the Renaissance and Classical periods, and it discusses the frame in which the conceptualisation of race was aesthetically assembled: ugliness. The Western aesthetic of ugliness is framed from what is known in Western culture and it says very little about the original civilisations in the Americas. Hieronymus Bosch's triptych *The Temptations of St. Anthony* presents a large inventory of medieval representations of ugliness through the monstrosity of hell's creatures.

Chapter 3 specifically discusses the first conceptualisation of race in colonisation utilising the larger frame of ugliness, *indigeneity*. Bosch's monstrous anthropocentric representations are the frame of the monstrous anthropology that determines the Western conceptualisation of indigeneity. Following this thread of monstrosity, the depiction of the cannibal is the first monstrous depiction of the first colonial experience. The monstrous depiction of the Indigenous civilisations of the Americas marks the way in which they would be interpreted: colonised and thereafter enslaved. Following the horrendous history of colonisation, enacted by the colonisers, monstrous anthropology becomes encoded in the narrative constituted by the narrative frames that develop into the first racial conceptualisation of indigeneity.

Chapter 4 discusses what becomes the next conceptualisation of race, *blackness*, and how it becomes encoded into the origins of race alongside indigeneity. The chapter begins in the time when blackness was not interchangeable with slavery, which occurred at the end of the 16th century; prior to this, skin colour only functioned, sometimes, as a descriptor for the religious identification of certain peoples. The institutions in power, such as the Catholic Church and the kingdoms, determined inequality, for which slavery was the crudest example. The chapter goes on and presents one of the most extreme examples of blackness at the historical fringes of indigeneity, slavery, and conquest: the story of Juan Garrido. Juan Garrido was the first documented black *conquistador*. The historical threshold of the interchangeability of blackness and slavery predicates the complicity of Western blackness and colonisation. The chapter concludes by describing a set of the linking aesthetic processes of blackness with indigeneity, the most important one being 'colouring', which refers to the set of contrasting processes to a determined set of base colours. The formation of indigeneity and blackness is described using one of the first recorded painting in the Americas: *Los Tres Mulatos de Esmeralda* (Zambo Chiefs) which was painted in 1599 by Adrian Sánchez Galque. This is used as an illustrative case study because it was sent to the Kingdom of Spain to showcase the *mulatos* (of Indigenous and African descent) 'chiefs', and it illustrates the constituted discursive Western imagery of indigeneity and blackness.

Part 2 shifts its unearthing to the following layer of colonisation, in accordance with the epistemological shift from the Classical period to the Modernity period, to the operation of colonisation as a pure function. Chapter 5 discusses the larger frame of the discourse of philosophical anthropology and how it encodes the aesthetic conceptualisation of race into a focus on form, represented in the inequality of human races and in biopolitics. The chapter discusses what the episteme of Modernity means for race, form of governance, and colonisation in general. The chapter discusses the shift from the Classical period to the Modernity period, the shift from sovereign power to biopower, and the shift of inequality from being determined by institutions to races.

Chapter 6 situates the book in local grounds, specifically Queensland, Australia, through a case study of the Aboriginals Protection and Restriction of the Sale of Opium Act 1897 (1897 Act) and the way that this Act created the conditions of possibilities in which Indigenous Australian peoples in Queensland could be governed. The chapter analyses the local command of colonisation through the 1897 Act, in other words, the techno-political administrative function of the 1897 Act, through mapping its historicity, where both indigeneity and blackness are used as racial markers for a specific type of biopolitical governance, the *Blanket Approach*, that operates through the specific triple function of totalisation, multiplicity, and the creation of desire.

Chapter 7 further analyses this case study and elaborates on how the 1897 Act operated as a system that saw the operation of what may be called a 'state of exception', which is a similar legal mechanism used in the wake of the Jewish Holocaust in World War II. It critically assesses how emerging Western geopolitical assemblages, particularly the state of exception within biopolitics, could have recursively influenced the local Blanket Approach operation of colonisation in Queensland. The chapter reexamines Agamben's notion of state of exception through briefly reviewing colonial history as one of the main conceptual sources of the emergence of such biopolitical devices.

Chapter 8 reviews the constitution of colonisation and its intricate relationship with race through aesthetic contemporary views. It brings us back to the blue and white transfer in how colonisation is transfigured through aesthetic logics and how thinking through art can look like. It also reexamines decolonial aesthetics in the way colonisation can be viewed from a chaos that has a codification. This chapter closes the book by way of an invitation to review colonisation and race from the logics of aesthetics, rather than from the logic of the discourse of anthropology.

The reader of this historical-philosophical investigation will note that a clear subject position is not articulated for the author, despite colonisation affecting various facets of the author's life. Similarly, this work does not abide by strict conceptual or historical global and local foci, and some might regard the attention to specific local events, policies, or individual historical figures as arbitrary or even superfluous. I[5] can assure the reader that the micro-histories examined in this book are, directly or indirectly, an important part of the colonial 'wound' that affects me and all other subjects directly or indirectly linked by colonisation: each event, historical figure or local policy exemplifies specific key dimensions of the constitution of the history of colonisation at large.

However, it is not the author's intention to establish a synthesis of a global and local history of colonisation, but rather the intention is to carve a path that makes the transition between the macro and micro histories intelligible. Individually, and even collectively, it is impossible to claim to be able to neutralise colonisation and racism with the 'stroke of a pen'; the colonised can never forget. As an author endeavouring to archaeologically unearth this path in colonisation between these two scale registers, it becomes necessary to suspend individual-anthropocentric discourse and to explore using a counter-anthropocentric attitude. The convoluted history of colonisation certainly begins and ends in the body, but the process that constitutes it is weaved by discourses and institutions using the fabric of culture. One can aim to counteract the immediate influence of colonisation or coloniality and racism through self-affirmation in writing or elsewhere, yet the cultural sphere in which the colonised inhabits continues to be the context that surrounds him or her. A counter-anthropocentric attitude shifts the focus from the person to the place and space that breaches the realm of the colonised self to engage in a reflective balance between the self and history, subalternisation and power, and materiality and conceptualisation. In this sense, the imaginary realm can concede a sense of freedom by establishing a perpetual and real contradiction between history and life that can then be dissolved in the infinite possibilities of the Real. In *Poetics of Relation* (1997), Édouard Glissant illustrates this attitude to elicit this perpetual contradiction, particularly in this fragment:

> And now what they tell me is, 'You calmly pack your poetics into these craters of opacity to rise so serenely beyond the prodigiously elucidating work that the West has complished, but there you go talking nonstop about this West.'— 'And what would you rather I talk about at the beginning, if not this transparency whose aim was to reduce us? Because, if I don't begin there, you will see me consumed with the sullen jabber of childish refusal, convulsive and powerless. This is where I start. As for my identity, I'll take care of that myself.' There has to be dialogue with the West, which, moreover is contradictory in itself (usually this is the argument raised when I talk about cultures of the One); the complementary discourse of whoever wants to give-on-and-with must be added to the West. And can you not see that we are implicated in its evolution? (Glissant, 1997, pp. 190–191)

At this point, then, my subject position can be certainly constituted by my identity(ies), but at the same time potentially augmented by the endless global elements that preexist.

NOTES

1. A more elaborate discussion on archaeology is presented in following sections.
2. The intention of unearthing the origins of colonisation located in the objects that it 'spoke of' is not to define these conceptualisations but to present the processes that historically constituted and animated the *praxis* of colonisation.
3. Colonization [Def. 1]. (n.d.). In *Merriam-Webster*, Retrieved November 20, 2016, from http://merriam-webster.com/dictionary/colonization.
4. Torres Strait Islanders are Indigenous peoples located in the islands between the north part of Queensland and New Guinea. The 1897 Act applied to Torres Strait Islanders from 1906 and then a specific 'protectionist' policy was assembled for this territory of Queensland in 1933.
5. I am intentionally switching from third to first person because I am attempting to showcase the necessarily occasional surfacing of the author as a comment on the opaque position that an author is located in, when in a given text.

Part 1

Origins: Colonial Aesthetics (The Caribbean)

WORKING NOTIONS: WESTERN CULTURE

Western culture means the place where Eurocentrism is located and produced, simultaneously considering that this place is constituted by peoples and nationalities that do not limit it. However, culture has many definitions and, as Rothman notes, 'it is more than the sum of its definitions' (2014, p. 4). Therefore, culture will be understood as Michel Foucault explained to Alan Badiou during an interview in 1965: 'By culture, I understand, given a determined cultural form, with specific forms of knowing and specific institutions; there is liberated a language that is proper to it, eventually a certain type of discursive practise is enabled' (1965). This apparently circular definition speaks to culture being the relational link that enables a set of discourses, institutions, and *epistemes*. Thus, Western culture is the whole and the links of a given civilisation; in this case, a history of a civilisation that emerges in Europe, which metanarrative is predicated by Modernity (Harvey, 1990; Lyotard, 1987), and it's at the centre of capitalism and patriarchy, and that leads the ongoing process of colonisation (Dussel, 1993; Grosfoguel, 2003; Mignolo, 1996; Quijano, 2000).

DISCOURSE OF PHILOSOPHICAL ANTHROPOLOGY

The discourse of philosophical anthropology refers to the way Western culture (at least) engages with the world through making meaning from an anthropocentric perspective. At the centre of this discourse is the personification of how modern 'man'—with all its patriarchal dimensions—ought to be: 'organised into a distinctive whole and set contrastively against such wholes and against social and natural background is' (Geertz, 1979, p. 229). Anthropocentrism is characteristic of the period when colonisation first occurred (the 15th and 16th centuries) and its knowledge making was dominated by institutions, particularly those of Christianity. Foucault argued that Kant solidified this method through which Western culture conceptualised its ontology in his institution of philosophical anthropology in *The Critique of Pure Reason*, but Kant stated it better in a short paper published in 1784 entitled *What is Aufkärung?* Foucault elaborates further on this paper in many of his works, but it can be found clearly in *The Politics of Truth* (2007). He explains that Kant's philosophical anthropology is the solidification of Modernity and the birth of the modern technology of the self that is defined by modern philosophical anthropology. When explaining this operation, he states:

> Even if it is relatively and necessarily vague, the Enlightenment period is certainly designed as a formative stage for modern humanity. This is anthropology in the *Aufkärung* in the wide sense of the term to which Kant, Weber, etc. referred, a period without fixed dates, with multiple points of entry since one can also define it by the formation of capitalism, the constitution of the modern man (defined by the bourgeois world), the establishment of nation-state systems, the foundation of modern science. (Foucault, 2007, p. 57)

Therefore, the discourse of anthropology refers to the 'man' of Modernity that is produced by capitalism, Modernity, and patriarchy.

AESTHETIC DISCOURSE

Aesthetic discourse refers to the limits of language where text focusses on the symbolic and not on the literal; thus, the limits of communication and representation are suspended to allow a certain freedom of interpretation and sensing (Eco, 2010; Kant & Pluhar, 2010; Nietzsche, 1995). Eco states that, 'Aesthetic discourse involves to some extent a rupture with (or a departure from) the linguistic system of probability, which serves to convey established meaning, in order to increase the signifying potential of the message' (Eco, 2010, p. 56). This is the case of the founding 'openness' of all types of arts (visual arts, prose, poetry, etc.). However, this openness is not completely free, as it is determined by the historical processes of the time, its epistemological period, and certain categories employed by a given culture. For example, in Western culture, ugliness and beauty are large categories. Thus, when referring from aesthetic ideas of, for instance, beauty, this work does not begin with universal ideas of beauty (such as the universal definitions of beauty that Kant proposes throughout his *Critique of Judgement*), but this part understands aesthetic discourse to be conditional to certain historical periods and not completely immune to underlying narratives that may occupy meanings and interpretations. In sum, whilst aesthetic discourse is located at the limits of linear interpretation or where literality and multiple interpretations are possible, aesthetic discourse remains highly codified and determined by a given history of a culture where communication and representation occur in a more multi-layered signification process.

EXPLAINING PURE FUNCTION OR INCOMMENSURABLE OPERATIONS

It is important to consider that when explaining pure function or operations concepts such as the 'panopticon' or 'blanket' (in the case of this book) are not used simply as a metaphor or a symbolic transference to explain the operation of a given praxis, for instance colonisation, but as a *form of content* that captures the mechanism of colonisation. In a similar way, Foucault (1976) defined 'panopticism' as a form of content constituted by its pure function, as opposed to a form of expression or discursive practice; the pure function of a form of governance is defined as a form of content or an abstract machine that, referring to a given conceptualisation or discursive device, imposes a given identity practice on a given subjectivity. When explaining the link between Foucauldian archaeology and panopticism, Deleuze states:

> When Foucault defines Panopticism, either he specifically see it as an optical or luminous arrangement that characterizes prison, or he views it abstractly as a machine that not only affects visible matter in general (a workshop, barracks, school or hospital as much as a prison) but also in general passes through every articulable function. So the abstract formula of Panopticism is not only 'to see without being seen' but also *to impose a particular conduct on a particular human multiplicity.* (Deleuze, 1985, pp. 33–34, emphasis in original)

Penal law feeds into the confirmation of the assemblage of the prison and the prison feeds into the forms of expression of the penal law. The discursive and non-discursive practices continually feed from each other, refer to each other, and are, at times, in explicit contact.

Chapter Two

Aesthetics of Ugliness

To begin to answer Cesaire's burning question of, 'what, fundamentally, is colonization?' we need to start from its origins; colonisation starts from the end of the 15th century in the Caribbean where a whole set of discourses start to be assembled from the epistemological conditions of possibility of the time. Darwinism and its generalisations into the realm of the social was born out of the Enlightenment period (mainly 18th century). Domination justified by 'superior' civilisations, cultures, or races, and informed by the human sciences would happen hundreds of years after 1492. Michel Foucault when unearthing of Western knowledge in *The Order of Things* maps the epistemological topology of the Classical and Renaissance periods, according to him 15th- and 16th-century western peoples navigated reality through systems of representations in which the image had a protagonist role. In reexamining the first texts of colonisation—diaries, chronicles, 'natural histories', and so on—drawings, engravings, and imagery at large (considered texts) had a specific explicative power that sparked my interest to examine colonisation within a different discursive space: to view colonisation from an aesthetics discourse would tell a different story of race, domination, and inequality.

Colonisation begins in the fringes of the Renaissance and Classical periods, 15th and 16th centuries. In the Renaissance period, words fitted to things inasmuch they are part of the grand story of the world written by the hidden hand of God, or the 'prose of the world' (Foucault, 1973). The world here is an ever-expanding story that cannot be fully read by Western culture. Resemblance then becomes the way to understand objects in the grand story of the world. Thus, aesthetics here functions as a way to apprehend all objects to the grand narrative of Western culture. The Classical period focus, in the other hand, is representation. Here, text becomes foundational to transparent-

ly represent this grand narrative of the world, specifically a specific system
of classification that has a given order by God. Resemblances here turn into
the transparent system of classification that binds a given order that also
discriminates them or differentiates them. This system of classification does
imply a certain order that can be understood as hierarchical, such as Carl
Linnaeus' taxonomy system where some have argued is where Social Darwinism takes its form from. However, at the point of the Classical period the
system of classification was given by the grand narrative of God that trans-
lates into a hierarchy, in the case of social hierarchies, dictated by the main
institution of the time, the Catholic Church. Thus, it is in this aesthetic
discourse focus that the Renaissance and the Classical periods where colonisation takes place through the realms of prose, narratives, and imageries.
However, how does this aesthetic logic looks like in Western culture at large
and as it relates to colonisation?

USING AESTHETICS TO PROBLEMATISE WESTERN DISCOURSES

While approaching the discourse of aesthetics as a frame to view concepts
one can find that views critical of Western culture and anti-colonial works
have deployed aesthetics in various ways. It was Friedrich Nietzsche, particularly in his *Birth of Tragedy* from within metaphysics, who first problema-
tized Western rationality through aesthetics and proposed that humans are
first and foremost creators and not rational beings, stating that it was in arts
where one can find the productive source and sense of the history of cultures.
At least Aimé Cesaire, Édouard Glissant, Cornel West, and Walter Mignolo
would similarly problematise aesthetics and propose, and even produce, decolonial aesthetics. These authors and others will be discussed later in the
book in relation to an elaborated decolonial aesthetics. Against the Western
history of philosophy as metaphysics, and Western rationality by extension,
Nietzsche inverts the dominance of reason in metaphysics, in order to highlight the role of art and aesthetics in navigating and, ultimately, understanding Being and the (Western) World—that is, ontology. According to Plato,
who was one of the founders of metaphysics, the foundation of reality is the
intelligibility of ideas, because the way 'man' knows the world is through the
senses, and these ontologically and epistemologically depend on ideas, on
idealism. In Plato, we have things and ideas of things in the world, and art is
simply copies of those ideas—copies of copies: in art we only find representations of the empirical world. On the other hand, the world of ideas is
universal, eternal, and stable; that is, it is valid for everyone, everywhere, and
always, and the only way to access ideas is through reason and rationality.
Following this logic, if we want to live well and in control, we need to live
targeting and engaging directly with ideas. Subsequently, the virtue is reason,

to know, given that it can directly access ideas and knowledge. This is why Plato evicts the artists from the Republic, because artists do not use reason; instead they mostly use imagination and produce copies of ideas that are far from the ultimate accessible reality. Nietzsche effectively reverses this metaphysics, not only arguing that it is in art what allows cultures to live well by serving the function of 'transfiguring reality' from its meaninglessness and chaos, but it also suggests that the true capacity of 'man' is creativity and not reason. For Nietzsche, humans are all creators given that they craft concepts to interpret the world every day and instrumentally find ways to embrace the unity of the world through music, poetry, dance, and other aesthetic activities. Nietzsche therefore rejects idealism and empiricism, notoriously stating that there are no facts but rather only interpretations, and that ideas are not the ontological starting point of reality but the point at which cultures transfix reality for self-preservation reasons: aesthetics and art become key.

In the context of his *Genealogy of Modern Racism* in 1984, Cornell West (2002) first established that '[t]he role of classical aesthetic and cultural norms in the emergence of the idea of white supremacy as an object of modern discourse cannot be underestimated' (p. 56). West's affirmation of the importance of white interpretations of aesthetics as models or, more accurately, imagined attributions of whiteness in Greek aesthetics as the ideological origin of white supremacy and of Social Darwinist measures supports the link between race and aesthetics within the standards of Western culture. This genealogy of modern racism powerfully targets the way in which Social Darwinism is constructed, i.e., the Western assemblage of racism through a discursive construction of an 'inequality of human races',[1] however, it focuses on the structural built ideological hierarchy and not on the aesthetic production of race. That is, West (2002) critiques modern racism through the metaphysical-empirically scientific lens, even when he argues that 'classical aesthetics', i.e., the category of race, stems from the categorical representations of 'Africans, Orientals, Europeans, and Lapps'. His approach still appears to stem from a reexamination of the anthropological view and not one that goes to the accepted root or origins, i.e., the aesthetic construction of race and the model measured against white supremacy. Later, in chapter 5, it will be argued that, overall, racism and colonisation in Modernity is best reexamined when aware of its supremacy but focused on its pure function, which is incommensurable, through a biopolitics that uses colonial aesthetics as markers for governance.

Fanon, Cesaire, Glissant, and other anti-colonial and critical race academics from the 1950s onwards have used aesthetics' form, not its discursive content, to also 'speak back' and reexamine the complexities of racism and colonisation. At least two aesthetic discursive strands were constructed and commented on the complexities of black and colonial aesthetics during the global anti-colonial movement in the middle of the twentieth century; one

aimed to construct an aesthetic discourse that represented black consciousness through the arts and the other endeavoured to display the complexities
and heterogeneity of colonisation and racial dynamics in practice. The former effort can be seen in the decolonial black aesthetics of the Harlem
Renaissance, *Présence Africaine*, and more specifically in the literary works
of Cesaire. The latter interestingly refers predominantly to the works of
Fanon where *Black Skin, White Masks* and *The Wretched of the Earth* use an
indeterminate prose and writing style that allow for the heterogeneous complexities of race and colonisation be best expressed (Oto, 2003). That is,
Fanon is well cited as a source of black and anti-colonial radicalism, and is
also engaged with a critique of Western master–slave dialects and phenomenology, which largely demonstrates how these approaches are insufficient to
think about the black, colonial, and Caribbean conditions, but he is not often
acknowledged for his use of literary aesthetic discourse to critique racism
and colonisation.[2] Beyond the fact that there was a lack of concepts that
could properly address the complexities of racism, blackness, colonisation,
and more in the 1950s, Fanon engaged in a type of almost poetic prose that
figured the form and style, i.e., aesthetic features, that allowed his works to
be a poetic performance of critique that arose from the zone of non-being,
because no argumentative form in a history of ideas or historical investigation that engaged with complex ideas like colonisation and race could be
restrained in a closed register of thinking. Scholars including Alejandro de
Otto and Maldonado-Torres, among others, argue that Fanon proposed that
the zone of non-being, or *damné*, contains an aesthetics of tragedy, in the
Greek sense of the genre, that does not only refer to a territorial negation to
the colonised in the political sphere, but also the non-being space where
freedom can be politically engaged. Whilst Glissant, Cessaire, and many
other Caribbean and Creole thinkers depart from the aesthetics of verse and
prose to build a language for the *damné* through specific 'places' (inspired by
the history of the Caribbean islands), it is Fanon in *Black Skin, White Masks*
who powerfully departed from an aesthetic discourse to question and make
polyphonic statements using a poetic prose style. If Fanon's aesthetically
informed writing form and style pertains to a more fitting discursive space of
decolonial critique, then Anzaldúa's *Borderlands* can be another example of
the importance of aesthetics in reexamining colonisation given the many
literary figures and imagery that she deploys to make sense of the embodied
'borderlands' of *meztizaje* subjectivity. Aesthetic discourse as a medium has
enabled colonisation studies' authors to be able to communicate the sometimes incommensurable processes that constitute the complexities within colonisation as a form of governance.

While the aforementioned works stand out in their deployment of aesthetic style and critique to address colonisation, very few works do this in direct
opposition to the discourse of philosophy and are often deployed from the

17th- and 18th-century episteme of philosophical anthropology (henceforth, the discourse of anthropology) or the episteme of Modernity, which is a historical miscalculation. That is, if colonisation is to be examined from where it originated and was created at the end of the 15th and the beginning of the 16th centuries, then it must consider the Western historical epoch that colonisation was built upon: an epoch where discursive similarities through imagery assembled how Westerners understood their limited world, and later others, at the time.

As previously stated, part 1 follows the historical footsteps that informed the emergence of colonisation centring its episteme through similarities, which is a discursive space identified by another 'master of suspicion'—as per Michel Foucault in his *Order of Things*—where we immediately find that imagery occupies a central role in many discursive and non-discursive practices. Beyond the fact that conservative estimates establish that less than one-fifth of the European population in the 16th century could read (Ramírez-Alvarado, 2015), imagery conveyed messages that bypassed representation of the real. Thus, Western aesthetics through a specific interplay within imageries were able to communicate the source of resemblances in the episteme of the Renaissance period and the source of the Classical period's episteme, i.e., representation. In other words, in the origins of colonisation there appears to be an intersection between what Foucault called the 'prose of the world' episteme where Western resemblances operate to capture the Caribbean into the totality of the Western world as text to be endlessly weaved into the holy perpetual grand narrative written by God, and the emergence of representation that hides the hierarchal organisational logic that founds it (Foucault, 1973). Thus, the importance of aesthetics in both the Renaissance and Classical periods appears to be the place where a reasonable space should illuminate the epistemological birth of colonisation as a result of the historical importance of the grand narratives, interpretation, representation, and classification in those periods. The intersection of the Renaissance and Classical periods during the beginnings of colonisation (i.e., the end of the 15th and the beginning of the 16th centuries) allows for a mixture of processes from both periods to occur in colonisation given that these epistemological shifts in Western history never occur in a clear-cut manner.

AESTHETICS OF UGLINESS

If the modern judgement of the inferiority–superiority binary conception of race and civilisations are removed, few ways are left to understand how Western culture first understood different societies and civilisations. That is, given that most views that aim to understand colonisation are produced from the discourse of anthropology, it is difficult to paint an understanding of

colonisation unlike this mostly rational approach. What follows is an unearthing of aesthetic discourse, as opposed to a universal (art) history of
aesthetic judgement, in Western history that enveloped the origins of colonisation focussing on the epistemological space in which Western culture
conceptualized Indigenous peoples in an aesthetic of ugliness where a monstrous anthropology is created.

In his works entitled *On Beauty* (2010) and, of particular relevance here,
On Ugliness (2007), Eco stated that aesthetic judgements vary according to
time periods and that while the Western history of ugliness shares common
characteristics with the Western history of beauty, they display different
features according to the social context in which these judgements are
passed. The epistemological time periods of the origins of colonisation are
distinguished by aesthetic features, such as the Renaissance episteme that
through resemblance a great narrative of the world can be elucidated and the
Classical episteme that encodes classification systems through representation. The Western history of the aesthetics of beauty and ugliness can provide
a foundational pathway into what was 'seen' in the first encounters that
framed colonisation. In particular, ugliness provides an unexplored frame of
analysis that can assist in determining a different perspective through which
the Western culture understood Indigenous societies in the 15th and 16th
centuries in their first encounters in the Americas. In Western culture, ugliness is a space where the socio-political conditions are symbolically manifested (Eco, 2007; Marx, 2002), and it also manifested the moralisation of
Western society (Rosenkrantz, 1853). Finally, ugliness is all too human
(Nietzsche, 2014) for Western culture as it is the mirror of what it can be and,
to an extent, what it is. That is, ugliness is all too Western and it becomes a
manifestation of its own anthropocentrism.

While many writings about Western aesthetics exist, such as *Aesthetics*
by Hegel and *Critique of Judgement* by Kant, these all focus on the idea of
beauty and only rarely mention ugliness.[3] The first comprehensive written
elaboration of ugliness was composed by Rosenkrantz in 1853 in his book
entitled *Aesthetic of Ugliness*. Rosenkrantz theorises ugliness from a framework in which it autonomously moralises ugliness assuming that beauty
already has its own autonomous moralisation. Eco explains:

> Rosenkrantz performs a meticulous analysis of ugliness in nature, spiritual
> ugliness, ugliness in art (and the various forms of artistic incorrectness), the
> absence of form, asymmetry, disharmony, disfigurement, and deformation (*the
> wretched,* the vile, the banal, the fortuitous and the arbitrary, the gross), the
> various forms of the repugnant (the ungainly, death and the void, the horren-
> dous, the vacuous, the sickening, the felonious, the spectral, the demoniac, the
> witchlike and the satanic). Too much to allow us to carry on saying that
> ugliness is merely the opposite of beauty understood as harmony, proportion,
> or integrity. (Eco, 2007, p. 16, emphasis added)

Rosenkrantz argues that ugliness has a complexity of its own and is not fully dependant on beauty. This complexity is nothing other than the autonomy of the moralisation that Eco proposes that ugliness can be equivalent to evil. Rosenkrantz's (1853) argument assumes that aesthetics is the manifestation of a form of moralisation: that ugliness can be equivalent to evil. Therefore, for him, evil manifests in ugliness and, contrastingly, goodness and virtue manifest in beauty. Rosenkrantz rejects the idea that ugliness is morally dependent on beauty; if he is right, then virtue is dependent on evil and vice versa. Therefore, he attempts to unravel the complexity of ugliness in order to distinguish it from beauty and to demonstrate that these concepts are not dependent on each other.[4] In 1852, Rosenkrantz wrote:

> The inferno is not only ethical and religious, it is also aesthetic. We are steeped in evil and in sin, but also in ugliness. The terror of the formless and of deformity, of vulgarity and atrocity surrounds us in innumerable figures, from pygmies to those gigantic deformities from which hellish evil observes us, gnashing its teeth. It is into this inferno of Beauty that we wish to descend. And it is impossible to do so without entering at the same time the inferno of evil, the real inferno, because the ugliest ugliness is not that which disgusts us in nature—swamps . . . it is the egoism that manifests its folly in perfidious and frivolous deeds, in the wrinkled lines of passion, in grim looks and in crime. (as cited in Eco, 2010, p. 135)

In contrast, Eco (2007) argues that, outside moralization as a pathway to develop the 'nature' of ugliness, the lack of theoretical appreciation of ugliness can stem from it being historically less examined, less written about, and therefore less researched.

Marx (as cited in Eco, 2007, p. 116) stated that ugliness and beauty are often determined by 'socio-economic and political conditions'. Marx (2002) did not only refer to the power to buy that which could be the tools to become beautiful, but he also referred to beauty itself being an ideology that is constituted by the hidden interest of capital. This suggests that, in reality, ugliness is part of the ideology of the binary of beauty and ugliness. From this understanding, Eco states that Marx intimated that a materialist dialectic is manifested in a symbolic form through the beauty–ugliness binary. That is, the symbols manifested in beauty are represented in the buying power of the bourgeois position (and everything that surrounds that position), and the symbols manifested in ugliness are represented in the proletariat position. The ugliness of the proletariat position is characterised by an ideology of the need for consumption, which attempts to possess that which could function as an antidote to the ugliness-proletariat position. Beauty and ugliness become the symbolic tension that recursively confirms inequality.

In his piece entitled *Twilight of the Idols*, Nietzsche (2014) provides a more interesting account of ugliness predicated on a kind of anthropocentrism that is dialectically narcissistic. He states:

> Ugliness is seen as a sign and a symptom of degeneration . . . Every suggestion of exhaustion, heaviness, senility, fatigue, any sort of lack of freedom, like convulsions or paralysis . . . all this provokes an identical reaction [just before he was discussing narcissism], the value judgement 'ugly' . . . What does man hate? There is no doubt about this: he hates the twilight of his own type. (Nietzsche 2014, p. 78)

Ugliness, in Nietzsche, is the parallax reflection of the Western notion of beauty. The twilight of humanity in Western aesthetics is ugliness, and this is an important part of what defines Western history (Eco, 2007). The value judgement of ugly is only understood from a judgement defined by a history that values vigour over exhaustion, lightness over heaviness, youth over senility, strength over weakness, and movement over paralysis. This history is Western culture's history. From this perspective, ugliness is as much part of the West as all that it deems to be beautiful because it is produced and reproduced through the value judgement of beauty. Ugliness is not hidden: it is *not* as if ugliness needs to be decoded in order to find a treasure—it is there to be seen, but it is not exposed as much as beauty is exposed. If beauty is historically (and therefore socially) defined, then the same applies to ugliness. This indicates that the framing and mind-set that makes us see beauty also makes us see ugliness. Moreover, beauty and ugliness do not refer to inherent attributes or all elements of that which is beautiful or that which is ugly. If anything, the attributes that define beauty or ugliness are inherent elements of the culture in question: in this case, the Western culture. For example, Western culture often regards the desert as rough, lifeless, and sometimes ugly. However, these descriptions often convey very little about the desert itself (assuming a distinction between desert and jungle, or valley, or forest, or any other landscape), but rather it conveys what the West values. It values that landscapes have smoothness and ease, and that do not pose a threat to the way in which Western societies live. Moreover, it values abundance of what Western culture wants to 'see'. The desert certainly has the aforementioned attributes and more, but not within the frame of Western culture. Therefore, a desert that is sometimes classified as ugly and is often regarded to have low value can reveal more about the Western frame of classification than about the desert itself. Through ugliness, we can understand Western Culture's frame of classification, which is to understand the West's mind-set including that which is highly valued and that which is poorly valued. In this sense, a history of ugliness in the West is a history of ugliness of Western Culture's framework and not the history of the object that it calls 'ugly'.

As an inquiry pathway, Western ugliness provides an obscured and often ignored account of its intrinsic history (Eco, 2007). Through the realm of Western ugliness and motivated by domination, peoples were conceptualised in, and therefore captured into, the Western framework. For this reason, this framework is important to consider in order to elaborate on how the West historically engaged in practices that continued to form and reproduce the first colonial discourses. These first European frames were deployed almost immediately to what were mostly unknown civilisations[5] at the moment of first contact. These conceptualising practices were first manifested in writing and drawing in the colonial records of the diaries or 'chronicles' (*crónicas*) of the *conquistadores*.[6] These recorded what they saw, but they also formed what became known as indigeneity in the 17th and 18th centuries, and even today. However, where can imagery references be located that convey how the ugliness of the unknown was represented in the late 15th century and the beginning of the 16th century?

Thus, the focus of the Western origins of colonisation is on how race, through an aesthetics of ugliness, was a prominent colonial discursive device was conceptualised, particularly of whom it spoke of, in the knowledge grids of the end of the Renaissance and Classical periods. This is not to suggest that the hierarchisation of 'human races' assembled by the discourse of anthropology did not have a vital effect in the way post-Enlightenment colonisation forms were enacted—colonisation as a form of governance is still distinguished by this *pure function* as I will argue later on. What this part establishes is that the conceptual markers that highlighted and then carved the bodies of colonisation's subjects are not assembled from a Social Darwinist logic, but are assembled by the imageries of colonial aesthetics because aesthetics informed much of what counted as 'truth' in the disciplines and social practices of the time. Furthermore, this part shows that the Western conceptualisation of peoples through aesthetic discourse and how, from 'human sciences', the focus of colonisation imprinted specific narratives through Western aesthetic forms of representation.

MONSTERS: BOSCH'S TRIPTYCH *THE TEMPTATIONS OF ST. ANTHONY*

'The great multitude of men,' wrote Henry Power, an English follower of Descartes, 'resembles rather Descartes' automata, as they lack any reasoning power, and only as a metaphor can be called men' (Easlea 1980: 140). The 'better sorts' agreed that the proletariat appeared as a 'great beast', a 'many-headed monster', wild, vociferous, given to any ritual vocabulary identified with the masses as purely instinctual beings. —Silvia Fedirici in *Caliban and the Witch Women: The Body and Primitive Accumulation* (2010, p. 152)

On the basis of the power of the continuum held by nature, the monster ensures the emergence of difference . . . the monster is the root-stock of specification, but it is only a sub-species itself in the stubbornly slow stream of history. — Michel Foucault in *The Order of Things* (1973, p. 151)

Monster is one of the concepts in Western culture where we find the point in which the 'unnatural' is framed as ugliness in parallax reflection to the 'natural', which is understood in its highest form as beauty. It is the location where not only the 'metaphor [that] can be called men' is a formless conceptualisation of ugliness, but where the transfiguration of beauty in Western culture's 'man' creates a parallel space on the opposite side of the grid of its own type in the greater classification system in which man were located in the Classical period. Monster becomes the conceptual space sitting beside Western man yet in the opposite direction, both created by the larger holy narrative of the 'universal plan' as Saint Thomas Aquinas would write in his *City of God*. Bosch's triptych *The Temptations of St. Anthony* (1505–1506) will be used in this chapter to map the framework of the aesthetic of ugliness of the 15th and 16th centuries because it has a rich representation of a taxonomy of monstrosity alongside 'man', due to the period in which it was produced, and because it was one of the few paintings that also has a larger narrative painting version alongside the triptych *The Garden of Earthly De-lights* (hereafter *Earthly Delights*; 1506). *The Temptations of St. Anthony* functions as a standalone detail of the narrative represented in the section the monsters are on Earth as opposed to the hell section in *Earthly Delights*. In general, the triptych *Earthly Delights* functions as a representation of the Western great narrative of beyond the world (paradise and hell) and *The Temptations of St. Anthony* represents the immersion of monsters into the world. Conversely, *Earthly Delights* suggests a *telos* or an 'end' (utopia) of what the universal history should look like according to Western culture. Notably, the monstrous-cannibalistic characteristics of the creatures in the triptych's section of hell echo the way monstrosity features in colonisation.

This brief description of Bosch's triptych *The Temptations of St. Anthony* is not intended to decode the complex artwork or rigorously describe the denotative elements of the triptych. This beautiful piece is suspiciously complicit and relevant to Western culture's depiction of the assembled frame of ugliness in the conceptualisation of indigeneity in the first colonial experience of the Americas. The construction of ugliness by the colonial West to the Indigenous civilisations of the Americas was a monstrous one. Bosch's painting describes better than words the ugliness of monstrosity in the 15th and 16th centuries. Hieronymus Bosch (1450–1516) did not live to experience the Reformation in full; therefore, Eco states that he is a 'son of his epoch' (2007, p. 102).[7] When theorising about *The Temptations of St. Anthony*, Eco also states:

His infernal creatures are hybrids reminiscent of the diabolical collages in Baldus . . . They do not spring from a combination of 'known' animal features but have their own nightmarish independence, and we do not know whether they come from the Abyss or whether they live, unobserved in our world. (Eco, 2007, p. 101)

What we do know is that the natures of these unknown monstrous creatures, the unknown feature, is crucial given that it is the space in which Western culture attempted to conceptualise what was new to them. That is, that which was new or simply unknown had to be grasped and conceptualised using a set of existing imageries that Bosch introduced in this painting. The monstrous creatures, almost naturally in a battle with man, are odd, strange, and at times horrendous, terribly, and explicitly evil. The suggested attributes of having a hierarchal organisation, a class differentiation, and even the capacity to fight a battle using Western standards are characteristics that come from Western culture and are therefore cultural anthropomorphisms. The creatures from hell are the product of 'man' (Western culture) because they are similar to them, culturally and politically. In other words, this triptych was chosen as a rich chart of monstrosity enclosed in a given set of narratives. This brief description will follow the narratives from the left panel to the right panel to highlight specific imageries but also to describe its potential narratives. The identified imageries will be considered as the arrangement for the conceptualisation (discursive devices) of indigeneity and the rules of formation that sketch the underlying narratives of this conceptualisation. Therefore, this mapping will start from an aesthetics of ugliness focussed on monstrosity to follow the conceptual arrangement of these imageries and narratives.

FIRST PANEL (LEFT TO RIGHT): REPRESENTATIONS OF FEAR

Hieronymus Bosch's triptych of *The Temptations of St. Anthony* (1505–1506) starts with a narrative representation of horror through the anxieties of wondering what the outcome will be of the invasion by an army of the monstrous. In the first panel on the left, and from the top to the bottom, the calmness is immediately disturbed by flying sea voyages that are being attacked by fish-like creatures. One fish-like religious man is praying, but his body is horizontal. On top of this man, there are wolf-like creatures that reassure the imminence of danger. Similar indescribable images disturb the calmness of the horizon, which indicates a stable past. Focusing on the upper middle part of the first panel, the calmness precipitates the depiction of the aftermath of the battle in the second panel. The pale and dry colours in the first panel indicate death, the end, and a lack of hope. Then, the dark gradients of black, brown, and red in the first panel alter the perspective to an

Figure 2.1. **Hieronymus Bosch's triptych of *The Temptations of St. Anthony* (1505–1506). Modified picture by author.**

imagery that suggests a closer experience of 'seeing'. There are numerous possible interpretations of the situations depicted in the painting, and as the focus moves to the bottom of the first panel, the perception changes and it makes us believe that we are inside a wall. Then, it is clearly seen that two men are helping a third, apparently injured, man and they are all walking on a boarded walkway. These images suggest that they are moving away from the battle scene, perhaps to a safer area. However, on their left, there is a blackness that suggests that anything could intercept them on their way to safety and put them in further danger. In the bottom right, closer to the viewer, there is an indescribable bird-like creature. It is dressed in soldier's armour and its dark eyes penetrate the viewer. In the painting, it is uncertain whether this creature is malicious or not, dangerous or not, but the monster is from hell and therefore must be one of the Devil's servants. The image depicts the creature to be from hell, but in a more odd than terrifying manner. The creature is handing a document in the direction of a representative of the Catholic Church. This man of the cloth is discreetly reading another document. He is hiding below the boarded walkway with other indescribable things in the same blackness on the left of the three men walking on the walkway. The fish-like monsters, the wolf-like monsters, the creature being used as a carriage, the non-Christian priest-like creatures, and the hatching egg giving birth to a bird, with a bird-fish-like creature on top: these images and imagery suggest that these monster-like creatures are not to be worried about just now and thank goodness because they look terrifying. However, some are being represented as having the ability to attack, which indicates that an attack is imminent.

SECOND PANEL (LEFT TO RIGHT): REPRESENTATIONS OF THE TERROR OF WAR

The second panel represents the terror of war and conquest, a display of a 'battle to the death'. Fire, blackness, armoured ships, destruction, beasts, more strange creatures, men from the Church, an owl, a bird, crosses, an evil fish-like creature, giant rodents, dogs, soldiers, and a crucified Jesus Christ are the representations that aid the imagery of war. Combined, this imagery also attempts to highlight the chaos of war. With the same perspective as the first panel, the second panel moves from being distant from the battle to being in the midst of it. It appears to suggest a double movement that simultaneously depicts a far view and a close view. The last movement has the effect of bringing the viewer inside the picture. The truth is even further contested in this panel through the highlighting of the strangeness, with hell being the most feared form of monstrosity in that time period, and a recomposition of Western objects of war (e.g., ships, carriages, armour) that are unique and had never been seen before this painting.

A representation that is prominent in the second panel is the fish-like creature with the red cloth and a machine on top. This is the second creature in red that is prominent due to the intense red colour in comparison to the gloomy grey and black colours that saturate the three panels of the triptych. This fish-like creature (with its part machine) converses with the bird-like creature and the man in red. At this point, red appears to communicate a form of noble distinction in men, while the red colour for the (monster-like) creatures suggests a high-ranking command in the forces of hell by Western standards. The strangeness of the bird-like and fish-like creatures also appear to be important in the ranks of creatures from hell, which indicates that hell's creatures have a similar organisation to those of Westerners.

The colour red operates as a representation of battle, and it explicitly refers to blood, but it also refers to importance, officialdom, and hierarchy. The blood colour is shared by both humans and non-human creatures alike. The non-human creatures appear to have a degree of Western sophistication and intelligence, or simply Western similarity. The red colour appears to be a form of anthropomorphism rather than the mark of violence, of hierarchy, and of sophisticated civilisation. The representations indicate leadership, titles, and differentiation from other creatures of hell, which are anthropomorphisms. The hell creatures that bear red are 'civilised' by Western standards and are not savages in the sense that is understood today.

THIRD PANEL (LEFT TO RIGHT): REPRESENTATIONS OF THE TRAGEDY OF CONQUEST

The third panel in the triptych has less darkness. Faded pastel colours comprise at least one-third of the picture. However, there is more blood red coloured imagery than in the previous two panels. The third panel presents the aftermath of a great and tragic battle, the aftermath of chaos. A flying fish-creature takes a man from the ground from right to left, which suggests that they are moving away from the battle towards sundown in the west. It is the third time that the city is represented, and it is depicted as an invaded city with the visible remnants of a battle, with death very visible, and with many other postwar objects and activities. In the centre of the panel, an old woman, similar to the Virgin Mary, is pouring blood into a cup for the Anti-Christ, who can be seen as an infant. A sizable red cloth covers part of the infant; the cloth covers more than 10 percent of the picture and connects with other strange creatures. Also, there is a man under a dark cloth looking at the viewer. He is hiding his intentions of reading a book; in the context of the image, it suggests that the book is a religious book. At his feet lay blood and dead bodies of both humans and the monstrous creatures from hell. At first glance, the triptych as a whole gives a sensation of hopelessness. However, the aforementioned man, hiding in the black cloth and looking at the viewer, provides a sensation of action: an invitation, an announcement of action, and perhaps a clue that the war is not over. The man appears to suggest that this is a never-ending battle of good against evil, or Western man against Bosch's creatures from hell; a necessary fate and thus in the realm of a tragic narrative. Men respond to the holy story and command of being made from the image of God, and this carries with it a large responsibility that very well could mean the end of their lives, a battle to the death.

As seen in Bosch's *The Temptations of St. Anthony*, the Western taxonomy of an aesthetic of monstrosity at the end of the 15th century and the beginning of the 16th century, which is around the times of the origins of colonisation, displays a narrative that predicated an anthropocentric view of what 'men' feared and hated from themselves; the Western culture's capacity to engage in a tragic and horrendous war for the purpose of conquest where two armies battle to the death. The non-human creatures from hell are monsters because they are not human and not known creatures, even if they have animalistic features. The representation here and the creation of others, particularly of the monsters, is framed within the confines of what is available in the culture's imagination. Bosch's *The Temptations of St. Anthony* shows the narrative frame in which representation encodes Western culture's anthropocentric view of difference, taking its image as the centre of its 'universe'. How does this anthropocentric view of fictional creatures from hell specifically become relevant to the immersion and colonisation of the Americas by the West? How does this Christian fictionalisation relate to what would become known as the 'New World'?

NOTES

1. This phrase is referring to Arthur De Gobineau's 1852 book of the same title.
2. Explained examples will be seen in later chapters throughout the book.
3. For example, in *Critique of Judgement*, Kant writes only a few lines regarding ugliness that obtusely attempts to address ugliness in art without neglecting his obsession with beauty: 'Only one kind of ugliness can be represented in conformity with nature without destroying all aesthetic pleasure, and therefore artistic beauty; namely, that which arouses disgust. For, in this singular sensation that depends solely on the imagination, the object is represented—so to speak—our enjoyment of it were obligatory, while we reject it violently: thus, as far as our sensation is concerned, the artificial representation of the object may no longer be distinguished from the nature of the object itself, and hence it cannot possibly be considered beautiful' (p. 48).
4. Eco's and my reading of Rosenkranz differ from a more recent translation and critical introduction to *Aesthetic of Ugliness* by Andrei Pop and Metchild Widrich (Rosenkranz, Pop, & Widrich, 2017), because it claims that ugliness in this text cannot be reducible to any kind of moralization only. The debate of the moralization of ugliness could add another interesting perspective in the discussion of an analytic of ugliness, yet I found that it did not add an analytic dimension to the origins of colonisation.
5. Marco Polo and other incursions can be considered as preexistent historical processes that are prior to the frame of the Western narrative and therefore have an influence in the colonial narratives; see Federici (2010) and Sáez-López (2011) for further discussion on this.
6. *Conquistadores* was a specific term that was instituted by the Kingdom of Spain to differentiate the first colonisers that participated in the first wars, particularly in México, from the colonisers that continued to arrive from the Americas towards the end of the 16th century (Alegría, 1990).
7. This does not go against the art theory and art appreciation claims that Bosch was very influential in the Surrealism movement in the 20th century (Breton, 1929).

Chapter Three

Monstrous Anthropology

CALIBAN: All right, I'm going . . . but this is the last time. It's the last time, do you hear me? Oh . . . I forgot: I've got something important to tell you.

PROSPERO: Important? Well, out with it.

CALIBAN: It's this: I've decided I don't want to be called Caliban any longer.

PROSPERO: What kind of rot is that? I don't understand.

CALIBAN: Put it this way: I'm *telling* you that from now on I won't answer to the name Caliban.

PROSPERO: Where did you get that idea?

CALIBAN: Well, because Caliban *isn't* my name. It's as simple as that.

PROSPERO: Oh, I suppose it's mine!

CALIBAN: It's a name *given me by your hatred*, and every time it's spoken it's an insult.

PROSPERO: My, aren't we getting sensitive! All right, suggest something else . . . I've got to call you something. What will it be? Cannibal would suit you, but I'm sure you wouldn't like that, would you? Let's see . . . what about Hannibal? That fits. And why not . . . they all seem to like historical names.

CALIBAN: Call me X. That would be best. Like a man without a name. Or, to be more precise, a man whose name has been stolen. You talk about history . . . well, that's history, and everyone knows it! Every time you summon me it reminds me of a basic fact, the fact that you've stolen everything from me, even

my identity! Uhuru! (*He exits*). (*A Tempest* by Aime Cesaire originally published in 1969 [165–185])

THE CANNIBAL

According to the French historian Jules Michelet (1798–1874), 'the real discovery of men started when Christopher Columbus arrived to the islands of
the Caribbean in 1492' (cited in Sáez-López, 2010, p. 470). The importance
of this 'discovery of men' (men here could be used interchangeably with
Western culture) was expressed shortly after 1492. In his dedication in *General History of the Indies* (1522), Francisco López de Gómara said, 'the
discovery of the Américas was the biggest event since the creation of the
world' (p. 156). Furthermore, Fernando de Oviedo was considered to be the
first *cronista* (an early historian) of the Americas who captured what he was
experiencing through both words and images. De Oviedo also felt that he had
to capture everything in drawings and images of the marvels he had seen. He
states: '[i]t is like seeing painted by a *Berruguete*[1] or another great painter
like Leonardo Da Vinci . . . or other famous painters I met in Italy that words
cannot fully describe their pieces . . . all this is better seen that written' (de
Oviedo, 1533, Fol. 91, in Alegría, 1978, p. 312). Many *cronistas* agreed that
the power of words was unable to fully describe this 'New World' that they
were colonising. As a result, the *cronistas* drew images alongside their words
in their diaries[2] that would end up being reproduced as engravings in Europe
and distributed there. These images provided a different account of how
Western culture understood or wanted to understand the Americas, and particularly their peoples. Many images were produced depicting Indigenous
peoples from the Americas, and in the beginning from the Caribbean, as
early as 1493 (Ramírez-Alvarado, 2015) and these drawings were then reproduced as engravings (xylographs or chalcographies)[3] and distributed to most
of Europe from the end of the 15th century onwards. The following three
images in this section are from the beginning of the 16th century, and they
were some of the first drawings of the Indigenous civilisations from Western
culture's perspective. In the obscured history of the ugliness and monstrosity
of the Americas, the method of framing monstrosity was through cannibalism. It is immediately noticeable that the styles of the drawings can be
readily compared with Bosch's creatures in *The Temptations of St. Anthony*
and cannibalism already imagined in the hell section in *Earthy Delights*.
Similarly, yet 100 years later, Shakespeare would write *The Tempest*
(1610–1611)—a play that features Caliban who is a character that has been
associated with the representation of the uncivilized, and even the colonised,
through monstrosity. This section depicts the type of monstrous representations of the Indigenous peoples within the aesthetic discourse: the cannibal.

The first time that the word 'cannibal' was written in the Americas by Western culture (in the Spanish language) was on November 23, 1492. In Christopher Columbus's diaries, he writes: *'y otros se llamaban canibales, a quien mostraban tener un gran miedo. Y desde que vieron que lleva este camino, dice que no podían hablar, porque, los comían y que son gente muy armada'* (de Las Casas, 1522 in Alegría, 1978).[4] In this fragment of Columbus's diaries, it is important to highlight that what he emphasizes is a tone of fear, the practice of eating human flesh, and the alleged presence of armed peoples. The narrative that Columbus presented was already a prelude to a battle against armed and flesh-eating peoples that set the scene for them to be considered monsters. This description is not far from Bosch's depiction of the monsters from hell in both of the aforementioned triptychs. Columbus further attests this point in the days leading up to this entry on November 4, 1492, when interpreting the descriptions of these peoples who attacked the Indigenous peoples from the Caribbean: *'gente que tenía un ojo en la frente . . . entendió también que lexos de allí avía hombres de un ojo y otros con hocicos de perros . . . criaturas monstruosas'* (in Varela, 1984).[5] This description is quite similar to the drawing in figure 3.1 of an Indigenous group capturing and preparing a man to be eaten. In this drawing, which was

Figure 3.1.   Lorenz Fries, *Auslegung der Carta Marina* (Estrasburgo, Johannes Grieninger, 1525).

finalised in 1525, Indigenous men are depicted with inhuman heads, i.e., dog-like heads, but with human bodies. From left to right, one of the creatures is riding a llama with a captured Indigenous man. He holds a whip for the llama. In the centre, another creature (a cannibal) is chopping a man into parts. The cannibal creature is using a cleaver to chop the body parts. The body parts that are hanging above him suggest that they are being preserved as Europeans would preserve meats (using salt) to be eaten later. Another cannibal Indigenous creature is helping with related chores. At the extreme right, a fourth cannibal Indigenous creature is observing the chores being done while eating a human body part, an arm, under a wooden structure. These monstrous creatures inspire fear and sorrow for the fate of the victims represented in this drawing.

It is very likely that representations of cannibalism in indigeneity are inherited from representations of witchcraft in Europe, suggesting a link between conceptual formations of race in colonisation, and gender in earlier Western culture. This linkage is not the focus of this chapter or book, however we must stop at this topic to augment the arguments of this book. Representations of witchcraft in Europe have been a common theme in the language of imagery since the 14th century and some argue that witchcraft imagery, in woodcuts, books, and in many other types of engravings, represented a specific projection that operated as a mechanism of control over women in Europe (Zika, 2009). Charles Zika's work, particularly in his book *The Appearance of Witchcraft*, narrates the history from the 14th to the 17th centuries of this changing witchcraft imagery that is characterised by, wearing loosened hair (similar to prostitutes of the time), displaying hyper sexual drive to animals, monstrous creatures and the Devil, taking male role activities or even completely emasculating men—stories were displayed of witches castrating men and keeping their phallus, and riding phallic objects such as agricultural tools and them domestic ones—later cannibalism, and many more. At one point in the 16th century, witch's representation used the relationship with the devil and the Roman god Saturn interchangeably, where cannibalism features as one his noteworthy myths. Zika states:

> [*The Three-Fold Idolatry of the Roman Church*, a woodcut by Matthias Gerung], . . . this gruesome figure seems to represent a combination of the ancient planetary gods Saturn and mars, and the Canaanite god Moloch. All three were associated with different forms of violence . . . Saturn with cannibalism . . . In the deep left background, a woman kneels before a cauldron on a flaming fire, in which one can see a skull; and beside her on the ground are human limbs she is cooking up. The cauldron in this case specifically emphasizes the physical violence of witchcraft; it suggest the dismemberment of human bodies and acts of cannibalism—themes which . . . only gained prominence in the second half of the sixteen century. (Zika, 2009, pp. 95–96)

Indigenous peoples are also presented with Saturn practising cannibalism in, for instance, the engraving entitled *Novus Orbis* by Johann Huttich and Simon Grynaeus of 1532, where a possible link can be argued. Witches in Eco's work on ugliness (Eco, 2007) is classified along the lines of a monstrosity of Satanism and sadism as well, also where collective rites represented in dances with the devil further added a specific monstrous motif to conceptualisations as mechanism of control, also seen with representations of indigeneity. It also should be highlighted that there was no evidence of witchcraft as a religion until the 18th century, suggesting these representations were mainly fictional to communicate a specific narrative for a specific purpose (Zika, 2009).

The 'authenticity' of Indigenous objects, peoples, practices, and cultural elements in the Caribbean and the Americas is the subject of debate in other works (Alegría, 1978; Chicangana-Bayona, 2008; Robiou, 2008), yet mentioning them here can help further illustrate the Western historical formation of the imageries and narratives of indigeneity. It is noticeable that a cleaver (or a metal knife) is used to cut the body parts, and it is well known that metal was not used for cutting devices in any recorded Indigenous group in the Americas (Alegría, 1978; Federici, 2010). Furthermore, another historical error can be seen in the practice of hanging meat for preservation and the use of a whip to ride the llama. The preservation of meat, the use of the whip, and the metal knives are all distinctive objects and practices from the colonial West in medieval times. This early depiction of cannibalism depicts more than an explicit attempt to Westernise cannibal Indigenous peoples and more than the fantasies of sailors who undertook long voyages on the high seas. Instead, it depicts a preconceived style of illustrating how Europe understood and conceptualised Indigenous peoples in the first colonial experience. That is, this image depicts what Europe was bluntly imagining and conceptualising when they experienced the civilisations of the Americas.

The portrayal of Indigenous peoples here is evidently outside the 'civilised' and 'uncivilised' hierarchal logic. This is seen above and in the picture through assigning Western cultural attributes such as similar cultural objects (metal knives, wooden hut, etc.) and similar quotidian practices (hanging meat for preservation, the way the captured person as carried using the llama, etc.). The Western attribution to the cannibal Indigenous peoples can be compared with the portrayal of the creatures from hell in *The Temptations of St. Anthony* because Western culture is the point of reference in which these monstrosities are described. The cannibal illustration demonstrates how Western culture is the point of reference even in completely different civilisations, and it goes as far as recording historical errors. The monstrous cannibal creatures are not uncivilised or inferior; the West illustrated them with similar cultural practices, almost all identical except that they were monstrous creatures.

The beginning of the use of the term 'cannibal' by Spanish colonisers occurred only one month after the arrival of Europeans in the Americas. The narrative of feared Indigenous peoples began in the description of the first day of arrival in the Americas on October 12, 1492: '*Ellos todos a una mano son de buena estatura de grandeza y Buenos gestos, bien hechos. Yo vi algunos que tenían señales de heridas en sus cuerpos, y les hice señas de qué era aquello, y ellos me mostraron como allí vienen de tierra firme a tomarlos por cautivos*'.[6] It is important to highlight that from the first moment of colonisation, Western culture framed two distinct groups of Indigenous peoples: those that collaborated with the Spanish *conquistadores* and those who appeared to be a menace to their conquest by fighting back.

The drawing in figure 3.2 was finalised in 1505 and it is considered to be one of the first drawings of Indigenous peoples in the Americas (Alegría, 1978; Sáez-López, 2011). The drawing is thought to have been drawn by Americo Vespucio, but this has not been confirmed (Alegría as cited in Sáez, 2010). This is a simpler representation of the Indigenous civilisation of the Tupinamba: an Indigenous man roasting another man. The drawing itself is a map, and at the bottom the man is using a rotating device to cook another whole man over a relatively intense fire. Given the white skin colour of the victim, it is believed that he is European (Chicangana-Bayona, 2008; Ramírez-Alvarado, 2015; Sáez-López, 2011). Therefore, this functioned as a warning to mainly Western peoples, and it was a sign of the narrative around the dangers that needed to be addressed through defending themselves against the cannibals. Furthermore, this illustration is the first depiction of

Figure 3.2.   Map Kunstmann II, ca. 1505, Bayerische Staatsbibliothek, Múnich (Cod. Icon. 133).

the immersion of West as actors in a narrative of a possible tragedy in the Americas. As in the previous picture, the debate around the factual inconsistencies is not the focus of this book, yet the picture is a useful tool to highlight that the roasting method depicted is a European one. However, this again demonstrates the West's cultural anthropocentric attributions to the Indigenous civilisations of the Americas; furthermore, it again depicts Indigenous peoples as a menace to the colonisers.

In the illustration in figure 3.3, which has not been preserved well, there is a later depiction of the 'cannibal' Indigenous peoples in the Americas. It is a group feasting on human body parts while cooking another human. From left to right, the integration of a woman in the practices of cannibalism can also be seen. In the background, there is a depiction of Indigenous houses in the Americas called them *bohíos* (Alegría, 1978). In the middle of the illustration, there are some men devouring the human flesh after it has been cooked. Men of all ages are represented here: a bearded men (suggesting the image of Saturn, the Roman god that castrates his father and eats his sons), bald men (suggesting middle aged), and young men. Notably, they all are effectively naked, but their appearances resemble the physical appearance of Europeans portrayed in the religious paintings of the time. In the middle, there are human body parts cut in pieces that resemble the way a chicken is cut by a butcher. The human body parts are on top of a roasting device that is fuelled by an intense fire and it is being kept intense using a fan that another Indige-

Figure 3.3.   *Wahrhaftige History* (Hans Staden, Marburg, 1557).

nous man is holding. In the bottom right, there is a child eating a small piece of the cooked human. The child also resembles the religious paintings of children or angels of the Renaissance. However, in this picture, this representation of innocence is disturbing given the context.

The imagery in this picture appears to be less Westernised given that the bodies are represented without Western conceptions of clothes, their houses resemble the structures that existed in the Americas at the time (of which some remain today), and the drawings suggest movement that feels like a foreign celebration or a foreign type of feast. However, Westernised attributions remain: they appear to be located in the bodies and in the roasting device. The monstrous communication of this picture lies in the feast of human flesh. Notably, the picture also highlights a child eating the human flesh, which projects pure evil as depicted by the hell section of Bosch's *Earthy Delights*. This imagery of Indigenous peoples in this cannibal feast presents a conceptualisation that is determined by a knot of horror and tragedy.

Around the same time as this engraving, the priest Fray Bartolomé de las Casas, who was a *cronista* and the first advocate for Indigenous human rights, wrote a letter to the Spanish Crown entitled *Brevísimo en relación a la destrucción de las Indias*.[7] This letter was a summarised account of the situation of the Americas that highlighted the horrible events caused by the Spanish *conquistadores*. In one part, when he describes the actions of an unnamed captain of the kingdom of *Guatimala* (today Guatemala), he writes:

> *Tenía éste esta costumbre: que cuando iba a hacer guerra a algunos pueblos o provincias, llevaba de los ya sojuzgados indios cuantos podía que hiciesen guerra a los otros; e como no les daba de comer a diez y a veinte mil hombres que llevaba, consentíales que comiesen a los indios que tomaban. Y así había en su real solemnísima carnecería de carne humana, donde en su presencia se mataban los niños y se asaban, y mataban el hombre por solas las manos y pies, que tenían por los mejores bocados. Y con estas inhumanidades, oyéndolas todas las otras gentes de las otras tierras, no sabían dónde se meter de espanto.* (de las Casas, 1552 in Alegría, 1978, folio VIII)[8]

This account (and much of de las Casas's letter) tells a different story that portrays a picture of terror, of chaos, and of monstrosity as the context and as the underlying narrative; yet, this was produced by colonisation and not by the Indigenous peoples. It is not that the Indigenous peoples were good or bad in Western culture's terms. Many stories tell the history of the Indigenous peoples being portrayed as victims of the *conquistadores*, and therefore being shown as in the famous description of the 'noble savage' (Alegría, 1978). Even the heroic narratives of certain Indigenous peoples, such as the narratives of Tupac Amaru and Lautaro, among others, appear to follow the 'noble savage' narrative given that even these Indigenous warriors alongside their Indigenous resistance groups only went to war with the Spanish, the Portuguese, the French, the Dutch, and the British, in sum with the West of that time, for valid reasons according to the Western framework (Sued-Badillo, 2003). This horrendous narration from a position that condemns the colonisers appears to escape the monstrous conceptualisation of indigeneity, blaming the Spanish. However, it illustrates that even in the 'reality' of this tragic situation, a different view will conceptualise the situation of indigeneity in horrendous terms.

The aesthetic monstrous anthropology of the cannibal framed the manner in which First Peoples of the Americas were conceived and therefore treated in colonisation. There is research in colonial aesthetics, from Mannoni's controversial analysis of the figure of Caliban (Fanon, 2008) to the recent analyses of Western culture's art history tropes of colonialism focusing on cannibalism (for example, see Schreffler, 2005). However, much of the analysis does not go far enough in addressing the critical cultural studies' issues in the socio-cultural codification of these discursive practices and their effects in the operation of colonisation. There is very little doubt that the first colonial experience was a genocide and a crime against humanity, starting with the enslavement of Indigenous peoples. Moreover, the historical process of tragedy and horror appears to stem from the framework of monstrous anthropology and not the other way around. In other words, Western culture framed *indigeneity* in the great narrative of, in the Nietzschean sense, an 'all too human' monstrosity that existed well before colonisation in the hellish history of European culture where colonisers constructed an imagery that represented what they imagined from their aesthetic discursive repertoire and, to an extent, what they desired to see in the Americas instead of a significant inter-cultural exchange that would shed light of the ancestral cultures of the Arawak and Indigenous peoples at large in this 'new world'.

'THE FABLE OF THE *CARIBES*'

aunque dice que el comienzo fue sobre el habla de los Caniba, que ellos llaman caribes, que los vienen a tomar, y traen arcos y flechas sin hierro, que en todas aquellas tierras no había memoria de él ni de otro metal, salvo de oro y cobre, aunque cobre no había visto sino poco el Almirante. El Almirante le dijo por señas que los Reyes de Castilla mandarían destruir a los caribes y que a todos se los mandarían traer las manos atadas[9] December 26, 1493, Christopher Columbus's diaries. (de las Casas & Sanderlin, 1552/1971)

Sued-Badillo (2003) states that the idea of the Americas starts in the Caribbean. 'America' was prominently imagined alongside the monstrous anthropological imagery of the cannibal from its first Western conceptualisation. Also, one must remember that many Indigenous peoples referred and still

AMERICA.

*Eſtrix dira hominum ſcatet auro America: pollet
Arcu: psittacum alit: phomea ſerta gerit,*

Figure 3.4.   *America* **(Galle, Antwerp, 1590–1600).**

refer to the continent today named 'Americas' as Abya Yala. On December 26, 1492, one month after the first written use of the word cannibal and two months after Columbus arrived on the first island of the Caribbean in the Americas, the term *Caribe* was written as a way to correct the supposedly Arawak word *caniba*.[10] The West gave a name to the cannibals, and they grouped the cannibals in the term *Caribe*. Furthermore, Columbus promised to capture the *Caribes* because it appeared that they were the evil Indigenous peoples that needed to be stopped. The *Caribes* are depicted as warrior tribes that raped and pillaged the first Indigenous peoples in the Caribbean. According to mainstream history, the *Caribes* were a warrior tribe that historically had an ancestral grudge against all the *Arawak* group, which were mainly located but not limited to the north of South America (Alegría, 1990; Robiou, 2008). The Indigenous peoples that Columbus first interviewed were called *Taínos*, who are an Indigenous group within the larger *Arawak* group, located in what is known today as Puerto Rico, the Dominican Republic, Haiti, Guadalupe, Jamaica, Cuba, and the Bahamas (Sued-Badillo, 2003). The *Caribes* would sail at specific times of the year, according to specific astrological constellation beliefs, and go to war capturing women and men. They would keep the women as slaves and marry them. The men were sacrificed in very elaborate ceremonies to honour their ancestral rivalries with the *Arawak* groups (Robiou, 2008). They lived in the smaller islands of the Caribbean including what is today called Martinique (Robiou, 2008). According to various historians (such as Alegría, 1978, and Robiou, 2008), the *Caribes* not only practiced ceremonies that involved the sacrifice of captured peoples, but they also practiced ritualistic consumption of human flesh (Alegría, 1990; Robiou, 2008). The *Caribes* also played ritualistic ball games in which the winners would be sacrificed as well (Robiou, 2008). However, the existence of the *Caribes* as a distinctive tribe separate to the *Arawak* is an ongoing debate (Alegría, 1990; Robiou, 2008; Sued-Badillo, 2003). Later in this section, the first argument against their existence is presented.

The *Caribes* were depicted early on as the monstrous creatures of these new lands, and the first Indigenous peoples in contact with Columbus, i.e., the *Taínos*, were depicted as the good Indigenous peoples, or at least the ones who could be 'saved'. This statement is true to the point of being manifested in the naming of the 'good' Indigenous peoples that 'informed' Columbus of the existence of these cannibals. The word *tainú*, and later known as *Taíno*, was the word used in the *Arawak* language to mean 'the good ones', and the Indigenous peoples from Puerto Rico, the Dominican Republic, and Cuba were known (and today are still referred to) as *Taíno* (Alegría, 1978). The *Caribes* appeared to become the explicit conceptualisation space where the West conceptualised all creatures from hell, as in *The Temptations of St. Anthony*, and to justify going to war with them, capturing them, and using them as slaves for mining gold and silver (Sued-Badillo, 2003). That is, the *Caribes* is where the conceptualisation of monstrosity began and followed through historically. Thus, it is from this point that its 'othering' and evolving processes must be examined.

In 1884, Juan Ignacio de Armas, who was a Cuban anthropologist, published an essay entitled *The Fable of the Caribes* that, for the first time, critically analysed the concept of the *Caribes*. This essay has spurred a long debate in many social sciences, and the latest research has supported the essay's argument by stating from analysis of Caribe's diet archaeologists found no evidence that they ate human flesh. Handy (April 27, 2018) showed that, after analysing centuries-old food remains in the Caribbean islands, there was no evidence of human remains that would indicate any sort of cannibalism. In his essay at the end of the 19th century, de Armas argued that the famous tribe called the *Caribes* was a myth created in order to justify the enslavement of Indigenous peoples in the Americas (Alegría, 1990; de Armas, 1884; Sued-Badillo, 2003). De Armas supported this argument first through demonstrating that the Indigenous peoples only ate plants and small animals (*frujívoros*), second through arguing that the kingdom of Spain passed a royal decree (*Real Cédula de Gracia* 1503 in Alegría, 1978) ordering the *conquistadores* to not enslave the Indigenous peoples unless they committed an unforgivable sin such as cannibalism, and third through exhibiting linguistic parallelisms with other known ancient groups in European history and literature that suggested that the name *Caribe* was plagiarised from other stories and myths. After elaborating on these arguments, he concluded that: '*No había dos razas en las Antillas sino una sola . . . La fábula de los Caribes fue al principio un error jeográfico, luego una alusinación y después una calumnia*' (de Armas, 1884, p. 34).[11] De Armas's essay had been mostly ignored until the late 1970s (Alegría 1978; Robiou, 2008; Sued-Badillo, 2003). Although it is located in the modern anthropological discursive space, this essay presented an explicit critical illustration of the monstrous anthropological conceptualisation: because it discussed the key points of the *Caribes* in relation to the capture and slavery of Indigenous peoples, it contested the process in which the West imagined the *Caribes* as cannibals and it presented an argument of how this Indigenous group was an imagined category, in an anthropocentric manner.

De Armas's first argument stated that the stomachs of the *conquistadores* were accustomed to meat and cannibalism was a practice that historically was an extreme act for Europeans (mainly sailors) to satisfy the apparent need for flesh (de Armas, 1884). The Indigenous peoples did not possess the material conditions to be accustomed to eating meat and therefore did not have the organic capacity to crave, consume, and digest meat. When setting up this argument, de Armas suggested that the only ones that could actually have practiced cannibalism were the Spanish *conquistadores* and not any type of Indigenous people in the Antilles:

> *Los únicos casos auténticos de antropofajia en la conquista, fueron cometidos por los mismos conquistadores; porque el estómago de éstos, mui diferente en*

condiciones dijestivas al de los sóbrios i frujívoros indios, no pudo soportar
algunas veces la carencia de carne . . . Los mismos infelices que injustamente
acusados de antropófagos llevaba Colón a España . . . estuvieron a punto de
ser devorados por la tripulación (13).[12] (de Armas, 1884, p. 15)[13]

de Armas argued that the Spanish were the only ones that were capable of eating human flesh when meat was not available. Therefore, this convenient accusation arose from the behaviour of the accusers in relation to what the colonisers could interpret in what they observed from their anthropocentric perspective. Based on a careful revision of the diaries of some of the men on the voyages, some historians (primarily critical historians) support this account of the authenticity of Indigenous cannibalism and they called for historical revisionism; Chicangana-Bayona, 2003; Schreffler, 2005). Notably, the underlying tone of horror and tragedy appeared to be present in the storyline of the *conquistadores* and the Indigenous peoples: from the position of the colonisers through depicting Indigenous peoples as monstrous cannibal creatures that terrorised other Indigenous groups and potentially the colonisers or from other positions, like the arguments of de las Casas and de Armas, that depicted Indigenous peoples as the victims of the carnages of the Spanish.

De Armas (1884) narrated how Columbus in 1493 captured 23 Indigenous persons to sell as slaves: 'Seven from San Salvador, and 16 from Cuba' (de Armas, 1884, p. 24). Only ten survived the voyage, and he sold four in Seville and took the remaining six to the Catholic king of Spain. The king and queen ordered Columbus to return the Indigenous persons back to their lands. However, it was reported that most died during the second voyage back to the Americas and he used the remaining two as interpreters, in effective disobedience to the order from the kingdom of Spain. During the second voyage in 1493, Columbus sent a full ship of Indigenous 'slaves' (700 in total) to be sold in Spain and he justified this action by stating: '*lo han liberado de los antropófagos y ahora los pueblos indígenas podían estar en paz*' (de las Casas, 1495, cited in de Armas, 1884, p. 26).[14] The kingdom of Spain also forbade this. De Armas (1884) stated that Columbus proposed a slave trade, like that emerging from Africa commanded by the Portuguese. The kingdom commanded the 700 aboard the second ship to be freed. However, this proved to be a futile action given that the Indigenous peoples ended up being slaves in Europe where the kingdom of Spain did not have immediate influence. In August 1503, Queen Isabel I signed a royal decree (*Real Cédula*) that allowed licenses to sell African slaves and that, in the case of the Indigenous peoples, only the *Caribes* or other cannibal groups could be captured and sold as slaves: '*y contra los caribes y negros, de acá se pueden, con el nombre de la Santísima Trinidad, eviarlos todos como esclavos que se podrán vender 4,000*' (1503, in Acosta 1589).[15] With allusion to the *Real*

Cédula, de Armas strongly suggested that the *Caribe* tribe was an invention to capture and enslave the Indigenous peoples of the Americas. This royal decree is important because it institutes the historical process of capturing and enslaving Indigenous peoples in the Caribbean through the historical process of cannibalism at least 30 years before Indigenous slavery was solidified after the conquest of Mexico.

The *Caribes* were presented as a warrior tribe and horrifying group that captured other Indigenous peoples without provocation. However, de Armas suggested the opposite, for which he declared that there was more historical justification that the creation of this monstrous Indigenous imagery was for the purpose of justifying the beginnings of Indigenous slavery. The complicit relationship between the monstrous cannibal imagery provides the grounds for instituting the process of horror and tragedy, which followed the process of capturing and slavery using a rationale that cannibals could be enslaved according to God and the kingdom of Spain, which also institutes the narrative frames of capture.

Furthermore, the essence of de Armas's argument lies on the 'fable' part of his title. He concluded that the *Caribes* were nothing more than a myth, a story: something legendary that repeats itself in ancient Western culture's history. He located this fable three times in Western culture's history. The first time he located the story in Armenia, a tribe that Herodotus (the Greek historian, 485–425 BC) described in the ancient times of 400 BC (de Armas, 1884) called the *Calibes* or *Armeno-calibes*. The second location was in Homer's *Iliad*, where it retells a story about the *Alibes* and the *Alizonas*, which indicates parallelism with the word *Amazonas* and *Caribes* (*Ilíada* II, 856 cited in de Armas, 1884). In the third historical location, the same word *calibe* appears in Spain: '*según Justino, había un pueblo de Calibes; por lo cual, por las diverjencias anteriormente notadas, puede creerse que ese nombre, que en griego significa hierro, se dió indistintamente a varios pueblos fuertes e industriales del antiguo mundo*' (Jutino, lib. 44, cap. 3 in de Armas, 1884, p. 4).[16] From here, de Armas undermined the credibility of the existence of a group that had a suspiciously traceable history in ancient Western writings. Therefore, this completes the circle that returns us to the beginning of this chapter where the Western culture frame of reference is located in Bosch's *The Temptations of St. Anthony* and in the imagined creatures in the hell section of *Earthly Delights*. The narrative of the frame of the *Caribes* appears to have a preexisting reference. As mentioned before, the fictionalisation of Western culture's conceptualisation of indigeneity is not judged on its falseness or on its truthfulness; rather, it is judged on its presence or absence, or its positivity. The positivity of the narrative of the frame of the *Caribes* lies in a mythical Western group that may or may not have existed, but that is certainly located in a history of Europe as a narrative that assists in the formation in ways to talk about peoples, i.e., as a language that can form a conceptualisation.

The line of thinking that debates that the *Caribes* was a fable or a myth in factual terms is inconsequential for this part; the importance of this argument's discussion lies on the Europe-based narrative that constituted the discourse the West used to interpret the Americas and its peoples. Certainly, as early as in the 1884, de Armas built a strong case to question the intention behind the story of the existence of the *Caribes*, yet other academics built a strong case in favour of the *Caribes* existence, not necessarily based on cannibalism (Alegría, 1990; Robiou, 2008). The information on both sides illustrates the assemblage of the conceptualisation that Western culture used to construct the narrative frame that is the grounds in which colonisation launched its enterprise of conceptualising the object that it spoke of.

NARRATIVES THAT CONSTITUTE THE WESTERN DISCURSIVE DEVICE OF INDIGENEITY

Western indigeneity as a discursive device became the conceptual grounds to launch colonisation, and one of the first moments that race became weaponised by the West against another culture. At this point, it should become apparent that this 'otherness' was not initially encoded in a Social Darwinist inferiority–superiority dichotomous logic with an absence of complex narratives encoded into the way the discursive device of race was initiated in colonisation: the device of Western indigeneity. The codification of the Western narrative frames of indigeneity are not premised by Enlightenment logic, but rather are conceptualised in storylines that became the rules of formation of colonial representations. In other words, Western representations of indigeneity are not encoded logically but aesthetically. The overarching metanarrative that appears to be at the foundation of this discursive device is a monstrous anthropological metanarrative, constituted by four rules of formations or narrative frames: (1) terror, horror, and tragedy, (2) capturing and enslavement, (3) similarity and anthropocentrism, and (4) conquest.

The first narrative frame or rule of formation allows for certain actions to be justified, e.g., wars, enslavement, assassinations, or any form of degradation, because that which is strange and monstrous holds a non-human quality and for this reason the rules of humanity are applied in a negative sense, i.e., the formation of the rules of non-humanity. These rules of non-humanity initiated the pathway from the first day that Christopher Columbus saw the Indigenous groups and wrote that the Indigenous groups he first encountered said that other evil Indigenous peoples who ate human flesh were attacking them. The cannibal Indigenous person, i.e., the *Caribes* in the first years of colonisation, was the discursive means for a conceptualisation that would aid domination in colonisation. The first colonial encounter was predetermined by an expectation of the relatively known civilisation or culture of the Indies. When Christopher Columbus and the fleet of three boats realised that these cultures were completely unknown, they painted them in their minds with what they already knew as they thought they have arrived to the *'Indies'*. The conceptualisation of un-Christianised creatures determined the 'side' and the narrative in which these creatures were framed; indigeneity needed to mainly occupy the space of otherness. They were a civilisation of dark and irreligious creatures. The Spanish described the Indigenous peoples as very generous at first, but the dangerous ones, i.e., the ones who were not welcoming and resisted colonisation from the perspective of the Europeans, were described with more detail. They were described with monstrous features and characteristics to commit the most horrid nightmares of any being: they ate human flesh (which was something commonly recorded in long voyages such as those from Spain to the Americas). *Therefore, Europeans, in the Freudian sense, projected onto the First Peoples of the Americas the horrors they were capable of and how they imagined how peoples should look if they were to carry out such monstrous actions.* The narrative process of tragedy allowed for some Indigenous peoples to be portrayed as the 'noble creatures' (because savagery was not yet a descriptor) and others as the cannibals, given the narrative allowances that the tragic narrative genre provides—tragedies featuring the coexistence of good and evil as conceptualised by Western culture. This process planted a seed that grew in many narratives of Indigenous martyrs that only fought to continue to live 'peacefully' and it simultaneously grew narratives of 'senseless' warrior groups who inexplicably cooked and sacrificed outsiders, from the *Caribes* to South Pacific First Peoples, such as the 'head hunters' in south Papua New Guinea and the Torres Strait Islands (Nakata, 2007).

This seed of the narrative frame at its core provided the method through which the Western conceptualisation of indigeneity would always be sensed as the 'other' belonging in a 'dark-monstrous' realm. The realm of Western culture is where 'proper' life could be lived and, in contrast, every other realm must have another narrative opposed and therefore predicated to the Western realm. People can 'overcome' this narrative, but the very word 'overcome' relates back—in opposition—to a preexisting narrative of tragedy, of hardship, and mainly of 'otherness' predicated by the dominating storyline of Western culture. Furthermore, Europeans invited these fantastically dangerous storylines, because in medieval times there was an appreciation of extreme situations because they assisted in creating seducing stories of the first *conquistador* and coloniser heroes who experienced fantastic adventures. The narrative frame of horror, terror, and tragedy provides allowances for the characterisation of 'heroes', but these stories were nothing but an imposed self-serving fictional genre. However, the effect of these story-lines was the creation of a space where narratives of tragedy functioned as a monstrous anthropological generator of a Western framing of peoples in the Americas through the racial discursive device of indigeneity.

The second narrative frame is the narrative of capturing and enslavement. Slavery starts with the First Peoples in the Americas.[17] Slavery was the crudest form of capture; the process of capture meant bringing these peoples into the gaze, and therefore into the course of conceptualisation, of the West. The initial motivator of colonisation was extracting all possible 'goods' from the Americas: Christopher Columbus took all that he could carry in the first voyages and Indigenous peoples were not an exception. Europeans captured anything of value, and then they captured the lands, which was not the original intention. Anything that opposed the West was captured with incredible force through enslavement, or worse. However, this process did not only use the means of enslavement, but it also used luring techniques such as titles, mandatory mixing of races, and promises of safety (which were often broken by Europeans). Slowly but surely, the capturing also meant the pacification and settlement-occupation of the Americas; it also meant the transformation of the way in which the Americas were 'seen'. The process of capture does not only refer to explicit enslavement, but it also refers to the control of worldview perspectives. Christianisation, pacification, and later 'civilisation' were a few ways through which to achieve this. For example, the capturing process reframed the ancestral understanding of gold into a Western culture worldview; it reframed human sacrifice into an European worldview of morals; and it allowed for one understanding of individuality and made indiscernible different appropriations of what the Western culture referred to as individuality (Dussel, 1993; Geertz, 1979; Grosfoguel, 2003). Colonisation and enslavement are intrinsically complicit because the latter historically constituted the former, from the capture of peoples to the arrest of worldview perspectives.

The historical process of capturing and enslaving from the *Caribes* and then the Aztecs, and later most other Indigenous peoples, not only integrated the idea of Indigenous cultures into the West's understanding but also brought them into the space of Western culture's system of inequality, which started in the position of slavery if the West did not recognise their previous social status. To bring indigeneity into the Western colonial narrative was to physically capture and enslave. This was the method of bringing *indigeneity* into the light of Western history, where a position in Western space could be provided. Slavery was not the only status provided in the capturing and enslavement process: titles were provided to *caciques* or Indigenous leaders, nobility, and acknowledgements in the colonial endeavour to both Indigenous men and women. In the early 16th century, it was institutionalised that Spanish and other Europeans should marry Indigenous peoples, for example

Hernan Cortes demanded that all colonisers in Mexico to 'marry' Indigenous women, primarily to seize and conquer using the *mestizaje* or mixed races (Alegría, 1990). The capturing process was manifested more explicitly in slavery, but it was not limited to this social status.

The third narrative frame of anthropocentrism, which refers to Westernisation and the idea of 'man' at the centre and processes content through similarities, is closely related to capturing yet it refers to similarity in the anthropocentric sense. In this process, the interpretation of similar representations to the signs and symbols of Western culture is read in the Renaissance and Classical episteme narratives that man is the centre of the universe. That is, the interpretation was from the assumed Western culture's vantage point where everything serves a purpose in an anthropocentric universe, primarily because God created the world and men were created in God's image. Therefore, God's main creatures must have a central role in the universe. Yet everything outside the centrality of God is positioned in the space commanded by the negative image of him, the Devil. This negative space maintains the centrality of God and of men because the position of the Devil and that which is monstrous is in reference to this centrality. The 'discovery of men' that colonisation inspired refers to the discovery of the potential extension of the anthropocentric interpretations of a new and vast space, and for it to be captured. This means that the frameset of Western culture, which interpreted everything in their terms only, was extended to its fullest at the time of the colonisation of the Americas. As the years passed, this anthropocentric similarity system formed a *logos*, or an anthropology, because the readily available known references of the West were not sufficient. An extended language of anthropocentrism had to be created in order to make sense of the overwhelming diversity that the colonisers were encountering in the Americas. The process of anthropocentrism was the underlying position in which anthropology could emerge to conceptualise indigeneity.

Different, and even monstrous, civilisations were conceptualised using the same instruments for cooking, similar political organisations, and similar cultural practices, among other practices that are distinctive of the West but had to be captured through this anthropocentric gaze. This anthropocentric perspective process had not yet been linked to a hierarchal inequality that would make *see* other civilisations in the binary of inferiority–superiority such as Social Darwinism. This happened later when anthropocentrism became constituted as *logos* in philosophical anthropological discourse by Immanuel Kant (Foucault, 2009). The anthropocentric gaze *sees* that which is familiar to Western culture, interprets that which is unfamiliar to the West, and it becomes reconfigured as familiar, and that which is uncaptured remains invisible to the eyes of anthropocentrism. Thus, anthropocentrism is a location in which the visibilities are constantly captured from a position that is not subjective but is very clearly grounded as the centre of the gravitational space, as conceptualised by Western culture. Western culture is the centre of the world and then everything is interpreted in reference to what the West 'knows' and anything outside of the 'known' becomes and is made invisible.

The fourth narrative frame is conquest and it is at the core of the chain of processes of the conceptualisation of indigeneity. It is thus at the heart of monstrous anthropology, because it is the force that makes interpretation possible and skews it to monstrosity when domination is required. The process of conquest is the seed of colonisation and what makes this conceptualisation its instrument as the colonial history solidified it. The first colonial experience began as a mistake. Christopher Columbus and the kingdom of Spain intended to find a new route to the Indies. The first year (1492) in the Americas was characterised by a desire to extract everything possible, which was inspired by the imperial imperative to strengthen the kingdom against possible invaders (Foucault, 2005). However, imperialism turned into colonisation as a result of this will to conquer or to completely own (culturally, physically, epistemologically, etc.) the places it conquered. The Spanish, Portuguese, and French *conquistadores* and colonisers searched for everything that was of value according to the West. The 'pacification' of the Aztec Empire marked a transition between the extraction of goods for the Spanish and other Kingdoms, and the expansion of the West into a never-ending movement of complete conquest for the sake of conquest. The horrific first war against the Aztec Empire explicitly revealed the monstrous anthropology chain through illustrating tragedy, capture, and enslavement, which are the gravitational centre of the 'winning' West and pure conquest. Yet the historical threshold in which the conceptualisation of indigeneity was formed and became consolidated was when the colonisers first arrived, in the Caribbean (mainly what is currently known as Cuba, the Dominican Republic, Haiti, Jamaica, and Puerto Rico) from c. 1492 to 1525. The former three processes preceded later endeavours of conquest that confirmed and folded the conceptualisation of indigeneity. That is, the explicit invasion of the American mainland from 1521 with the 'pacification of Mexico' (see the following chapter, *Blackness*, for more details) added to the process of conquest, which sealed the first conceptualisation of indigeneity.

The monstrous anthropological meta-narrative frame of indigeneity is constituted by the narrative grids of tragedy-capture-anthropocentrism-conquest. The Western conception of indigeneity designed for and within the emergence of colonisation as discursive racial device was crafted historically from an aesthetic discourse perspective and within the historical epistemological stages of the end of the Renaissance episteme and the beginning of the Classical episteme. It can be said that the emergence of representation in the Classical episteme of Western culture as a way to understand the world was inspired by the 'discovery of a new world' and the push to appropriate it aesthetically. It is not coincidental that after the beginning of colonisation cultural-shifting Western writers (e.g., Shakespeare, Hobbes, Prévost, Rousseau, Goethe, Schiller) and visual artists (e.g., Goya, Girodet, Diderot, Delacroix, Doré) who never crossed the Atlantic at times made explicit references to colonial imageries and narratives. Classical epistemological representation was born heavily aided by the emergence of the monstrous and meticulous representation of otherness a refractive inquiry into Western culture's own horrors.

NOTES

1. Alonso Berruguete was a Spanish painter (1488–1561).
2. The drawings made by the *cronistas* were later redrawn by artists usually located in Spain or in other European countries. The *cronistas* did not have authorship other than in the books that were later published (Alegría, 1978; Sued Badillo, 2003).
3. The research for this book included over 70 images of representations of Indigenous peoples from the 15th and 16th centuries by European authors, some of whom never visited the Americas (Ramirez-Alvarado, 2015; Sáez-López, 2011).
4. And others were called *cannibals* to whom they showed great fear. And since they observed that we shared the same route, they said that they could not say a word about them, because they could be eaten (by the cannibals) and that they were very armed people.
5. One-eyed people . . . he understood from those languages that they were men with only one eye and others with dog-like muzzles . . . monstrous creatures . . .
6. They all had good height and made proper face gestures. I saw that some had signs of injuries, and I asked them in signals that what have caused the injuries, and they showed me how other peoples would come and try to capture them.
7. *A short letter about the destruction of the Indies*: an extensive letter in fact with more than 100 pages long.
8. This person had this practice: that when he went to war against any people or province, he took as many indigenous peoples he could so they could fight against them; and since he would not give them any food, 10 and even 20 thousand at a time, he persuaded them to eat the other indigenous people they would capture. Then, he witnessed a brutal butchery of human flesh, that in front of him infants were killed and roasted, and they killed men only to eat their hands and feet, which were regarded as the most delicious parts. When the other peoples would hear these inhumanities, they could not hide their fear.
9. Although he said that they were called *Caniba*, that they call *caribes*, the ones who come to take them, and whom are equipped with bows and arrows not made of steel, that in all that land there is no memory of another type of metal, other than gold and copper, although copper was not so much seen. Columbus communicated through sign language that the kingdom of Castilla would order the destruction of the *caribes* and would have them all bound by their hands.
10. Ramírez-Alvarado (2015) states that Christopher Columbus understood that *caniba* was a *Taíno* reference to followers of Great Khan.
11. In the Antilles there was only one race and not two . . . The fable of the *Caribes* was in the beginning a geographical mistake, then a hallucination, and then slander.
12. The footnote in the essay refers to the diaries of Fernando Colón in which he describes how the men were about to eat the Indigenous people that Columbus had captured to take as an offering to the kingdom of Spain.
13. The only authentic cases of *anthropophagia* in the conquest were committed by the *conquistadores*; as a result of their stomach, they had very different digestive conditions from the sober and *frujíveros* indigenous peoples, and they could not manage the lack of meat . . . The same damned people who were accused of cannibalism that where on the voyage with Columbus to Spain . . . they were almost devoured by the men on the voyage.
14. We have freed them from the cannibals and now the indigenous groups can be in peace.

15. And against the *Caribes y negros*, from now on they can, in the name of the Holy Trinity, send them all as slaves that can be sold 4,000 . . .

16. According to Justino a group of *Calibes*; because the aforementioned divergences, it can be believed that this name, which in Greek means 'steel', was given to many groups that were regarded as industrious and strong from the ancient world.

17. Slavery and its links with the Western conceptualisation of blackness, which is the next important discursive origin in the beginnings of colonisation, are discussed in the next chapter.

Chapter Four

Blackness

Clearly, not all Blacks are Africans, and not all Africans are Blacks. But it matters little where they are located. As objects of discourse and objects of knowledge, Africa and Blackness have, since the beginning of the modern age, plunged the theory of the names as well as the status and function of the sign and of representation into deep crisis. The same was true of the relation between being and appearance, truth and falsehood, reason and unreason, even language and life. Every time it confronted the question of Blacks and Africa, reason found itself ruined and emptied, turning constantly in on itself, shipwrecked in a seemingly inaccessible place where language was destroyed and words themselves no longer had memory. (Achille Mbmembe in *Critique of Black Reason*, 2017, p. 12)

The second chapter of the history of colonisation in the 15th and 16th centuries focused on the second stage of slavery and how the conceptualisation of *blackness*[1] was entangled with slavery. It is important to distinguish blackness from slavery, as they were not the same even within Europe, Africa, and Asia (Frankopan, 2015). In the Americas, the history of Western blackness is often told from the perspective of Modernity or the discourse of anthropology, in a progressive manner where the abolition of African slavery is the climax and the centre of the narrative. This history is dominated by the United States' account of Western blackness (Ocasio, 2011; Sued-Badillo, 2008). Within colonisation in the Americas, the first stage of slavery was the enslavement of Indigenous peoples, which is widely documented and has been persuasively argued (Alegría, 1978; Katz, 2003; Mann, 2006; Weber, 2007). The periods of Indigenous and African slavery are closely linked, but they do not occur in a successive fashion. In chronological terms, both slaveries occur almost simultaneously in the 15th and 16th centuries. If the history of slavery from the 9th and 10th centuries in Europe and the East is accounted for, the story becomes more convoluted and freed from the racial narrative (yet no less cruel, of course). Grounded in the history of colonisation and specifically in the conceptualisation of Western indigeneity, the visible processes of slavery are found that function as the fuel for conquest. In these colonial grounds, it is also found that Indigenous slavery, African slave trade, and Western blackness begin to be conceptualised in the way that these conceptualisations are known today.

This chapter elucidates a pathway to the often forgotten history of the relationship between the Western conceptualisations of *indigeneity* and *blackness* that inaugurated the discursive tool of race in colonisation and, to an extent, in Western culture's history. The aesthetic conceptualisation of Western *indigeneity* defined by monstrous anthropology and institutionalised by 'royal decree' through slavery has a common thread with the conceptualisation of Western *blackness*. Similar to *indigeneity*, *blackness* as a racial discursive tool is not only informed by a 'natural history' of a classification system that would then lead to Social Darwinism because there is a long-standing history of *blackness* in Europe that is not directly linked to slavery or even phenotypic inferiority. That is, slavery until the 15th century was not dominated by those of African descent, and there had been a long-standing record of African peoples in Europe, among other historical threads that will be elaborated in this chapter. The assemblage of *blackness* as a racial discursive, and therefore a colonial tool, is built in parallel with and on the grounds of monstrous anthropology. However, at the same time, it is seen differently when considered alongside the discursive formation of *indigeneity*. In other words, at this point of the book and in this chapter in particular, it is argued that the historical proximity of the formation of *blackness* and that of *indigeneity* (and its direct relationship with slavery) in the first colonial experience resulted in the first vector (or diagonal) relationship that constituted the larger frame of the discursive tool of race. This is not to suggest that Western conceptualisations of *blackness* and *indigeneity* are the same—they are both graphed in different vectoral directions; however, they have a very close relationship that is not linear, but rather diagonal. By a diagonal relationship, I mean a relationship that adds space to the linearity of time (history) and thus is able to connect two points in a plane that whilst they do not share the same 'line', as in the case of *indigeneity* and *blackness*, they can have a relationship relative to its direction in a given system in a plane (Deleuze, 1985). In the case of the racial discursive conceptualisations of Western *indigeneity* and *blackness*, this chapter will illustrate that they share a distinct relationship in the frame or discursive tool of race, within the plane of colonisation.

Both Western conceptualisations of indigeneity and blackness spiral in the current of the history of colonisation, cross over each other at times, find themselves moving side-by-side, and, at one point in the history of colonisation, they converge into a created (infinite) multiplicity provided, no longer by royal decree, but by the sophisticated grids of the discourse of anthropology. The historical threshold of the interchangeability of blackness and slavery predicates the complicity of Western blackness and colonisation. This threshold is defined by the history that occurred in the years before slavery in the Americas turned into slavery fuelled by African peoples. In this space, the close relationship of slavery, the conceptualisation of indigeneity, and the conceptualisation of blackness are seen more evidently than in other accounts of the history of the West. This is not to say that this research states or suggests a history of the causes or roots of colonial contexts around the world. Such a claim could not be achieved in the scope and perspective that this book provides. The only claim that this book makes is that the conceptualisation of blackness and of indigeneity are the grounds on which Western culture built the first primitive representation of race: it being from its very beginning both fictive and true at once (as Mbembe [2017] notes). Furthermore, what follows in this chapter is not only the mapping of blackness, which authors like Mbembe have done all too well recently, but the mapping of the genesis of this conceptualisation in the context of colonisation and its concatenating relationship—from its origins—with indigeneity.

Analogous to indigeneity, blackness in colonisation becomes enthralled in the narrative plane of colonisation, not through the inferiority–superiority Social Darwinist logic (and this chapter will illustrate that this is less the case with blackness) but through a codified narrative that eventually frames blackness aesthetically. Unlike indigeneity, blackness was visible in Western culture given that is was 'seen' in the 'everyday' in medieval times in Europe, as opposed to being seen as a parallax projection of Western image. Therefore, the canvas of Western blackness needs to be painted using the narratives of colonisation. The aesthetic character of blackness will emerge from the existing narrative colours of colonisation; then, the narrative colours of the history of blackness in colonisation will be added as the pure representation of the first racial discourse is fully painted. Before it became discursively and historically interchangeable with slavery in specific colonial places and later nation-states or diaspora characters—simultaneously being imagined as displaced and of the birthplace of humanity, Africa—blackness as we know it did not exist.

Early colonial history interacted with Western blackness in a porous manner because, differing to the conceptualisation of indigeneity, there was a familiarity with blackness and slavery in the 15th and 16th centuries. Slavery carried a non-black dominant history that began its trans-Atlantic link with the Americas through its Indigenous peoples. In contrast, blackness had no specific classificatory meaning in the 15th century and the beginning of the 16th century, as many black peoples (as long as they were Christians) could occupy various roles in Western culture and in the colonisation of the Americas, which they did. The example of a short history of one man, Juan Garrido, provides an account of blackness inside colonial history and as an active participant in colonisation, as opposed to being the subject of colonisation as a slave or worse. After the second half of the 16th century, a formal slave trade was imposed in the Americas, which resulted in the African slave trade that lasted for more than 300 years. In the context of the slave trade, Western indigeneity, slavery, and blackness assembled the discursive tool or the colonial conceptualisation of race.

In the 16th century, and in the following centuries, it is very difficult to separate blackness, slavery, and colonisation because they are entangled in a convoluted history that is not a linear narrative. Therefore, it is very tempting to follow the pre-drawn historical direct pathway of Western blackness that Western culture provided that flattens its history through equating blackness with slavery, and vice versa. Through providing a broader account of the history of Western blackness, the arbitrary nature of Western blackness will become more palpable and how the currents of the history of colonisation pushed it towards the direction that it took in order to assemble the tool or conceptualisation that functioned as part of the operation of colonisation.

BLACKNESS AND SLAVERY: PARALLEL PATHWAYS

On May 29, 1453, Constantinople, the last Greek and Roman bastion of the Christian West, fell into the hands of the Muslim Ottoman Empire (Alegría, 1990); it was known as the *Basileuousa Polis* or 'the Queen of Cities' (Hochschild, 1998) and what today is known as Istanbul. Constantinople was strategically located between the Golden Horn and the Marmara Sea, and it was the crossroads for Western commerce between Asia, Europe, and Africa. Europe did not have gold mines; therefore, when Constantinople fell, a shortage of the precious metal was quickly reported (Hochschild, 1998). Gold was the principal currency material; however, other products were used for exchange such as spices, silver, and other objects (Alegría, 1990). Almost intuitively anticipating this crisis in the 1440s, the prince of Portugal, Enrique '*El navegante*', initiated expeditions to find alternative routes to Africa (Alegria, 1990; Frankopan, 2015). When Constantinople fell, Portugal had already established political relationships with some African kingdoms. Towards the end of the 15th century, Portugal dominated most routes to Africa and, by extension, most commercial relationships between Europe and Africa. Europe exchanged firearms, gunpowder, horses, textiles, and other European products for African spices, gold, ivory, and slaves (Frankopan, 2015). Soon, all other European kingdoms had to recognise Portugal's monopoly in order to participate in the trade with fair prices. The first kingdom to recognise Portugal's monopoly was Spain in 1479, primarily due to the alliance that they had across lineages that lasted until 1580 (Saco, 1879). As the commercial trade grew, the only trade ports were the Port of Lisbon and the Port of Seville (Mann, 2006).

Alvise Cadamoso, who was a Venetian trader, mentioned in his trade records what they exchanged: 'intercambiábamos buques caragados de paños, tela, trigos en abundancia y otros efectos por oro y negros' (Mann, 2006, p. 171).[2] This is not surprising given that Venice was built upon the wealth of the slave trade as early as in the 10th century, or as Frankopan writes:

> Among those with no compunction about human trafficking [in Christian Europe in the 10th century] were the inhabitants of an unpromising lagoon located at the northern point of the Adriatic. The wealth it accumulated from slave trading and human suffering was to lay the basis for its transformation into one of the crown jewels of the medieval Mediterranean: Venice. (Frankopan, 2015, p. 119)

From early on in the ninth century, slaves appeared to be a luxurious enterprise that was comparable to gold in Asia, Northern Africa, and Europe. Venice was not the only city that benefited from the slave trade: from Northern Europe (Viking Rus' and Scandinavia) to Eastern Europe and Western Asia also gained great wealth in selling humans for an array of purposes including wars and personal servants, and slaves were even given as a rare and 'expensive gift' (Frankopan, 2015). In this context, slavery was widely present and yet industries in Europe were not dependant on slave work like what would occur in the Americas for a brief period in the mining industry and later in the sugar cane industry from the late 16th century onwards. Furthermore, until the beginning of the 16th century, slaves in Europe were Slavic, Irish, Scandinavian, North African, Greek, and of many other types of descent, and not exclusively African or 'black'.

A black-skinned person was not something unseen in Europe, especially in Spain. In the eighth century, Muslims from the north of Africa invaded most of the kingdom of Spain. From the 13th to the 15th centuries, large segments of the population of Lisbon, Seville, and other cities were black because many roads were opened from Africa as an outcome of this invasion (Alegría, 1990). This can be seen not only in the different records of trade, contracts, decrees, and other legal documents, but also in the emerging literature of the time. For example, in the Golden Age of Spanish literature during the 15th and 16th centuries, many characters in novels were described as black. Authors including Miguel de Cervantes in his works *El coloquio de los perros* and *El celoso extremeño*, and Lope de Vega in his *La Dorotea* and *Servir a señor discrete*, among others, described the non-slave black presence in everyday society in Europe (Alegría, 1990). Similarly, important figures in Europe were of African descent,[3] for example Alessandro de'Medici (first Duke of Florence), Juan de Pareja (Diego de Velázquez's assistant), and bishops and priests from Ethiopia and Congo would also be appointed by the Vatican.

In Africa, Portugal established close bonds that guaranteed a monopoly of the commercial routes. In 1489, the kingdom of Portugal established a very close relationship with the kingdom of Congo, particularly with their ruler Nzinga Mbemba (Alegría, 1990). In order to honour this friendship and to be accepted in the eyes of the Western kingdoms (particularly in the eyes of the Vatican), Nzinga Mbemba converted to Christianity in 1490 (Hochschild, 1998). He was given the Christian name Alfonso I. After this, he became the first king to bring Christianity to the African continent. Soon after, Nzinga had created a full Catholic infrastructure that had direct links with the Vatican in Rome. After the kingdom of Congo was recognised as a Catholic kingdom by Pope Alexander VII (Rodrigo Borgia, a former bishop from Spain), Nzinga sent clerics from Congo to the Vatican to serve as representatives of the kingdom of Congo. This was achieved as a result of the influence of Portugal over Spain, who was the Pope at that time (and who was one of the most controversial Popes in the history of the Vatican), and of the Borgia family being one of the most influential families in Europe at the time (Rolfe, 2010).

In this context, it was not rare to find black-skinned men arriving in the Americas in 1492–1493 who were not slaves. Out of an estimated figure of 90 sailors in the first ships that arrived in the Caribbean at the end of the 15th century, Alegría (1990) and Sued-Badillo (2008) identified at least 12 black-skinned men who were non-slaves with identified roles in the expedition. There could be more black-skinned men given that it was not necessary to record the sailors' skin colour as black. (However, this is how historians were able to identify some.) To identify black-skinned figures in history is a contemporary preoccupation. In the records of the 15th and 16th centuries, the term 'black skin' was usually found as a descriptor next to the name or in the identification details that might distinguish a subject in the same way the descriptors of handless, *buen mozo* (handsome), *el bello* (the beautiful one), *judío converso* (converted Jew), or *de Segovia* (from Segovia, a province in Spain) were used to describe people. The jobs of the black men identified by Alegría (1990) and Sued-Badillo (2008) varied from miners to merchants, from sailors to *conquistadores*, and from soldiers to scribes. The records describe that black-skinned slaves were only introduced towards the end of the 15th century in the Americas, but the records also described that the slaves were not exclusively black. Some records included slaves from other skin colours such as *pardos* (a form of brown). However, there were no records of white-skinned slaves introduced into the Americas (Sued-Badillo, 2008).

When the kingdom of Spain, and later other European kingdoms, arrived in the Americas, neither black skin nor a specific skin colour determined slavery. This is not to suggest that in the 15th and 16th centuries there was no inequality—it was a period distinguished by inequality—however, institutions[4] such as the Church or medieval aristocracy lineages determined that inequality. For example, inequality was fiercely practiced on non-Christian peoples, recently converted Christians, Jews, and Muslims, among other groups (Rolfe, 2010). In 1492, the kingdom of Spain issued an edict that all Jews should be driven out of the kingdom and their territories (Rolfe, 2010); Christopher Columbus narrated that this happened 'in the same month I was to undertake my expedition to the Indies' (July 30, 1492). Similarly, in that same year (1492), the fall of Granada ended the Muslim domination over the Iberian Peninsula (Alegría, 1990). These non-Christian categories, which constituted their relationships with the main institutions of Europe (such as the Vatican), determined social statuses, recognition of kingdoms by the Vatican, and recognition by other important kingdoms. This also sometimes determined the plausibility of invasions and it facilitated allegiances between kingdoms. Imperialism was a 'game of thrones' that resulted in a hierarchy of kingdoms confirmed by institutions such as the Catholic Church. If this social hierarchy with slavery at the bottom was not determined predominantly by skin colour during the period in which the first colonial experience occurred, then the formation of 'blackness' was predicated by a set of previous historical processes interwoven with discrete threads outside the modern racial categories and slavery rationalised by an inferiority–superiority binary of humans or Social Darwinism.

Slavery in the 14th and 15th centuries in Europe was primarily domestic and white: slaves were mostly women and the recorded preferences for slaves were the ones describes as 'not so rare' ('*no tan raras*' in Sued-Badillo, 2008). As mentioned above, slavery in Europe was a luxury; there was no recorded time in the 14th and 15th centuries where slavery had significant numbers in contrast to the Roman Empire and the ninth century in the caliphates in various cities in North Africa and in Spain (Alegría, 1990; Frankopan, 2015). Eastern Europe provided most of the slaves, but slavery was recorded across the periphery of the West (Sued-Badillo, 2008). For example, in the kingdom of Italy (particularly in Rome), the preference was for Greek slaves even though the Vatican forbade this from the 10th century onwards (Sued-Badillo, 2008). Christopher Columbus's voyage records[5] illustrated that when trade with Africa began in the mid-15th century, more black-skinned slaves were introduced. Furthermore, Columbus was from Genoa, a maritime state that had ties with Venice and Northern Africa, which had histories built on the wealth of slave trade. Alegría (1990) and Sued-Badillo (2008) argued that slaves from Africa were usually captured enemies or the product of internal conflicts and interests in African kingdoms. Through slavery, these conflicts found a way to send people out of Africa, and some of those persons were key figures in African politics. Some records recount stories of captured African royalty with claims of important statutes, including claims to African thrones (Alegría, 1990), who were sold as slaves in order for others to make those claims. While the luxurious slave trade was mostly white in the 14th and 15th centuries, the African slave trade existed, including black-skinned slaves, yet these were not interchangeable with slavery as would happen with the slave trade to the Americas starting from the mid to late 16th century.

In Europe, slaves were accustomed to having a degree of freedom in the contexts in which they worked (Alegría, 1978). For example, domestic slaves were allowed to have their own time after their working hours finished (Sued-Badillo, 2003); other slaves would not see their 'owner' for months at a time, and when they met it was only to divide the profits that the slave had made as a product of his or her work. These and other arrangements were characteristic of *ladino* (urban or city) slaves. The *ladino* slaves were the first slaves that arrived in the Americas (Alegría, 1990; Sued-Badillo, 2008). For these slaves, the changes in working conditions were very dramatic when they moved from Europe to the Americas. From living in houses or flats, they had to sleep in the open or under a tree in the lands of the Americas, lands that were often tropical jungles. From primarily working in domestic or artisanal industries, the *ladinos* were forced to work in dangerous industries including mining, which involved very manual labour such as heavy lifting and transporting heavy precious metals from the mountain rivers (where gold was first found in the Caribbean) to the improvised ports on the coastlines, and using very rustic tools to find the gold and other precious metals. These severe working situations provided the conditions for the first *ladino*-led slave rebellion in 1514 (the first black slave rebellion in colonial times) on the island of San Juan, which is Puerto Rico today (Alegría, 1990; Sued-Badillo, 2008).

At this point, it should be apparent that blackness at the beginning of colonisation was not interchangeable with slavery, that inequality was determined by the otherness which institutions such as the Church or aristocratic family lineages decided, and that the slave trade was very profitable due to its luxurious characteristics. These origin histories of blackness in colonisation are important in order to see the contrasting grounds in which blackness was then built upon before the slave trade emerged in the Americas and lasted for over 300 years. The contrasting grounds in which Western blackness emerged in colonisation helps us see the canvas in which this imagery was painted. In the next section, through the story of Juan Garrido, we will see a short example of how blackness is described at the end of the 15th and the beginning of the 16th centuries in complete opposition to slavery.

JUAN GARRIDO, THE BLACK *CONQUISTADOR*

I, Juan Garrido, black resident of this city, appear before Your Mercy and state that I am in need of making a *probanza* to the perpetuity of the king, a report on how I served Your Majesty in the conquest and pacification on this New Spain, from the time when the Marqués del Valle entered it; and in his company I was present at all the invasions and conquests and pacifications which were carried out, always with the said Marqués, all of which I did at my own expense without either salary or allotment of aboriginal people or anything else. As I am married and a resident of this city, where I have always lived; and also as I went with the Marqués del Valle to discover the islands which are in that part of the southern sea where there was much hunger and privation; and also as I went to discover and pacify the islands of San Juan de Buriquén de Puerto Rico; and also as I went on the pacification and conquest of the island of Cuba with the *adelantado* Diego Velazquez; in all these ways for thirty years have I served and continue to serve Your Majesty. For these reasons stated above do I petition Your Mercy. And also because I was the first to have the inspiration to sow wheat here in New Spain and to see if it took; I did this and experimented at my own expense. (Juan Garrido, 1538, Folio I).[6]
(Probanza de Juan Garrido, 1538)[7]

A clear example of a history of blackness that is in complete opposition to slavery in the context of colonial times in the 15th and 16th centuries in the Americas is perhaps the first recorded history of the black *conquistador* Juan Garrido. The *Probanza of Juan Garrido* in 1538 is the first historical material of a black man in the Americas that includes interviews with witnesses answering questions about Juan Garrido. The story of Juan Garrido is isolated from slavery and provides an individual historical account of blackness in the beginnings of the colonisation process that does not only demonstrate the arbitrary relationship between skin colour and inequality, i.e., black skin and slavery, but also showcases the practice of colonisation in its individual form before the function of colour.

Other examples of black men could be cited, for instance the history of Miguel Enriquez who was a rich merchant of the Americas (Lopez-Cantos, 1998), and at least nine other black *conquistadores* have been identified in the 16th century in Peru, Venezuela, Costa Rica, Honduras, and Panama.[8] However, Juan Garrido's story is the first illustrative example of blackness not being indistinguishably interchangeable with slavery in the 15th century and most of the 16th century. It is also an illustration of blackness on the other side of subjugation. This opposite of subjugation does not suggest a contradiction that nullifies the merits of any claim regarding the horrors of slavery or a distance from colonised peoples due to the apparent historical divergence. Quite the opposite: it illustrates a nonlinear relationship that positions the history of Juan Garrido all too closely to the historical process of slavery, Western (conceptualisations of) blackness, and colonisation.[9]

What is known of Juan Garrido is predominantly derived from the histori-cal document *Probanza de Juan Garrido del 27 de septiembre de 1538*. One of the first publications of Juan Garrido's story was the 1978 article by Peter Gerhard entitled 'A Black Conquistador in Mexico', and then in 1990 in a book by Ricardo Alegría entitled *Juan Garrido: A black conquistador*. Both publications used the *probanza* from 1538 as their primary historical source. In the *probanza*, Garrido outlines his contributions to the colonisation of the Americas from 1501 to the 1530s, notably the contributions of the colonisa-tion of San Juan, Florida, and Mexico, and also his contribution of being the first person to introduce wheat to the Americas. The *probanza* tells the story through ten questions in interview format that are then answered by seven well-respected witnesses. The first question asks if the witness knows Juan Garrido and the next nine questions are asked with the intention to confirm his contributions and to verify the living conditions of Juan Garrido at the time of the *probanza*. Each witness answers every question; if the witness has no knowledge of what is being asked, this is recorded. Each witness is presumably a distinguished person of the time; the witnesses include Alonso Escobar, El Bachiller Alonso Pérez, Rodrigo Salbatierra, Alonso Martin de Xerez, Juan Gonzalez de León, and Pedro de Vargas. In the content of the questions, Juan Garrido attempts to demonstrate that he was in the first colonisation process alongside important colonisers including Juan Ponce de León, Diego Velázquez, and Hernan Cortés in the Great War against the Aztec Empire, which occurred inside and around the city of Tenochtitlan.

Juan Garrido was originally from Africa; however, the specific place and kingdom to which he belonged is not clear (Alegría, 1990). It is known that Garrido was converted to Christianity in Lisbon sometime before 1494. The first record of Garrido residing somewhere was in 1494 in Seville (Gerhard, 1978). Sometime between the years 1499 and 1501, Garrido crossed the Atlantic and arrived on the island called La Española (today, Haiti and the Dominican Republic). La Española was the most important island for the colonisers at that time as Spain's colonised territory was primarily concen-trated in the main islands of the Caribbean; the mainland of the Americas would not be formally occupied for another 30 years. Juan Garrido came into contact with Nicolás de Ovando who was the representative of the kingdom of Spain in the 'Indies' at the time. From 1501 to 1508, there is very little record of what Garrido did in La Española. Historians speculate that, like most colonisers at that time, he organised expeditions to find and mine gold in the rivers located in the heart of most Caribbean islands (Sued-Badillo, 2008). In 1508, Juan Ponce de Leon was appointed to officially occupy the island of San Juan (Puerto Rico today), and Juan Garrido was part of the expedition to colonise the island. There, he helped to 'pacify' the island and protect it from the attacks from Indigenous peoples, many of which were recorded to be attacks from the *Caribes*. Garrido participated in the defence, construction, and reconstruction of different settlements in Puerto Rico. There, Garrido extracted a considerable quantity of gold as well. This is known because it was mandatory to give 20 percent of the gold found as a tax contribution to the kingdom of Spain and his name was on the royal tax records, which suggests that he had a mining group, which was typically composed of some colonisers and some Indigenous peoples from the island of Puerto Rico.

In 1513, Juan Garrido went with Juan Ponce de Leon and a small expedition to find the 'fountain of youth'. The Indigenous peoples from the island of San Juan and the island of Cuba had told a story to Juan Ponce de Leon that to the north of the Caribbean there was a place where the waters would make whoever bathed in them younger. It is unclear whether this story was told by the Indigenous peoples as a way of interesting the colonisers in other lands so they would leave the Caribbean, or whether it was a fictionalisation imagined by Ponce de Leon as a reason to expand the invasion to the north (Alegría, 1990). The small expedition sailed to the north and did not find the fountain of youth or the land described by the Indigenous peoples, but they found a vast land they later named *La Florida* (today, the US state of Florida). This was the first time that Western culture made contact with North America. Ponce de Leon, Garrido, and the rest of the expedition sailed back to San Juan. Ponce de Leon immediately asked the kingdom of Spain to fund a large expedition to find this fountain of youth and to colonise the vast land of La Florida. The historical gossip stated that Ponce de Leon knew that the king of Spain had recently married a much younger queen and that a fountain of youth would interest him (Alegría, 1990). In 1521, Ponce de Leon received authorisation from the kingdom of Spain and resources for a large expedition to find the fountain of youth. Garrido helped organise the expedition and went with Ponce de Leon as one of the highest-ranking soldiers.

On the way, the expedition stopped in the islands of Guadalupe and Martinique where the *Caribes* lived, or so the records stated,[10] and they helped 'pacify' the islands in order to facilitate their settlement. These islands were very small, but it was where many ships would stop to replenish their water rations before heading to Europe, and also when they arrived in the Americas from Europe. When the expedition arrived in La Florida, they were viciously attacked by the Indigenous peoples, as if the Indigenous peoples were expecting them. The expedition could not even leave their ships and go ashore. In the battle, Ponce de Leon was badly injured, and the expedition withdrew, failing to colonise the area at that time (Alegría, 1990). Ponce de Leon had sustained a deadly wound and Garrido took him to the island of Cuba, where Ponce de Leon wanted to die. Ponce de Leon died in July of that year and asked Garrido to sell his properties and give the money to his family.

In Cuba, Garrido was informed that Hernan Cortes was about to conquer the great city of Tenochtitlan. Cortes gathered all the Spanish forces he could and also looked for support from the Indigenous nations in the areas surrounding Tenochtitlan. These Indigenous nations had been enemies of the Aztecs for many years, and some were sources for slavery for the Aztec empire but did not have sufficient strength to fight them alone (Iglesia, 1942). Cortes promised these Indigenous nations that they would take the city and give them their part; however, history proved that this was a lie. Garrido found Cortes in Veracruz in 1521 and quickly became a very important soldier in his ranks. The great battle started in that same year in August and lasted for more than two months. The Spanish side had close to 200,000 soldiers and the Aztecs had 300,000 (Iglesia, 1942; Solís, 2004). Garrido fought alongside Cortes in many battles. He even participated in the great battle at Montezuma Temple, which was the foundation of the Tenochtitlan empire (Alegría, 1990). After the great battle at Montezuma Temple, Tenochtitlan fell and the Spanish took Mexico. They renamed it *Nueva España* (New Spain). In Garrido's *probanza*, he asked all witnesses:

> 4. Yten si saben etc que yo pase a esta nueva España en compañia del Marques del Valle don Hernando Cortes y estuve con el syempre hasta que se conquisto e pacifyco toda la tierra e me halle y estuve presente en la conquista de T ascala hasta tanto que se dieron de paz.
> 5. Yten si saben que despuesde pacificada la provincia de Tascala el dicho marques se vino a esta cibdad de Mexico y estando en ella los naturales de la tierra herharon della al dicho Marques y españoles que con el estavan y le mataron mucha gentes.[11]

El Bachiller Alonso Perez answered:

> A la quarta pregunta dixo este testigo que estando sobre esta en . . . [roto] . . . el marques del Valle en la calzada de Acachinango como el dicho Juan Garrido de color negro andava syrbiendo en lo que le mandava velando e yendo a los lugares . . . [roto]. . . mandavan como lo otros conquistadores lo hazian e que esto vida este testigo y siempre lo tubo por conquistador al dicho Juan . . . Juan Garrido fue desta ciudad con el marques del Valle a las yslas que descubrio e bolvio perdido a esta cibdad e que esto sabe.[12]

When Spain aimed to colonise Mexico, it was expected that those who participated in this war would be rewarded (Iglesia, 1942; Solís, 2004). However, new colonisers continued to arrive from Europe to participate in the invasion and the pilfering of the resources of the Americas. The first colonisers felt that they were entitled more recognition and lands than the new colonisers that arrived after the first wars against the Indigenous peoples. Therefore, the kingdom of Spain acknowledged the first colonisers through creating the title of *conquistador* that held a higher position in the lands of the Americas (Alegría, 1947).[13] El Bachiller Alonso Perez speaks to this recognition and testifies how Juan Garrido was recognised in the Americas with the title of *conquistador* giving evidence of the lands that Garrido held in Mexico City next to Hernan Cortes's lands.

The last story that Garrido was known for in Mexico was that he was the first person to introduce wheat to the Americas. In the colonisation of the lands of Americas, colonisers wanted to introduce the farming products that were the basis of the European diets, particularly products from Spain. Plants and animals were introduced in the Americas in order to test the fertility of the lands. The first grounds that were tested were those in the islands of the Caribbean. However, due to the tropical nature of these islands, the attempts to grow wheat were futile. Wheat was very important for the colonial West given that it was the basis for products such as bread, and flour was used as a means of exchange. By the beginning of the 16th century, the colonisers had attempted to grow wheat numerous times, but they were unsuccessful. One day, Juan Garrido opened a bag of rice and he found three wheat seeds. He planted them in his lands in Coyoacan, Mexico City, and they grew successfully. It is recorded in the official history of Mexico that Juan Garrido was the first person to grow wheat in the Americas, and it is depicted in some historic representations including the murals of Diego Rivera in the *Palacio Nacional* in Mexico City.

The intention of the *probanza* in 1538 was to demonstrate to the kingdom of Spain through respected witnesses that Garrido was a well-respected *conquistador* so he could request the entitlements that he deserved as a *conquistador*. Although he already had lands in Mexico City, he reported that he and his family 'were in need' ('*padece necesidad*'). The text suggests that he was not given a pension or the monetary entitlements that he deserved, and it is explicitly stated that he was not given Indigenous peoples (*indios*), the first slaves in the Americas.

The purpose of telling the story of Juan Garrido in this chapter is to describe the blank canvas in which blackness in colonisation was created. In the context of Juan Garrido, slavery becomes the absolute contrast of his story, similar to other *conquistadores* (the newly created social status in the Americas) yet not the same due to the unequal relationship that Garrido had with the Spanish Christian colonisers. Furthermore, Garrido is not the exception (of the time) as mentioned above, he just constituted a story that became minimised by the advent of a new system of social status created from the very bottom, starting from slavery.

SLAVERY

As highlighted so far in this book, the first period of slavery in colonisation was the enslavement of the Indigenous peoples of the Americas. It was almost unthinkable in the 15th century and in the early years of the 16th century to start a slave trade, as it was understood then, to the Americas primarily because slaves were so expensive. (Note that de Armas [1884] indicated that some had proposed a slave trade from the Americas during this time.) Conversely, to enslave the Indigenous peoples, with no need for long voyages across the Atlantic, was as profitable as the gold that Spain, and all of Europe, avidly wanted to extract not only because slavery provided the labour in this industry (and later others), but also because slaves were as valuable as other highly regarded merchandise that were used as currency from at least the eighth century in Europe. Slavery had an intrinsic value in itself: slaves were considered valuable assets because slaves represented pure value. This section aims to chart the value of the slave trade beyond slave labour, suggesting that slavery discursively threaded wealth into blackness, which added to the ferocious exploitation of the Americas.

The great quantity of gold, silver, lands, potential slaves, and other goods valued by Western culture legitimised the representation of the abundance of the Americas:[14] colonisers wanted Indigenous slavery to continue. In this context, de Armas's argument of the invention of the cannibal *Caribes* as a means to justify the enslavement of Indigenous peoples appears even more plausible. The first prohibition from the kingdom of Spain (in 1493) of the enslavement of Indigenous peoples was an obstacle to further capitalising what Western culture regarded as valuable 'resources'. There was a moral debate about the 'humanity' of Indigenous peoples and whether they could be considered 'human' (Christians), but clear exceptions to this consideration would be unforgivable sins such as cannibalism. For almost 100 years, colonisers benefited from the luxury of the 'free' slave labour of Indigenous peoples. Slave trade in Western culture has a long-standing history of generating wealth, and the important European families and kingdoms were well aware of this. Some suggest that it is suspicious that the humanist debates about Indigenous peoples were followed by an increase in the African slave trade that benefited important houses or influential families in Europe (Alegría, 1978; Frankopan, 2015). Yet free slavery in colonisation was not something that would only be enjoyed by colonisers in the Americas for too long: the regulation and imposition of the African slave trade would capitalise on its preexisting lucrativeness exponentially and it would transform into one of the most profitable industries in the history of Western culture.

In 1518–1523, Carlos V, the emperor of Spain and Holy Roman Empire, authorised the first license to sell a large number of slaves from Africa to the Americas (Alegría, 1990; Sued-Badillo, 2003). The license was given to the

Dutch Duke Lorenzo de Goredot for 4,000 slaves. Then, this license was distributed to other traffickers in the Americas, mainly to the principal colonies in the Caribbean. For example, 1,200 African slaves were sent to the island of San Juan (Alegría, 1990).[15] Many of the main *conquistadores* protested the introduction of this new market of slaves because they were forced to buy these very expensive slaves. In practice, the kingdom of Spain was regulating and institutionalising African slavery for the first time in Western history. Therefore, black slavery was forced upon the colonisers as they were expected to pay the full value of the slaves, between 100 pesos and 500 pesos[16] per slave, which was a very high price at that time (Inikori, 1976). This market regulation and institutionalisation would benefit the interests of many families and kingdoms in Europe given that it created a means to attain more profit than the gold and other goods that the colonisers were required to send back to Europe as tax. Some resistances to the regulation of slavery and the institutionalisation of African slavery in the Americas that are mentioned by historians such as Sued-Badillo (2003) include hiding the Indigenous peoples and declaring to the authorities that they had died of disease or that they had escaped to other islands or other unexplored places in the Americas. Some have argued that to conclude that Indigenous peoples, in many cases, died of introduced diseases is to not appreciate the complexity of this history (Alegría, 1978).

The introduction of African slavery occurred slowly but steadily in the Americas. There is relative consensus in the historian community that close to 13 million African peoples (mainly from the southwest part of the continent) were enslaved and shipped to the Americas (Ianni, 1976; King, 1943; Mintz, 1981). As listed in figure 4.1 from 1526 to 1575, more than 110,000 African slaves were trafficked and sent to the Americas (Ianni, 1976). It can also be seen that, in 1576, the African slave trade suddenly tripled in number compared with the figures in the previous years. From the end of the 16th century until almost the end of the 18th century, the slave trade continued to consistently increase from approximately 150,000 in the 16th century to a record high of 2 million in the 18th century (which was the period when the British Empire controlled the slave trade). Very few industries in Western capitalist history have registered an almost consistent incremental (and at times exponential) growth for almost 300 years.

In 2002, Jean-Pierre Tardieu expanded on the idea proposed by Sidney Mintz (1981) that theorised that slavery became the model of profit and production that significantly influenced capitalism. Tardieu (2002) stated, 'a black slave was worth because of his capacity to produce . . . early on slavery was constituted as a commodity' (p. 57). From the mid 16th century, the slaves in the Americas were used as collateral, were listed in wills to be inherited, and could be used to buy most things (Tardieu, 2002). Monetary amounts in today's currencies cannot determine the value of slaves in the

Años	Senegambia	Sierra Leona	Costa de Barlovento	Costa de Oro	Golfo de Benín	Golfo de Biafra	África centro-occidental	Sudeste de África	Totales
1501-1525	12726	0	0	0	0	0	637	0	13363
1526-1550	44458	0	0	0	0	2080	4225	0	50763
1551-1575	48319	1168	0	0	0	3383	8137	0	61007
1576-1600	41778	237	2482	0	0	2996	104879	0	152373
1601-1625	23862	0	0	68	3528	2921	322119	345	352843
1626-1650	30360	1372	0	2429	6080	33540	241269	0	315050
1651-1675	27741	906	351	30806	52768	80780	278079	16633	488064
1676-1700	54141	4565	999	75377	207436	69080	293340	14737	719674
1701-1725	55944	6585	8878	229239	378101	66833	331183	12146	1088909
1726-1750	87028	16637	37672	231418	356760	182066	556981	3162	1471725
1751-1775	135294	84069	169094	268228	288587	319709	654984	5348	1925314
1776-1800	84920	94694	73938	285643	261137	336008	822056	50274	2008670
1801-1825	91225	89326	37322	80895	201054	264834	929999	182338	1876992
1826-1850	17717	84416	6131	5219	209742	230328	989908	227518	1770979
1851-1866	0	4795	0	0	33867	2	156779	30167	225609
Totales	755513	388771	336868	1209321	1999060	1594560	5694574	542668	12521336

Figure 4.1.   Slave trade from Africa by region (Ianni [1976] in *Capitalismo y Esclavitud* [Capitalism and Slavery]).

16th century because it is difficult to calculate and define one currency that has a universal value, even gold and silver have an evasive universal exchange value (Frankopan, 2015). That is, many forms of exchange currencies were valid: land, timber, spices, meats, jewellery, weapons, gold, silver in its natural form, and certain foods like flour are some examples of objects that were used as means of exchange (Ianni, 1976). The history of the symbolic character of exchange value of certain currencies is characteristic of the classical period yet it remained in flux. Although the material conditions of the Americas were regarded as abundant, it was a crude abundance where at times the colonisers lacked the basic means of exchange, such as formal currencies (Mintz, 1981). Therefore, many types of valuable merchandise could be used as a means of exchange, including slaves.

The value of one slave fluctuated according to their inherent physical and personal characteristics (what would be understood today as personality traits), where they were from (*ladinos*, directly from a specific African kingdom, or born in America), age, physical capacities, gender, and previous work experiences (Frankopan, 2015; Tardieu, 2002). However, there is some agreement that the price fluctuated between 200 and 500 pesos in the 16th century (after which the price increased further), which was a very high price. Sometimes, if the slave was a *ladino* with 'good manners', male, in a productive age, and strong, the price could reach close to 700 pesos (Sempat-

Assadourian, 1969). In Mintz (1981, p. 111), some records of prices are stated as follows: 'March 7, 1597, in Cordoba de Tucuman (today Argentina) 6 Angolan slaves were sold for the total of 1125 and ½. 24 of July of 1598, Gasparde Quevedo bought in the name of the Attorney General of Santiago de Chile, 2 slaves with a golden chain which worth was estimated to be 450 pesos.' The record goes on detailing the slave trade of that wealthy trafficker and illustrating the volatility of the prices of slavery and the different means of currency exchange. It appears that the symbolic use of currencies was mixed with the symbolic meanings of what was exchanged. In the process of selling the representation of a wealthy merchant, gold, pesos, and other currencies, and the exchange of such amounts of money and blackness appeared to blend into a mix in which wealth and blackness could be regarded as interchangeable. In this context, *blackness* from Africa or Europe, filling the void of the representation of slavery at the time, was starting to have as much meaning in terms of wealth as gold, silver, pesos, and other goods in the Americas and the West. Thus, *blackness* was starting to represent pure *value* (exchange value and use value).

The currencies and different means of exchange used in the 16th century were being redefined in every region in this 'New World' that the West had coined the Americas. The idea that the chaotic process of redefinition of use value, currencies, and means of exchange in the first colonial experience, and then it becoming an incubator of capitalism as we know it today, is not a new one (Mignolo, 1996). At least Castro-Gómez (1996), Dussel (1993), Grosfoguel (2012), Mignolo (1996), and Quijano (2000), who are the major coloniality–decoloniality theorists, have explicitly stated that capitalism and Western civilisation were historically formed through the process of colonisation that began in the Americas. Similarly, some contemporary historians argue that modern European milestones would not have been possible without the wealth accumulated out of the colonisation of the Americas. Frankopan referring to colonisation states:

> The age of empire and the rise of the West were built upon the capacity to inflict violence on a major scale. The Enlightenment and the Age of Reason, the progression towards democracy, civil liberty and human rights, were not the result of an unseen chain linking back to Athens in antiquity or a natural state of affairs in Europe; they were the fruits of political, military and economic success in faraway continents. (Frankopan, 2015, p. 197)

However, this raises the question of which industry or industries in the colonial context more powerfully enabled the logics of democracy and even of capitalism to begin.

It is rightly argued that Western culture's period shifting events, such as the Industrial Revolution, French Revolution, and others, were materially made possible by the ransacking of the America's wealth: gold, silver, and

other precious stones were stolen and later industries such as mining, plantations, and others only profited colonisers (West, 2002). It is also argued that
Indigenous and African slavery provided the labour for most of these industries, yet the argument does not consider the previous historical implications
of slavery in Europe and in early colonial eras. Slavery and the African slave
trade not only provided the productive force or labour to bestow wealth on
Europe to constitute Western culture as a virtual dominating culture, but they
also showcased one of the model industries for capitalism, as illustrated
above in the figures of the African slave trade. Furthermore, the natural
progression of Tardieu's (2002) argument would have to conclude that the
value of African slavery in the Americas was not only constituted by a use
value, but also by a considerably present exchange value. A step even further
to this argument would be to consider the pure value of African slavery as a
constitutive connotative meaning in its interchangeability with *blackness*. In
other words, *blackness* inherits not only the connotation of the slave in its
dimension of forced labour, but its assemblage is also constituted by pure
value that includes use value and exchange value.

Moreover, the discursive mechanism functions as follows. If the African
slave trade was influential in the constitution of wealth, to the extent that it
represented wealth, it could therefore be argued that the symbolic value of
wealth and its closeness to slavery, and thus its interchangeability with *blackness*, could have a function close to the core of the means of exchange and
pure value. In the sense that gold arbitrarily has a pure value, as a result of
the Classical period's understanding of value that determined that it was this
metal's function as a sign of pure value, blackness had a role in the constitution of the long history of pure value closely related to the history of profit.
This has been confirmed in the Americas for over 300 years as shown in the
table above. Blackness's discursive representation of wealth is further confirmed in the Americas as African slaves continued to be used as a means of
exchange. *From a discursive standpoint—that does have real manifestations
and is no less grounded on material elements—blackness operates with a
pure value element at its heart fuelled by the 'black gold' of slavery that
Western culture built as a means to spur capitalism.*

I must reaffirm that it is insidious to put a value on human beings, even if
that value determined today is about the past. Furthermore, I must affirm that
slavery in all its forms and in all periods of the history of humanity is
genocide. The most horrible genocide in the history of humanity is the traf-
ficking of slaves from the 15th century to the 19th century. However, when
navigating through the dark corners of the history of Western culture, which
is ultimately part of the history of humanity, it is wretchedly necessary to
continually re-present, visibilise, and illuminate all dimensions of this bar-
barism.[17]

LOS TRES MULATOS DE ESMERALDAS: PROCESSES THAT CONSTITUTED THE CONCEPTUALISATION OF BLACKNESS

At the end of the 16th century, in 1599, Adrián Sánchez Gallque, an artist of Indigenous descent, painted one of the first recorded paintings in the Americas, entitled *Los tres mulatos de Esmeralda* in Quito (Gutierrez-Usillos, 2011); today, it is exhibited in *El Prado* Museum in Madrid. It is not a coincidence that this was arguably the first 'formal' representation of Western indigeneity and blackness in the Americas, and it serves as a cultural history text or material to showcase the aesthetic discursive rules of the first racial conceptualisations in colonisation. This painting will be used to illustrate the processes that constituted the Western conceptualisation of blackness, considering its overlap with the processes that constituted the monstrous anthropological conceptualisation of indigeneity. The Western conceptualisation of blackness has a historical overlap with the conceptualisation of indigeneity due to the link with slavery: Indigenous peoples were subjected to slavery in the Americas and the African slave trade would replace this. Therefore, considering the processes that constituted the conceptualisation of indigeneity, i.e., tragedy-capture-anthropocentrism-conquest, the conceptualisation of blackness is built in dialogue with these processes in order to assemble the set of processes of *colouring-cultural practice-social status-and-value*. In this sense, *Los tres mulatos de Esmeralda* (1599) showcases one of the main products of colonisation: the aesthetics of race as a discur-

Figure 4.2. *Los tres mulatos de Esmeralda* **(1599)**

sive tool or the aesthetic conceptualisation of race for the subjects it spoke of. That is, the birth of race as an aesthetic discursive tool.

The conceptualisation of indigeneity, which is defined using monstrous anthropology, was assembled through a set of historical moments for which Indigenous peoples were subjected to colonisation. That is, the conceptualisation of indigeneity in colonisation was built through the historical instances in which the colonisers spoke of it in order to dominate or colonise. As elaborated in the previous chapter, the processes that constitute this conceptualisation are tragedy and horror, which provide the narrative formation within the frame of the cannibal monstrosity form that it took in the Americas; capture, which provides a subjugation narrative formation within the frame of forced labour and slavery towards Indigenous peoples; anthropocentrism, which provides a stance formation within the narrative that Indigenous peoples (cannibals and non-cannibals) would be understood from projecting only a Western framework and not from an inferiority–superiority Social Darwinist hierarchy (which would begin later in the 17th and 18th centuries); and conquest, which rather than only extract all that was possible to make the kingdoms in Europe more powerful, it enabled a narrative of occupation of the territories, the lands, and the subjects that ignited the expansive movement that became characteristic of Western colonisation. The conceptualisation of blackness must be understood in the context of the assemblage of race as a discursive tool of colonisation; given the origins of race, it should also be understood as a specific tool for the purposes of colonisation. *In other words, race was born in colonisation from the aesthetic conceptualisation of indigeneity and blackness. Los tres mulatos de Esmeraldas* is grounded in the processes that constitute indigeneity, but it also showcases more explicitly the processes that constitute blackness. Therefore, it is used here to illustrate the processes that constitute the conceptualisation of blackness within the background of the conceptualisation of indigeneity.

This oil painting represents the three *caciques*, i.e., prominent leaders, of the Esmeraldas (today, Ecuador): Don Francisco de Arobe and his two sons, Don Pedro and Don Domingo, who are first generation descendants from African and Indigenous peoples in the Americas. The painting's title is a conceptual mistake—a fitting way to begin to address the painting—given that the represented *caciques* were (pejoratively) called *zambos*, *cambujos o lobos* and not called *mulatos* given that they were the successive union of Indigenous and African peoples; *mulatos* is a (despective) name used to refer to a successive union between a white European and a black person from African decent or origins (Gutierrez-Usillos, 2011; Sued-Badillo, 2008). Furthermore, the area was one of the first material and discursive crossroads or borderlands between the viceroyalty of Peru and that of Panama that resulted from the tumultuous activity between Indigenous and African groups, pirates from kingdoms of Britain and others in Europe, and the vivid cultural mixing among Indigenous nations of the area and African freed slaves. Regarding 'cultural mixing', the report that accompanied the painting stated that Indigenous and African groups:

> Los quales se mezclaron entre los dhos [dichos] yndios y tomaron sus rritos y/ ceremonias y traje y las mujeres que les pareció de las más princ/cipales y cacicas y se fueron apoderando y señoreando de aquella/tierra e yndios della, como lo an estado y están de más de sesenta años a esta parte. [Would be both mixed, the Indigenous and they took their rites and ceremonies, and clothing and women, what they thought would of most importance and their female leaders and they took and possessed those lands and their Indigenous peoples as a nation and they have retained it for more than sixty years.] (AGI, Quito 25, N25, 33, año 1600)

Their power in that area (and in other places in the Americas such as La Española) was such that these *caciques* claimed that they represented over 100,000 people in that region (Gutierrez-Usillos, 2011). They declared the area to be *The Republic of Zambos*. The painting was an offering to the kingdom of Spain that was sent alongside a report of the 'pacification' of the area (Descalzi, 1996). *Los tres mulatos de Esmeralda* is illustrative because it not only depicts a very important part of colonial history, but it also discursively depicts at least four denotative elements that are very visible: colour, cultural practices, value, and social status.

Firstly, the painting presents the advent of colour becoming more than just the descriptor to, at times, identify people (alongside their name), but it demonstrated to the kingdom of Spain who dominated the area and it verified their alliance. Skin colour, in reference to blackness, until the end of the 16th century would hold a descriptive quality and would not determine social statuses. Juan Garrido is the perfect example of how skin colour operated on the opposite side of colonisation, as he had an active role in the first colonial experience. The historical documents that speak of Juan Garrido provide evidence of his role in the colonisation process and no other narrative is deployed. However, in this painting, black skin is one of the primary signs deployed to confirm that the Republic of Zambos ruled Ecuador in 1599. *Cimarrones* were first Indigenous and then African slaves that escaped their slavery, and the offspring of peoples subjected to slavery, i.e., *mulatos*, are in charge of a colonised land. The monstrous anthropological conceptualisation process, through similarities to the process of anthropocentrism, was no longer alone given that the process of contrasting colour became a vectorial dimension to the framework of the narrative process of race. Colouring appears to begin the highlighting and contrasting[18] processes in all their possible combinations. The process of contrasts defines the relevance of colour.

When colouring, even if it is a piece of paper that is all one colour, it is visible only by its contrast. The piece of paper is regarded as though it was coloured due to the contrast of the former colour of the paper and the new colour. Furthermore, paintings are defined by the contrasting of colours, the limits of painted objects, and their colours; they can suggest texture, depth, and perspective. Colouring as a process of conceptualisation that implies a set of preexisting colours that functions to refer to each other. *Los tres mulatos de Esmeralda* presents blackness to communicate who rules over this territory: it would not have been necessary to send a painting to communicate that a coloniser rules a given territory in the Americas in the 16th century. Thus, contrasting in direct opposition, yet in a vectorial direction, to Western projections required confirmation by colour.

The cultural practices are illustrated symbolically with golden adjournments, weapons, clothing, and gestures of grace, which indicate a representation of cultural difference from Western culture and, at the same time, of specific cultural meanings to the various Indigenous and African peoples that the *caciques* unified. By the end of the 16th century, more than 150,000 African peoples had been brought to the Americas, mainly from the Yoruba peoples (where Nigeria is today) (Sued-Badillo, 2008), as *ladino* African slaves were too few to be imported at that rate. As illustrated above, an exponential increase of the African slave trade was imposed on the Americas, primarily focusing on the Caribbean, Brazil, and a few other places in South America. For example, in 1554, 1,500 slaves arrived in Lima and this later influenced the constitution of the Republic of Zambos (Guitierrez-Usillos, 2011). By 1599, a more elaborate conceptualisation of Indigenous civilisations had been achieved. Languages, rituals, weapons, appearances, and other elements were identified as 'Indigenous' or as 'African' (and were being identified as *mulato* or *zambo*). The painting presents the contrast of a canvas of a group of Indigenous and African *zambos* men coloured by the cultural practices as projected and thus represented by Western culture, even the Indigenous descent of Gallque could only draw from this newly formed aesthetic discourse of race.

In this painting, the new aesthetic discourse of race communicated that the three *caciques* are Indigenous men, from the Western conceptualisation of indigeneity, through illustrating their adornments and their bodies, but also through illustrating the difference of Western indigeneity by wearing gold, Spanish clothing, polished spears with metal heads, and gesturing using Western gestures of 'grace', which indicates a performance of leadership as conceptualised at the time, which was very closely related to nobility and aesthetically comparable with similar European paintings such as the portrait of *Don Sebastian King of Portugal* (1574–1578, also in the Prado Museum) among others (Gutierrez-Usillos, 2011). The highlighted contrasts between Western indigeneity and Western culture inverted the previous Western anthropocentrism attributions. The colonised would no longer be understood in Eurocentric or anthropocentric terms only, but also in contrasting terms that were visibly differentiated through cultural practices.

In this painting, value is presented most notably in the depiction of the type of clothing, in gold, and in other valuable objects such as the elaborate spears that each of the subjects holds. The colours of black, yellow (gold), white, and brown were used to indicate the spectrum of hierarchy that is illustrated in this painting: this hierarchy was defined through what is considered valuable for Western culture. The painting presents very bright and golden Indigenous adornments that demonstrate wealth but also tradition that distinguished the Indigenous peoples in the area of Ecuador. This colouring of value, with the very visible gold signifier, branded the conceptualisation of Western indigeneity and Western blackness as valuable. Adornments, indicating tradition, and the facial skin of the three men denote a positive relationship between pure value and Western blackness and indigeneity. In the conceptualisation of indigeneity, slavery continued to carry a meaning of luxury from Europe, and later in the imposition of the African slave trade, it became a means of exchange due not only to the labour but also to its pure value. It could be argued that the painting displayed not only yellow (gold) as cultural sign that could be associated with value, but also the value that is associated with the colour black could be linked to cultural practice as represented in its juxtaposition with culturally valuable objects. Colour and cultural practice in this painting operate in a process hinged in difference, but that is signified as a valuable resource and as a cultural commodity.

Lastly, the titles of *Don* were given to the *caciques* and this highlighted their social status as non-slaves (Gutierrez-Usillos, 2011; Sued-Badillo, 2003). This needed to be illustrated in order to distinguish them from the African slaves: a dialectic of social status is created constituting a new narrative. The visibility of blackness in the painting communicates that they were leaders with noble titles through communicating that it needed to demonstrate that they were not slaves. The title of *Don* was a feudal title given in the context of Spain that differentiated the dons from the rest of the population, as all titles did in medieval times. This illustration of nobility, in addition to denotatively communicating the granting of these titles, also shows the colouring process using these cultural devices, and how it was processed through proposing a Western social status device. This social status device was closer to a hierarchal system, and it moved away from a system of differentiation using titles. The social status device here was used to propose merit and acknowledgement of the power that they held in the area, and it suggested a possible 'promotion', even to the *zambos* from Indigenous and African backgrounds. This colouring referred to the hierarchies that one group of peoples, with the primary colours of Western indigeneity and Western blackness. The way that the painting presents the three *zambo* men—one depicted from one side, the other depicted the opposite side, and the front-facing man in the centre, the father—suggests an invitation to the viewer to inspect the subjects and confirm their social status. To colour using the colours of social status creates a spectrum of hierarchy in which its highest position is depicted before the eye of Western culture, establishing a given set of possibilities from above that were not all slave-like yet did not compare with the possibilities of being free from a dialectic of social status predicted by the newly formed skin of race.

Juan Garrido received the title of *conquistador* as a result of his protagonist role in the first years of colonisation. The precondition for this title was to be Christian, for which he was converted many years prior (1494). That is, Garrido would be judged because he was not Christian born. Therefore, inequality was predicated through being converted to a religion. This is a similar discursive formation or narrative as capture, where it allowed for a dichotomous system for which the subject it spoke of would be Christian or not and, if not, they could be enslaved. The conceptualisation of indigeneity had a capturing process for which it operated through framing a subject in a specific way in order that it could be captured, dominated, and (often) enslaved. The social status process allows for a more complex form of capturing for which a given spectrum of inequality was assembled, in which the historical foundation includes slavery. Here, the interchangeability of Western blackness and slavery embedded in the foundation of the social status spectrum and linked with colour and cultural practice as difference and value as a process that highlights the historical involvement with wealth. In *Los tres mulatos de Esmeralda*, the social status granted to the *caciques* was referenced to slavery, which indicates the end possible point of the social status spectrum. In other words, the social status narrative in Western blackness there is a capture in the dialectic of social status as given by the coloniser.

After 100 years of exposure, drawings, paintings, engravings, writing (diaries and books of 'General and Natural Histories'), and knowledge-making at large that aimed to capture Indigenous cultures in the Americas in an understandable frame of analysis, and of over 150,000 African slaves sent mostly to the Caribbean and South America by the end of the 16th century (Ianni, 1976), Western culture had elaborated a language to aid the identification of the subject it spoke of in colonisation: the language of cultural practice constituted by a necessary set of symbols to identify indigeneity and blackness. The symbols of cultural practice are only relevant to non-Western peoples, as colonisers did not need to identify themselves as such. Lastly, these cultural practices, symbols, and colour, within the spectrum of social status that begins with an underlying position of slavery, are mediated by a process of value that includes not only use value but also pure value. In the painting, the 'coloured' *zambos* were well represented in Western blackness and indigeneity, but also represented as peoples of social status, as *Dons*.

Here, the discourse of race was being conceptualised as resources or assets of the kingdom of Spain because an agreement had been reached with them, and they accepted the titles and recognition of Spain to become a republic (Descalzi, 1996) in Western terms.

In the end, Oviedo was correct in writing in 1533 'all this is better seen than written' (Oviedo in Sáez-López, 2011): the colonisation of the Americas through the first racial conceptual tools of Western indigeneity and blackness, as it is best seen in *Los tres mulatos de Esmeralda* (1599). This painting illustrates the first blueprint of the tools of colonisation, fully drawn, coloured, and assembled. The Western conceptualisations of indigeneity and blackness are the tools found in the painting, which also functions as a historical map of the processes that constituted these conceptualisations. The conceptualisations here are solidified and ready to be used for the purposes of colonisation. Notably, *Los tres mulatos de Esmeralda* less implicitly depicts the processes that constitute the conceptualisation of Western blackness: colouring-cultural practice-social status-value. The conceptualisation of Western blackness is vectorially related to the conceptualisation of indigeneity, linked through the historical plane of slavery and constituted by colonisation in the 15th and 16th centuries, mainly in the Caribbean areas. Rather than only mapping these conceptualisations using the clues from writings in diaries, chronicles, or history books, the conceptualisation of indigeneity and blackness can be revealed through imagery, through the logics of aesthetics. The conceptualisation of Western blackness finds its initial racial discursive solidification in the potentially first European-like painting of the Americas in 1599, *Los tres mulatos de Esmeralda*, displaying the links with the conceptualisation of indigeneity. Again, the history of the painting functions as an allegory to the argument of this chapter given that whilst the painting was shipped to be presented, alongside a report, to the Spanish King Felipe II, he died while the painting was travelling to Europe (Gutierrez-Usillos, 2011). Perhaps this could be interpreted as a presage of the death-driven pathway and fictive or virtual quality of the discourse of race yet as we know, with very real effects on people in colonisation and beyond.

NOTES

1. By blackness, I do not mean the concept utilised to create the Black Identity that has emerged in civil rights movements around the world. In order to avoid confusion, 'blackness' must be understood as it is accompanied by 'Western' in order to identify this conceptualisation as predominantly constituted by the West.

2. '[B]oats full of fabrics, textiles, wheat in abundance, and other products for gold and blacks'.

3. In the Harlem Renaissance, historians like Puerto Rican Arturo Schomburg tried to rescue important African and Black figures that were excluded from the discipline of history.

4. See chapter 5, -'The Inequality of Human Races', where inequality is discussed referring to the end of the period in which inequality was determined by institutions and the beginning of the period in which inequality was determined by race.

5. These records can be found in the Massachusetts Historical Society archives in the research notes of Alice Bache Gould (1868–1958).

6. Juan Garrido de color negro vesino desta cibdad paresco ante Vuestra merced e digo que yo tengo nescesidad de hazer una provanca a perpetuad rey memoria de como e servydo a V.M. en la conquista *e* pasificación desta Nueva España desde que pasó a ella el Marqués del Valle yen su compañia me halle presentt! a todas las enfradas e conquista e pacificaciones que se an hecho syempre con el dicho Marques todo lo qual e hecho a mi costa syn me dar salaryo ny repartimiento de indios ni otra cosa slendo como soy casado e vecino desta cibdad que syempre e ressedido en ella y asi mismo fue e pase a descobrir con el Marques del Valle las que estan desa parte de la mar del sur donde pase muchas hambres e nescEsidades y asi mismo fue a descobrir e pacificar a las Islas de San Juan de Buriquén de Puerto Rico y asi mismo fue en la pasyficadón y con· Quista de la Isla de Cuba con el adelantado Diego Velazques en todo lo qual a treynta años que yo e servydo e syrvo a S.M. por ende a vuestra merced pido que avyda ynforrnacion de lo susodicho e de como yo fui el primero que hizo la **ysplrielcia** en esta Nueva España para sembrar [rigo *e* ver si se dava en ella lo qual hizo) espirimente fado a mi cosra y as; hecha la dicha ynformacion vuestra merced me la mande dar synada.

7. This is the opening of Juan Garrido's *probanza*, which is a document that was used to prove merit that would justify an allotment or a specific grant for money, lands, and/or any other form of resources (Alegría, 1990; Gerhard, 1978).

8. Kellog and Restall (2001) lists most of the black *conquistadores* through accessing other sources in Latin America as well as in the Archive of the Indies in Seville. He names Sebastián Toral, Pedro Fulupo, Juan Bardales, Antonio Pérez, Juan Portuguéz, Juan García, Miguel Ruiz, Juan Valiente, and Juan Beltrán as black *conquistadores*.

9. It must be mentioned that scholars are increasingly aware of black roles and their suspicious absence from historical records. The current increase in the publication of colonisation accounts appears problematic, see for example Matthew Restall's *Maya Conquistador* (2001).

10. Historians including Cancel (2000) and Sued-Badillo (2003) have persuasively argued that the Indigenous peoples who were fighting against the Spanish colonisers sailed to these islands to temporarily stay and plan their attacks on the main islands. Cancel (2000) identified the reports of attacks on the main islands, analysed the attack practices of the Indigenous peoples, and drew parallels with the Indigenous civilisations in the main islands. He also identified the Indigenous peoples that the *Caribes* would 'capture', most of whom were Indigenous peoples in slavery conditions.

11. Translation: 4. And do you know that I arrived to this *Nueva España* alongside the Marques del Valle don Hernando Cortes and I was with him until it was conquered and until everywhere was pacified, and I was present in the conquest of Tascala (Tenochtitlan) until peace was pronounced? 5. And do you know that after the province of Tascala was pacified, I came with the aforementioned Marques to the city of Mexico with all the other Spanish soldiers that were with him in that battle where many others died? (Garrido, 1538, in Alegía, 1990, Folio 3).

12. To the fourth question, this witness said that being on the (broken) . . . the Marques del Valle (Hernan Cortes) in the top of Acachinango like Juan Garrido of black colour said was serving through being ordered to fight and go to places (broken) . . . and he was sent like all the other *conquistadores* and this witness always regarded the aforementioned Juan Garrido as a *conquistador* . . . Juan Garrido was always distinguished along side with the Marques del Valle and because all the islands he helped discovered which is known by us all (Perez in Garrido, 1538, Folio 8).

13. The title of *conquistador* included rights to lands of their choosing, as well as specific monetary and slave entitlements. This practice started after the great battle of Tenochtitlan and it was abolished in 1541 (Iglesia, 1947).

14. It should be remembered that when the West arrived in the Americas, they thought they had arrived in the Indies.

15. This is consistent with the later proportions that positioned the Caribbean second in the Atlantic slave trade (35%). The largest proportion went to Brazil with 40 percent (see the National Center for History Report on *Atlantic Slave Trade* published in 2000).

16. One *peso* was usually made of gold or silver, and each peso was equivalent to 8 or 9 *reales*. It is demonstrated later that it is very difficult to give a present day account of the value of a peso during that time.

17. I felt compelled to include this part in the text because I do not want my argument to be misunderstood: I am not arguing that peoples had or have determined prices. This chapter was particularly difficult for me to write given that I am also a descendant of African slaves.

18. Note that the word *contrast* is used and not *differentiation*. Differentiation is too open to describe this process given that there is a clear frame of reference that refers to a clear juxtaposition between one thing and the other.

Part 2

Command (Queensland, Australia)

Chapter Five

Biopolitics in Colonisation

The Inequality of Human Races

> It would be difficult to describe our feelings as we sailed towards that great land of *cannibals,* a land which, viewed from a scientific, political, commercial, or religious point of view, possesses an interest peculiarly its own. Whilst empires have risen, flourished, and decayed; whilst Christianity, science, and philosophy have been transforming nations, and travellers have been crossing polar seas and African deserts, and astonishing the world by their discoveries, New Guinea has remained the same . . . where the natives may be seen in the cocoanut groves [*sic*] mending their bows and poisoning their arrows, making their bamboo knives and spears, and revelling in *war and cannibalism* as they have been doing for ages. (MacFarlane, 1888 in Nakata, 2007, p. 16).

In part 1, this archaeology has unearthed the global aesthetic origins of the conceptualisation of *indigeneity* and *blackness*, or the conceptualisation of racial tools used from the 18th century onwards as markers for the local administrative functionality of the command of colonisation, as it is clearly still used in the above quote from the end of the 19th century, and is the object of critical inquiry by Professor and Indigenous scholar Martin Nakata. In *Disciplining the Savages, Savaging the Disciplines*, Nakata (2007) examines major publications and reports produced that continue the discursive evolution of *indigeneity* and *blackness* (which are interchangeable in many countries in the Pacific), such as *Among the Cannibals of New Guinea* (1888) by Reverend Samuel MacFarlane. Indeed, Nakata's archaeological[1] excavation into the 19th and 20th centuries of the Western system of thought, which was informed by a philosophical discourse of anthropology, argues that the previous discursive formations of *indigeneity* and *blackness* are ascribed to Torres Strait Islander peoples. The careful examination of texts such as the voluminous *Cambridge Anthropological Expedition* (1898) reports and many other publications of the London Missionary Society and government policies—and of particular importance here, the 1897 Aboriginal Protection and Restriction of the Sale of Opium Act—clearly illustrate that the ethnographical 'findings' and assumptions are mere parallax projections onto the monstrous other and are also inferiority inscriptions that belong to a system of inequality predicated by the now prevalent Social Darwinism. With Modernity and its episteme, i.e., the discourse of philosophical anthropology, a second fold emerges from the 18th century onwards as a second stage of the operation of colonisation that, in addition to projecting on its aesthetic content to speak of the colonised, inscribes an operational form predicated by a system of inequality for which its imagined 'highest degree' is its own maker, the Western man.

The following chapters present an illustration of how colonisation operated and functioned in the modern period. The question that guides this chapter is: if the focus of the Modernity episteme is its incommensurable hidden function that determines the relationship of objects in relation to other objects and no longer just the content of its (primarily aesthetic) representation, how was colonisation operationalised in Modernity? As highlighted in the introduction of this book, it seems that colonisation studies have transited between a local historical critique to a global historical one, e.g., coloniality and postcolonial studies critique, and settler colonial critique, as if these locations—the local and the global—are mutually exclusive and one being subsumed by the other. However, settler colonial or post-Enlightenment colonisations did not occur in a historical vacuum nor were they only located in a macroscopic world historical epoch where everything is subsumed by the laws of an overarching colonisation logic. At the same time, an archaeological approach would contain us to the historical period where the philosophical anthropological discourse (henceforth, discourse of anthropology) reigns and, thus, colonisation is formulated more as an operation yet not disconnected from the aesthetics conceptualisations of race forged in the 15th and 16th centuries. In Modernity, we find that the biopolitical character of colonisation focusing on its form of governance uses the aesthetic conceptualisation of race as the frame, as opposed to the content, for which peoples were to be managed as undesired races of the state. This chapter will set the scene for the excavation of colonisation in the post-Enlightenment period in the next two chapters. An illustrative example of the heterarchical operationalisation of colonisation will be reexamined using Queensland, Australia, as a case study focusing on the pure function of colonisation.

The pages that follow examine the operationalisation of the discursive device of race in its shifting focus from aesthetic content to form in order to function as a biopolitical marker to exert colonisation. It will be argued that race becomes explicitly tied to inequality through the epistemological and discursive function of the discourse of anthropology, as scholars such as Martin Nakata have intimated. This should not suggest that colonisation and race abandon aesthetics: here, it is assumed that race as a discursive forma- tion is assembled aesthetically not focussed in the narratives of a constituting history or, simply, the aesthetics of race no longer focusses on its content. From the 18th and 19th centuries onwards, there was a shift where inequal- ity, as the organiser of life and death, was no longer determined by institu- tions such as Christianity but by a conceptualisation that is more longstand- ing and effective in governing through the bodies of subjects: race. In order to arrive at this point, we must consider the epistemological period in which the 18th and 19th centuries were immersed in focussing on Modernity's pure function, and activate Martin Nakata's critiques to the discourse of anthro- pology displayed in the context of the Torres Straits in Australia. Then, we will briefly discuss the way in which Modernity governed utilising biopoli- tics. We will also examine the gap between biopolitics and the contemporary governance technique of necropolitics in order to explicate the way death was managed in a biopolitical code before it might become a necropower, as Achille Mbembe (2003) coins as a contemporary global form of governance. Lastly, the rationale of post-Enlightenment colonisation will be illuminated using the illustrative text of Joseph Arthur De Gobineau, *The Inequality of Human Races*. Given these incommensurable and biopolitical characteristics, the task to unearth colonisation during this period will be to describe its pure function as it relates to the aesthetic conceptualisation of race as this serves as the markers that project the parallax reflection of Western culture onto non-Western cultures in order to determine who should be the subjects of colonisation's form of governance.

COLONISATION'S PURE FUNCTION: THE ANALYTICS OF MODERNITY

'Dirty nigger!' Or simply, 'Look, a Negro!'
I came into the world imbued with the will to find meaning in things, my spirit filled with the desire to attain to the source of the world, and then I found that *I was an object in the midst of other objects*.
Sealed into that crushing objecthood, I turned beseechingly to others. Their attention was a liberation, running over my body suddenly abraded into nonbe- ing, endowing me once more with an agility that I had thought I lost, and by taking me out of the world, restoring me to it. But just as I reached the other side, I stumbled, and the movements, the attitudes, the glances of the other fixed me there, in the sense in which a chemical solution is fixed me there, in the sense in which a chemical solution is fixed by a dye. I was indignant; I demanded an explanation. Nothing happened. I burst apart. Now the fragments have been put together again by another self. —Franz Fanon, 2008, p. 82, emphasis added

The second part of colonisation's two-part period is unwrapped by describing its hidden source: colonisation's incommensurable, and thus non-discursive, function within the discourse of philosophical anthropology. We have seen that colonisation was inaugurated in the realm of an aesthetics of ugliness where race is born of the monstrous conceptualisations of Western indigeneity and blackness. This monstrous representation is a classification in the order of objects typically found in the Classical period where representation through imagery establishes the conditions of the possibilities to try to grasp the 'New World' and colonise it. However, with the fall of the Classical period and the emergence of Modernity—arguably facilitated by the world-scale project of colonisation—Western culture finds itself with a new world-view that would also affect the process of colonisation. The Modernity episteme description, unearthed by Foucault's archaeology of Western knowledge (Foucault, 1974), will be the starting place for this book to unearth the second movement of colonisation's conceptual constitution.

The epistemological shift from the Classical to the Modernity episteme is characterised by how knowledge was no longer only constituted by representations ordered in a divine system of classification where 'man' is an object among objects. In Modernity, knowledge becomes constituted by a human or Western system of classification constituted by the incommensurable entity of what is studied and the always finite approximation of empirical human sciences. An example that Foucault (1973) discusses in his *Order of Things* is the transition between the classical field of natural history to biology. In archaeological approaches, the transition between epistemes cannot be determined using a hierarchical progression in which one period is considered superior to another, but simply its description aligns with the epistemological conditions of the possibilities of that period; each epistemological period has a specific focus. Thus, modern biology's focus is not the order of objects represented in a system of classification given by God, but rather it focuses on attempting to theorize life itself. The focus on the description of the physical structure of beings can be represented as a result of its contrasting identities, but the source of life itself cannot be described because life itself is invisible or incommensurable. The focus of the Classical episteme was constituted representations but with visible juxtaposed differences; in Modernity, the focus became organised in a functional homogeneity that becomes its hidden foundation. In biology, the hidden source is life itself and the functional homogeneity becomes suspended for the capture of Western culture's interest; power and knowledge here become one.

The shift from the Classical period to Modernity does not mean that Western culture ceases to place particular importance on representation, specifically to imagery and aesthetics; it means that, epistemologically, the focus shifts from classification through representation, to the source of what is meant to represent imagery in the first place. That is, in Modernity, the emergence of human sciences aims to theorize, for instance in biology life itself, by attempting to capture the condition of possibilities for the existence of things, e.g., life in biology and production in economics. This is produced not solely by the emergence of technologies such as the microscope, but by the conditions of possibilities that went beyond the visible: that which is visible can be represented and therefore classified. The incommensurability of the source of things, such as life, production, power, and so on, is the target of the Modernity episteme finding its answers in the limits of the thoughts of humanity. This form of thought is seen persistently in Kant's writings, particularly around the theme of philosophical anthropology. Foucault mentions that:

> Accompanying the critique in favour of an anthropological teaching, that monotonous reference point in which Kant has doubled his efforts of a transcendental reflexion by lobbying for a consistent accumulation of empirical knowledge about people. His 25 years of teaching anthropology is related to the university context of the time; that obsession is linked to the very structure of the Kantian problem: How to think, analyse, justify and how to build finitude, inside a reflexion that cannot be thought from an infinity ontology, and doesn't regret a philosophy of the absolute? A question that effectively is within the realm of anthropology, but it can't form a genuine dimension, since it cannot be reflected by itself from an empirical form of thought. (Foucault, 2009, p. 217)

Before, in the Renaissance and Classical periods, the source of the answers of the aforementioned questions of the conditions of possibilities of all things was God. Western culture's man was just another object, capable of managing representations, in the great order of things given by God. However, in Modernity, the source or the condition of possibilities for the existence of things shifted from God to man. Western culture's man became the source of all things, not ontologically but epistemologically. Hence the quote 'God is dead': 'man' killed him.

Furthermore, with the collapse of the Classical period, man also became an object of study, particularly in the social sciences. In the aftermath of the death of God, (Western) man ceased to be only an object among objects in an order in which the source of existence is divine; man also became a subject among objects being able to examine his own existence. In other words, in Modernity, Western culture does not only try to understand the order of things, but also the nature of man as the processor of this order. Western culture's man became the subject and object of his own comprehension. This is the constitutive epistemological space of the philosophical discourse of anthropology in which many human sciences function from the starting point and as the source of and for Western culture. Thus, the discourse of anthropology does not only include the disciplines of anthropology, but also biology, psychiatry, psychology, and sociology, among others. In the Modernity episteme, they start from the source of what can be possible from the finitude or limitations of man functioning to assemble knowledge from the heart of Western culture man's understanding. It is not a coincidence that it is from the 18th century onwards that there is a flourishing of studies of emerging disciplines such as anthropology, biology, sociology, psychology, and so forth. For instance, Nakata writes:

> Psychology and anthropology, in this way, were considered by scientists like Jackson and Rivers [an evolutionary neurologist and a psychologist, respectively] to be intrinsically tied up with the biological sciences. The physiology and the psychology are part of the one process; racial superiority and racial difference can be seen in both biology and in culture. (Nakata, 2007, p. 44)

These Western disciplines were guided by the modern episteme of the discourse of anthropology and were being used to validate a system predicated on a narrative of 'development' or evolution that implied an inferiority–superiority organisation or an ontological inequality human order. No longer would inequality be contingent on alliances with specific institutions, such as the Catholic Church or kingdoms: within the grids of the discourse of anthropology, inequality becomes represented in the very content of the Western inscriptions on people's bodies to then fit into a given 'order' made in the image of Western culture. In the context of the Torres Strait Islands and the Cambridge Expedition, Nakata explains:

> It is important in the context of this book to stress that by no means were these Cambridge scientists testing and observing in a theoretical vacuum. They came from a university already hundreds of years old, a university that had seen the knowledge it was producing increasing exponentially during the nineteenth century. They left their book- lined libraries to travel halfway around the world to test their theories. And they returned to their libraries to assess their data, consult with the relevant literature on the subject and write their reports. They also lectured, debated and produced seminal works in developing disciplines. Their aim was to produce a comparative study—a sort of 'before and after' chapter of the human race . . . They inscribed the Torres Strait Islander in a particular and already prescribed relation with European people, with 'other savage people', and with European knowledge. In doing so, they embedded the Islanders in an evolutionary history that they felt explained the continuing inequality between the different racial groups of the world. It is this action, and the subsequent relation that it engendered at the level of knowledge which is with us still, that limits understandings about Islanders and defines the parameters of the position that was constructed for them. (Nakata, 2007, pp. 29–30)

The discourse of anthropology provided the conditions of possibilities for the construction and inception of a classification system that made Torres Strait

Islanders, and arguably all colonial subjects in a similar manner, slip into the hierarchy of racial inequality determined by the inequality system predicated by a body of disciplinary works revolving around the ideas of Social Darwinism. Iconic works of this era include Charles Darwin's *Origins of Species by Means of Natural Selection* (1859), Lewis Henry Morgan's *Ancient Society* (1877), Sigmund Freud's *The Interpretation of Dreams* (1899), and Joseph Arthur de Gobineau's *Inequality of Human Races* (1853–1855), among others. Nakata states that the purpose of disciplines informed by the discourse of anthropology was to objectively study colonial subject, yet it created the very object it aimed to understand; thus, objectification, or as Cesaire once said 'thingification', would be the guiding approach to understand, to capture, and to govern others, particularly in colonisation.

BIOPOLITICS, RACE, AND COLONISATION

And we can also understand why racism should have developed in modern societies that function in the biopower mode; we can understand why racism broke out at a number of privileged moments, and why they were precisely the moments when the right to take life was imperative. Racism first develops with colonization, or in other words, with colonizing genocide. (Foucault 2011, p. 257)

From the 18th century onwards, a new form of government emerged that proved to be more effective and efficient than previous forms: biopolitics. Before the Modernity episteme, the authority of European kingdoms was defined by the sovereign's authority to take his or her subjects' lives or grant pardons if any subject disobeyed the law. Not infrequently, there were violent displays of brutality exerted towards the body of subjects as Foucault (1975) describes in detail in the beginning of his book *Discipline and Punish: The Birth of the Prison.* However, this technology of government is constituted by the sovereign—Agamben reminds us that the literal meaning of sovereign is the right to kill—where the imperative is *to make die and to let live.* With the turn to Modernity, the epistemological conditions of possibilities allow the sovereign formulation to be inverted into a biopolitics imperative that becomes *to make live and to let die* (Foucault in Castro-Gómez, 2007). This creates the favourable social and environmental conditions that allow the subjects' bodies to become productive instruments of the state and in service of capitalism. Rather than governing through focusing on punishing bodies, using the governance technology of biopolitics in Modernity, the focus is on extracting the maximum amount of production from the bodies that is favourable for the state.

Moreover, within the episteme of Modernity, social evolutionism or Social Darwinism logics painted the picture of nation-states, specifically with the emergence the colonial product of the conceptualisation of race. With the emergence of biopolitics, racial exclusion constituted the nation-state from the 18th century onwards through violent exclusions that aimed to feed into the narrative of 'natural', or more precisely cultural, selection. That is, the nation-state in the biopolitical code aimed to develop or affirm superiority through racist discourse. At the heart of modern nation-states lies biological racial distinctions because in the newest form of government 'to make live' and 'to let die' implied a Manichean logic for which certain peoples constituted those favoured by the state and others were not. Thus, Foucault (2011) defines biopolitics as the form of governance that makes live the desired races—those desired by the state—and lets die the undesired races. For those subjects that serve the state and the capital, the state will 'make live' solely to increase their productivity. Through the state's control of health, births, and mortality, the desired subjects receive all possible conditions to maximise their productive potential, as long as it serves the state's moral and productive capital. Those who are dangerous or undesired subjects of the state, and therefore not necessarily productive, are 'let die'. Biopolitics is a technology of government that aims to control the vital processes of the population—such as reproduction, life expectancy, and illness—and optimise other conditions—such as sanitation, security, education, and economic conditions, among others—that allow people to have a 'productive' life in the function of capitalism. Foucault (Castro-Gómez, 2007; Foucault, 2011) argues that this technology aims to produce these conditions for a desired type, or an identified population, and through the violent exclusion of others. Biopolitics, then, declares a war against any race that does not adjust to the imposed norms of the desirable population. That is, biopolitics makes live those populations that are 'better adjusted' to this 'productive profile', and lets die those who are not adjusted and do not promote the ideals of productive work, economic development, and modernisation. Thus, racism becomes the way in which these undesired peoples are aesthetically marked to be managed on the side of the 'let die' biopolitical formulation.

For Foucault, racism appears to have two dimensions: one constituted by its discursive formation (something that is not elaborated in his work and that this book aims to address) and the other as a biopolitical device or apparatus. Racism as a biopolitical device functions as a marker that enables the inferior-superior binary that encodes the topology of populations and maps the pure function of the nation-state. In other words, racism in a biopolitical character colours the map for biopower's operation in which it indicates where the function of 'making live' should focus and where the function of 'letting die' should focus. In Modernity, by appealing to the anthropological and biological themes of evolutionism, racism kills through the apparent slow motion of 'letting die' and, at times, there are moments that racial genocide is perfectly justified: in the genealogical element of his study of biopolitics, Foucault identifies a handful of instances including the Holocaust exerted by Nazi Germany (Castro-Gómez, 2007; Foucault, 2011).

While tracing what Foucault had to say about colonisation is not the main objective of this section, it is important to highlight that he does theorize colonisation and its relationship with racism in at least three of his lectures at the Collège de France: 'Society Must be Defended', 'Security, Territory and Population', and 'The Birth of Biopolitics'. Foucault was highly aware of the importance of colonisation in constituting particular historical assemblages to make the exercise of power more efficient, as well as the use of these apparatuses, and he even argued that this was not limited to colonised countries (Foucault 2005). In 'Society Must be Defended', Foucault engages in a genealogy of racism in which he identifies from the 18th century onwards that racism manifested as 'boomerang' back to the West. Racism in Foucault is intimately tied to the emergence of biopolitics (Foucault 2005). He first identifies racism as a discourse that highlights the physical, ethnic, and moral superiorities over undesired races (Castro-Gómez 2007, Foucault 2005a). This will to superiority becomes a battle that can never end with a truce or any juridical mechanism (such as a treaty), but only when one is completely destroyed. Foucault is not interested in racism itself, but rather in its operation and how it presents the foundations of a new 'art of government': biopolitics. Conversely, the elaboration of race and racism is not Foucault's focus, his focus is on the discursive practice of racism used as a 'strategy of war' to eliminate the undesired races. It must be highlighted that Foucault's genealogy of racism primarily discussed in the lecture of March 17, 1976, in 'Society Must be Defended', focusses on the practice of racism as a biopolitical apparatus almost exclusively in the context of European history. The discourse of racism or the conceptualisation of race is not discussed in this genealogy because Foucault's object is how racism aids biopolitics in the context of Europe and not how racism began in colonisation, where he acknowledges it was formed. This would be Foucault's focus on the 'make live' part of the biopolitical technology of government; however, when we focus on the 'let die' component of biopolitics, history needs to include a reexamination of race and colonisation in the context of how the undesired races were managed to 'let die'.

NECROPOLITICS

To live under late modern occupation is to experience a permanent condition of 'being in pain': fortified structures, military posts, and roadblocks everywhere; buildings that bring back painful memories of humiliation, interrogations, and beatings; curfews that imprison hundreds of thousands in their cramped homes every night from dusk to daybreak; soldiers patrolling the unlit streets, frightened by their own shadows; children blinded by rubber

> bullets; parents shamed and beaten in front of their families; soldiers urinating
> on fences, shooting at the rooftop water tanks just for fun, chanting loud
> offensive slogans, pounding on fragile tin doors to frighten the children, con-
> fiscating papers, or dumping garbage in the middle of a residential neighbor-
> hood; border guards kicking over a vegetable stand or closing borders at
> whim; bones broken; shootings and fatalities—a certain kind of madness.
> (Mbembe, 2003, p. 39)

In this section, we abandon the 18th and 19th centuries in order to briefly discuss the current technology of government discussed by Mbembe in an attempt to examine the gap between biopolitics and necropolitics within colonisation. Foucault's notion of biopolitics has been used to interrogate and theorize mainstream Western governmentality practices: the focus has thus far been predominantly on the 'making live' proposition of the biopoliti-cal formula and not the 'let die' proposition. In the context of the 18th and 19th centuries, this omission in describing the ways in which the manage-ment of death of the undesired races can be a weakness in Foucault's concep-tion of biopower because, in colonisation, there are numerous examples and practices of letting die the Indigenous, African, and Coloured peoples; these processes can be very illuminating in understanding biopolitics more broad-ly. In particular, when contemporary scholars such as Achille Mbembe iden-tified that the contemporary technology of government (in the 20th and 21st centuries) can no longer be understood along the lines of biopolitics and only focuses on the management of death from a logic of destruction, it was conceptualised as necropolitics. Mbembe makes a significant contribution to understanding the way biopower might have transformed itself into a necro-power in contemporary times and describes the way in which it was founded in the heart of colonisation in the spaces of the plantations and the colonies.

To an extent, Mbembe's view leaves the governmental technology of the Classical and Renaissance art of government intact in its fundamental right to kill; he argues that, in contemporary times, the focus is on the management of death (as opposed to the management of life in Modernity through the old sovereign right of 'to let live' transformed into 'to make live') through prac-tices of destruction being the imperative view of Western governance. The scope of what this book examines cannot elaborate an argument that endorses or rejects necropolitics as a concept or praxis. However, its focus on the management of death is illuminating because necropolitics develops in co-lonisation and in the aspect of biopolitics that already managed the 'dying' of undesired races of Western States. While the 'let die' proposition of biopoli-tics is similar to Mbembe's (2003) concept of necropolitics, he argues that the Western contemporary forms of governance focus on the broad and glo-bal management of death that is predicated by the impulse of a 'war without end'. In other words, necropolitics governs by the logics of a death drive, yet it is able to articulate itself to a form of management that governs on a world scale. Mbembe's departure from one of Foucault's supporting theses for biopower can be seen here:

> The technologies which ended up producing Nazism should have originated in the plantation or in the colony or that, on the contrary—Foucault's thesis—Nazism and Stalinism did no more than amplify a series of mechanisms that already existed in Western European social and political formations (subjugation of the body, health regulations, social Darwinism, eugenics, medico-legal theories on heredity, degeneration, and race) is, in the end, irrelevant. A fact remains, though: in modern philosophical thought and European political practice and imaginary, the colony represents the site where sovereignty consists fundamentally in the exercise of a power outside the law (*ab legibus solutus*) and where 'peace' is more likely to take on the face of a 'war without end'. (Mbembe, 2003 p. 23)

After an extensive philosophical political review of forms of Western governance, Mbembe arrives at this point where notably the location of the plantation or the colony, or colonisation at large, becomes the founding figure of this technology of government constituted by necropower. The way in which this historical transition occurred in the colonial spaces of, particularly, the 18th and 19th centuries given its modern quality focusing on incommensurable pure function is not necessarily unpacked.[2] However, the *pathos* or direction that the war against undesired races in colonisation is present in this new form of government where racism serves as a war strategy predicated in the coloniser-colonised battle to the death that, in contemporary times, extends itself to a world-scale 'war without end'. Thus, in necropolitics, race and racism are the key igniters of this newer technology of government.

Mbembe's view of Foucault's understanding of the operation of racism was predicated, within a biopolitical governance, on the pure function 'to regulate the distribution of death and to make possible the murderous functions of the state' (Mbembe, 2003, p. 17). Thus, Mbembe acknowledges race as the space where the biopolitical management of death occurs. Furthermore, Mbembe explicates race and states that: 'the racial community was a community founded on the memory of loss—a community of kinless. It was a 'community of loss' in the way that Jean-Luc Nancy, dealing with community in general, has defined it: a space inseparable from death, since it is precisely through death that community reveals itself' (Mbembe, 2017, p. 34). The thanatological character of the space of race within biopolitics, forged in colonisation, is an important element of the later function of necropolitics. Yet the epistemological transition from post-Enlightenment colonisation's pure function informed by biopolitics and targeted using the aesthetic markers of race is not present, nor is the aesthetic conceptualisation of race that would inform the form of the space of race in its management of death. This is not a topic that necropolitics addresses. In order to arrive at the way in which colonisation was operationalised, we need to understand how Social Darwinism operated in the Modernity episteme through the function of race, considering that its form is predicated by its previously discussed aesthetic character. That is, the content of racism was predicated before the modern period using the Western aesthetic conceptualisations of indigeneity and blackness constituted by their narratives, but now its content forms the frame for which the function would operate, namely through the incommensurable management of death. What follows is one of the most explicit manifestations of philosophical anthropology's epistemological period, in the 18th and 19th centuries, and what would become biopower's primary weapon against undesired races through one of the works that informed the beginnings of anthropology as a discipline (as well as other disciplines) and anthropology as the discourse that positions race as an historical axiom: *The Inequality of Human Races* by Count Joseph Arthur De Gobineau.

THE INEQUALITY OF HUMAN RACES

> Oh! the racism of these gentlemen does not bother me. I do not become indignant over it. I merely examine it. I note it, and that is all. I am almost grateful to it for expressing itself openly and appearing in broad daylight, as a sign. A sign that the intrepid class which once stormed Bastilles is now hamstrung. A sign that it feels itself to be mortal. A sign that it feels to be a corpse. (Cesaire 1955, p. 49)

De Gobineau's book, *The Inequality of Human Races*, explicitly marks the end of the period when inequality was directly commanded by institutions, such as the Catholic Church, and the beginning of the period where inequality became naturalised (Kale, 2010; Sabine, 1998) in the aesthetic discursive space of race. That is, he stated that the inequality of the human races was not determined by royal decree that determined if someone would be a slave, a peasant, a count, a Christian, or any other social status, but that they were now determined by something more permanent: by racial differentiation predicated by skin colour. Biopolitics is heterarchically assembled by this inequality in the aesthetics of race where one race is to made to live and the races that do not serve the function of the state are left to die. This skin colour classification is the *content turned into form* from the aesthetic conceptualisation of race, and its function is to mark differentiation by projecting onto non-whites the parallax representation of what Western cultures want to be defined as. In this way, it establishes a world history of Western culture where the prehistory is determined by that which Western culture has left in a 'prehistorical' period. With colonisation as an instituting force of post-Enlightenment discourses and Modernity in general, the Western man continued to require its 'twilight figure' that had to be purged and projected onto the 'other'. The vessel for this purge was the aesthetic conceptualisation of race. Thus, the focus shifted from the content of the aesthetic conceptualisation of race to the form of it or became its frame; in other words, race became constituted more by sign than by meaning. The hidden foundation of the classification of races in social sciences, i.e., its pure function, is grounded in inequality: the incommensurability of race is founded on the hidden function of inequity. To what extent does this clear signal of Social Darwinism mark the point in which the aesthetics of race acquires this incommensurable functional character of Modernity? Furthermore, how does colonisation's functional character *use* the colonial conceptualisations of race?

The drive to dispel the clearly mistaken thesis of *The Inequality of Human Races* is enticing, yet it is critical to view the way this text uses race beyond this tautological exercise. We can start by firstly refusing that De Gobineau's theories were not considered as important in later academic discourse. A clear example of this is the article entitled 'The Drift of Modern Anthropology' from *The British Medical Journal* of 1927, in which Sir Arthur Keith writes:

> Dr. Dahl asks a question of the greatest interest to everyone, and returns an answer which, I think, most students of mankind will accept as true. Are the aborigines of Australia what they are for lack of opportunities, or are they what they are because of their mental outfit? Dr. Dahl sums up the evidence, and comes to the conclusion that is not possible, by any process of education whatsoever, to convert aboriginal tribe into a civilized community. Dr. Scheidt, if he knew of Dr. Dahl's opinion, would agree with it, for he realizes that we who form the nationalities of Europe come of an ancestry which has been sifted in the sieve of civilization for some two hundred generations . . . Dr. Scheidt is fully alive to the importance of Darwin's law of selection; but he lays even greater stress on Count Gobineau's doctrine of race. (49–50)

In this excerpt, the '[European] students of mankind' refer to the social sciences, primarily anthropology. This quote is just one of many that clearly demonstrates the influence of *The Inequality of Human Races* in social sciences discourses, and it becomes particularly illustrative given that the next chapter will use Australia as a case study for the modern operation of colonisation. Beyond *The Inequality of Human Races*' relatively recent discreditation from the general claims of anthropology as a discipline given its use in German Nazi to justify the Holocaust and its current use in white supremacist and neo-Nazi discourses, this text is an important discursive component in the constitution of the knowledge production of social sciences at large with particular attention to the debates constituted by a dialectic relationship among superior and 'inferior' civilisations, nations, or races in general.

De Gobineau's book marks the solidification of the discourse of anthropology, particularly in colonisation. After a review of various detailed theses about the examination of civilisations and races, he concludes his book with this statement:

> I have shown the unique place in the organic world occupied by the human species, the profound physical, as well as moral, differences separating it from all other kinds of living creatures. Considering it by itself, I have been able to distinguish, on physiological grounds alone, three great and clearly marked types, the black, the yellow, and the white. However uncertain the aims of physiology may be, however meagre its resources, however defective its methods, it can proceed thus far with absolute certainty. (De Gobineau 1852, p. 205)

However, De Gobineau did more than rigorously institute a racial hierarchy that still echoes today (in some social sciences and in everyday racism): he clearly manifested in the human sciences the anthropocentric parallax view that Western knowledge production is predicated on and instituted a Western-centric heterarchical inequality of races. This projection, which is regarded as knowledge of what is stated to be researched regardless of empirical data, operates to transfigure the function of the given discourse in which the subject is observed. For example, a common criticism of De Gobineau's work made by renowned anthropologist Franz Boas was that the empirical data collected from peoples rejected Social Darwinism (Geertz, 1979), which suggests that the Social Darwinism claims are not supported by 'hard ethnography'. Yet the Western-centric comparison dynamics continued to be the frame of analysis for the social sciences, particularly in anthropology in which its foundation was constituted by the formation of 'modern man', i.e., the Western definition of man. For instance, Nakata states that the dynamics of racial inequality was redressed in every policy that addressed Indigenous Australian issues, after: '[t]he discursive and material circumscription of the preceding century, when missionaries, scientists and government used racially based arguments to rationalise their decisions to separate and protect Islanders from the external influences encroaching on their living environments passed into "history"' (Nakata, 2007, p. 158). Thus, inequality as identified in *The Inequality of Human Races* operates in function through the frames of the hidden foundations of the human sciences, which are informed by the discourse of anthropology, despite the invisibility of explicitly racially based arguments. In fact, its unperceivable character or incommensurability is central for the effectiveness of this form of government of the colonised.

In this text, race is explicitly crafted into a tri-coloured overarching hierarchy (black, yellow, and white) in which indigeneity is explicitly excluded because De Gobineau assumed that this 'race' would die out (see p. 112 of *The Inequality of Human Races*). However, in practice, race is assembled in a bi-coloured relationship in which it uses whiteness to mark Western culture as a present outcome of history, and any other peoples are marked with colours that constitute them as an object of the pre-Western stage of world's history: this effectively colours non-Western peoples out of the present.[3] This pre-Western stage of history is not the history of the world, but rather the history of Western culture that is used as the frame in which other civilisations are coloured, based on what Western culture has 'transcended'. For instance, De Gobineau describes the Aztec Empire along the post-Enlightenment rejection of fanaticism:

> The Aztec Empire in America seems to have existed mainly 'for the greater glory' of fanaticism. I cannot imagine anything more fanatical than a society like that of the Aztecs, which rested on a religious foundation, continually watered by the blood of human sacrifice. It has been denied, perhaps with some truth, that the ancient peoples of Europe ever practised ritual murder on victims who were regarded as innocent, with the exception of shipwrecked sailors and prisoners of war . . . This did not prevent their [the Aztecs] being a powerful, industrious, and wealthy people, which would certainly for many ages have gone flourishing, reigning, and throat-cutting, had not the genius Hernando Cortes and the courage of his companions stepped in to put an end to the *monstrous* existence of such an Empire. (De Gobineau, 1884, p. 39)

While part of this quote exhibits significant knowledge of the historical events and concepts of the battle between the Aztec Empire and the Spanish, the shortcomings are not limited by the incorrect information that the text displays but by two non-Western cultural grounds. First, there is a clear absence of an analysis of Aztec worldview perspectives (in which fanaticism would not make sense) and, second, there is an explicit attack of the 'monstrosity' of fanaticism as it is understood and experienced by Western culture's history. The Aztec religious 'fanaticism' that led to their defeat by colonisers becomes one of the supporting statements of the argument for the superiority of the white race against Indigenous and all other non-pure white races. For De Gobineau, there is not a tri-coloured (aesthetic) classification of races, but a pre-Western man ideal that functions as the recipient in which Western history can deposit their projected 'ugliness' in the guise of inferiority.

Furthermore, the departure from institutional inequality to its individualised version, the inequality of human races, needed to focus on seemingly individual traits of blood purity and capacity to be 'civilised' (that is, the ability to become a Westerner), among other subjective characteristics that have a high status in Western culture. The biopolitical rationale of the constitution of race, populations, nations, and civilisations—and at the same time their implied hierarchies—required individual characteristics as a space to operate in order to establish this inequality. Thus, the nature of man is discursively situated on the hidden foundation of a classification system predicated by hierarchies or heterarchy; the inequality of human races was focussed on

individual characteristics where non-white peoples were projected with inferior individual characteristics as determined by Western culture. De Gobineau states that:

> The irreconcilable antagonism between different races and cultures is clearly
> established by history, and such innate repulsion must imply unlikeness and
> inequality. If it is admitted that the European cannot hope to civilize the negro,
> and manages to transmit to the mulatto only a very few of his own characteris-
> tics; if the children of a mulatto and a white woman cannot really understand
> anything better than a hybrid culture, a little nearer than their father's to the
> ideas of the white race,—in that case, I am right in saying that the different
> races are unequal in intelligence. (De Gobineau, 1852, p. 179)

The racialised individual, and by extension the racialised populations, nations, and civilisations, became the object and subject of what predicates the
underlying narrative of Western culture: differentiation is predicated by similarities with and differences to the Western man as the measure of 'civilisation'. In De Gobineau, we find the link between the carefully crafted Western
entity of the individual according to human sciences, in line with Foucault
(1973), and the constitution of populations using the aesthetic conceptualisation race crafted by colonisation's origins to now be used as the canvas to
paint non-white peoples.

The individualising character of modern inequality is even seen when
referring to the failure of institutions to 'civilise' others in colonisation. For
example, in arguing against the capacity of institutions to determine inequality, De Gobineau states: 'You may search through all the pages of history,
and you will not find a single people that has attained to European civilization by adopting Christianity, or has been brought by the great facts of its
conversion to civilize itself when it was not civilized already' (De Gobineau,
1852, p. 75). Through establishing that Christianity, the main institution that
established inequality before Modernity, is mutually exclusive of civilisation
(being the highest stage of racial superiority), De Gobineau successfully
eliminates inequality from institutions and reassembles it in individualism by
redefining civilisation from the racial viewpoint of Western man. This can be
clearly seen in his definition of civilisation: 'I may now sum up my view of
civilization by defining it as *a state of relative stability, where the mass of
men try to satisfy their wants by peaceful means, and are refined in their
conduct and intelligence*' (De Gobineau, 1852, p. 91, emphasis in original).
It is here where the institutional differences commanded by sovereign and
medieval kingdoms, such as governmental practices, cease to be the focus of
inequality. However, using the already instituted definition of civilisation,
nation-states or any 'superior' political formation constituted by the virtues
of Western man is the basis of an inequality that reconstitutes itself as superi-
or by crafting otherness with the projections of the negative fantasies of

Western civilisation. The hidden foundation of the inequality of human races is predicated by an inequality in favour of the definition of Western culture, which is constituted heterarchically by deploying a system of classifications defined by the projections of what Western men cannot be like and therefore what it has overcome in its version of world history.

At this point, we can view the picture in which post-Enlightenment colonisation was founded and the second fold of colonisation in general: the frame of the aesthetic conceptualisation of race functions to distinguish races in the way that Western culture biopolitically governs. This racial frame is reserved for the 'undesired races' where colonial narratives were assembled for the purpose of creating an inequality that leads to death. However, the way in which the undesired races are thanatologically managed remains not fully explicated. Globally, in the 18th and 19th centuries, the birth of Western biopolitics that was constituted—and some might argue that is constituted—by colonisation occurred. In order to view this process locally in action, we cannot only rely on the macroprocesses or only on the microprocesses or local processes of colonisation. In the next two chapters, we will explore how colonisation operated locally through the case study of Queensland, Australia. In order to paint a more complete picture of colonisation, we must remember that:

> Every society, and every individual, are thus plied by both segmentarities simultaneously: one molar, the other *molecular*. If they are distinct, it is because they do not have the same terms or the same relations or the same nature or even the same type of multiplicity. If they are inseparable, it is because they coexist and cross over into each other . . . In short, every-thing is political, but every politics is simultaneously a *macropolitics* and a *micropolitics*. (Deleuze and Guattari 1987, p. 213, emphasis in original)

The geopolitical operation of colonisation is thus not subsumed by the micropolitical operation of colonisation, and vice versa. This is the heart of this book. Perhaps the best transition to the following chapter, which focuses on a specific experience of a micropolitical operation of colonisation, is to appreciate the complexity of the type of governance from within through Nakata's critical examination:

> The basic democratic principles on which the government of other Australians rested were still not in evidence. The style of management that ensued was still firmly in place when I was growing up in the Torres Strait Islands in the 1960s and 1970s. 'Surveillance under the guise of informality' (Sharp, 1993, p. 217) became the key to a new disciplinary control. A sophisticated and not so subtle system emerged that depended on the Protector (or Manager as they became known) using direct personal contact and knowledge. (Nakata, 2007, p. 139)

NOTES

1. In the introduction, we saw that Nakata's methodological approach is a Foucauldian archaeological one, as is used in this book.

2. Note that there is a historical review on the way race is unpacked, not the function of colonisation within biopolitics and racism, in Mbembe's *Critique of Black Reason* (2017).

3. Moreton-Robinson (2015) would establish that this bi-polar relationship rests on the illegal white territorial possession and the willfull invisibility to Indigenous peoples corresponds to a repressed acknowledgement that this possession is in fact illegal in settler colonies.

Chapter Six

The Blanket Approach

Colonisation in Queensland, Australia

This [Indigenous] ontological relationship to land is one that the nation state has sought to diminish through its social, legal and cultural practices. The nation state's land-rights regime is still premised on the legal fiction of Terra Nullius . . . In Australia, Indigenous subjectivity operates through a doubling of marginality and centring, which produces an incommensurate subject that negotiates and manages disruption, dislocation and proximity to whiteness. This process does not erase Indigenous ontology; this suggests that Indigenous subjectivity is processual because it represents a dialectical unity between humans and the earth. It is a state of embodiment that continues to unsettle white Australians. (Moreton-Robinson, 2003, pp. 35–36)

The pages that follow will use the Queensland Aboriginal Protection and Restriction of the Sale of Opium Act 1897 (1897 Act) to showcase the local operationalisation of colonisation in Australia and to be a privileged laboratory for understanding modern forms of colonisation. The operationalisation of colonisation has little to do with the Indigenous peoples and their experience of tens of thousands of years in Australia as I clarified in the previous section. As Indigenous scholar and distinguished professor Aileen Moreton-Robinson (2003) establishes in the aforementioned quote, colonisation was unsuccessful in erasing the 'ontological relationship to land' and therefore it failed to obliterate Indigenous subjectivity. Moreton-Robinson's theories will be engaged with more fully in the following chapter. Conversely, and differing from part 1 of this book, the *focus* here is not the aesthetic but rather the functional considering the biopolitical features of the epoch of Modernity: 19th and 20th century colonisations assumed a vigorous discourse of anthropology that draws on, sometimes explicitly, the Social Darwinist trends of the time. The history of the function of the 1897 Act in Queensland, Australia, carries many explicit trademarks of Modernity in the history of colonisation. Firstly, not only is the language of the discourse of anthropology present in many legal documents in Australia but anthropologists also had leadership roles in the implementation of this Act, as it was in the case of anthropologist Dr. Walter Roth who was Chief Protector for the first years of the 1897 Act. Furthermore, Australia interchangeably used the racial discursive devices of *blackness* and *indigeneity*: Indigenous peoples were referred in the discourse of the time using words such as 'indigenous', 'blacks', and 'aboriginals' (among many other terms) at the same time, making this interchangeable racial conceptualisation rare case compared to other countries where blackness and indigeneity, for instance, be mutually exclusive. Many more reasons could be provided for this, but a key reason is the widely documented and explicit content of this colonial case in Australia that is starkly contrasted against the historical silence of the Frontier Wars between settlers and Indigenous peoples (Reynolds, 2013). Thus, the 1897 Act's operation will be visibilised and described in the context of the history of Australia.

The description of the local operation of the 1897 Act will be conceptualised as the *Blanket Approach*, defined as a form of content for the functionality of the relief item, which is a literal blanket. On one hand, this 'blanket' refers to the phrase that alludes to a policy that provides a discrete and total solution to very complex problems; on the other hand, it means that it covered every subject like the blankets that were distributed in the 19th century and in the beginning of the 20th century in Queensland. This mechanism operated using the triple function of totalisation, multiplicity, and the creation of desire. First, the process that determines everything, that which was listed in the Act and therefore does not determine anything, that was first determined by the protectorates in the institution and constitution of the 1897 Act is called totalisation. Second, the process that delivers this totalisation to each individual person is called multiplicity. Third, the process of creating needs, necessities, and desires, and through that imposing the enclosure and perpetual process of the process of colonisation, is called the creation of desire. These process threads were and are continually assembled in reference to the history of Western *indigeneity* and Western *blackness*, which have been discussed in the previous chapters.

The colonisation of Australia started well before the 1897 Act, through the international law doctrine of *Terra Nullius* at the end of the 18th century; the High Court of Australia found this legal mechanism to be unsubstantiated in the groundbreaking Mabo case in 1992. Put simply, the colonisation of Australia was illegal (Watson, 2016). While this analysis does not engage in the illegal, founding moment of the colonisation of Australia, it is nonetheless important to consider in order to contextualise the contradictory (yet very real) nature of the 1897 Act as it was operated in Queensland, Australia. The 1897 Act was the first comprehensive law from the government of the colony of Queensland that aimed to control every aspect of Aboriginal affairs, and later Torres Strait Islander affairs.

Many members of Parliament stated that the Indigenous 'problem' was far from being resolved. The 1897 Act covered three broad topics: it addressed opium and alcohol use, created institutions for Indigenous Australian peoples be subjected to (reserves or 'protectorates', and missions), and restricted and subjected Indigenous Australian peoples to the Western definition of an ideal life—which included labour, marriage, education, health, 'civility', and government—and the use and exclusion of objects (e.g., possum blankets were banned and cotton/wool blankets were imposed). Opium and alcohol were quickly controlled by the 1897 Act. This did not mean that their consumption was outlawed: for example, the use of alcohol was allowed, but the protectors of the reserves defined their acceptable use. The missions and protectorates aimed to visibilise and accurately account for the population of Indigenous Australian peoples. In her guide to the government records and archives, Frankland states:

> Regional administrative control of the Aboriginal and Torres Strait Islander population of the State was achieved by dividing the State into Protectorates. Each Protectorate was administered by a local Protector of Aboriginals who was a police officer in all cases except for Thursday Island. The appointment of local Protectors began in 1898. Local Protectors had many responsibilities including the administration of Aboriginal employment, wages, and savings bank accounts. Local Protectors also played a significant role in the removal of Aboriginal people to reserves. By 1932 there were 95 Protectorates and widespread corruption had emerged within the administrative practices of the local Protectors. (Frankland, 1994, p. 4)

These 'protectors' regulated and controlled marriages, removals, labour, employment and wages, education, and Indigenous industries; they reported deaths, specific diseases, crimes, and so on, and they defined what would constitute an Indigenous person who would be under the rule of the 1897 Act, not including those who would apply to be exempted from the 1897 Act. Very few cases would be granted exemptions (Frankland, 1994).

The protectors were police officers who were paid additional income to be the enforcers of the 1897 Act; they were responsible for the protectorates in any given region of Queensland. At first, the protectors reported to the Northern Chief Protector and the Southern Chief Protector, and then shortly after to only one Chief Protector who was responsible for all protectorates. One of the Chief Protector responsibilities was to directly report to the Home Secretary, who then reported to Queensland Parliament. It is important to note that the 1897 Act did not control all aspects of Indigenous Australian life, but that it aimed to cover Indigenous Australian peoples with a defined set of elements that were important to the colonial West. This means that every aspect, not any aspect, of life was defined by the colonial West and was no longer defined by Indigenous Australia. Note that I make a distinction between *every*-thing and *any*-thing, in the same manner that Levinas (1969) distinguishes between totality and infinity. This distinction will be further elaborated in the next chapter.

OPIUM?

The 1897 Act was developed to control the distribution of opium and Indigenous Australian people's labour, but it also became a mechanism for social engineering through regulating every aspect of their lives (Kidd, 1997). Every (and not just any) aspect of Indigenous Australian lives was defined by the Australian colonial West. Indigenous Australian labour had a protagonist role in building Queensland, and this labour was paid with tobacco, alcohol, and opium charcoal, as well as food, liquor, clothes, and blankets, among other exchange items (Gillett, 2011). In the 1897 Act, opium was used as a rhetorical device to institute a point of entry to regulate Indigenous Australian populations. Opium was also used as a scapegoat to constitute an illustrative example of colonial domination in Australia (Gillett, 2011).

The use of opium in Australia was documented well before the institution of the 1897 Act and it was usually associated with Chinese people, trade, and cultural practices. Before the 1897 Act, opium was legal and Australians consumed it in large quantities. The government of the colonies of Australia enjoyed a very healthy revenue from the taxes that opium paid. Using today's values, opium contributed an estimated $2.5 million annually to the government (Berridge and Griffith, 1999). In the late 19th century, opium began to become more regulated and its use was registered by race, e.g., the Annual Reports present tables of opium offences reporting the offenders' names and their races such as Chinese, Malay, White European; however, it remained associated with questionable pay for labour and sex (Evans, 2007). The first formal attempt by the Queensland government to regulate opium occurred in the context of the global movement against opium (Berridge and Griffith, 1999). In the 1890s, the global war on opium had replaced the abolitionist (abolition against slavery) movement because it was considered that slavery had been abolished. However, in the 1890s, the opium 'problem' was disappearing in Australia (Gillett, 2011). According to both unofficial reports and official government reports, opium remained present, but the latter reported a significant decrease (Evans 2007). Gillett (2011) argued that for the younger generations of Chinese in Australia, opium was considered passé or something that only older people would do, even though opium use in China was rising. The use of opium by Indigenous Australian peoples was reported to be limited to opium charcoal, which is the opium residue after it was smoked (Kidd, 1997). The opium charcoal was consumed through diluting it in a large quantity of water and then this water was consumed. The drinking of the opium charcoal water was reported to be a distinctive social activity (Gillett, 2011). However, as early as 1902, the protectors under the 1897 Act were reporting the following:

> 'In the neighbourhood of towns where there are police stations the supply of opium, although not entirely stopped, is considerably checked.' —Protector Martin, Mackay, 1902.
> 'The blacks in these districts are not much addicted to opium smoking, as it is confined mostly to the elder people, and the younger ones evidently perceive that opium has been killing their race, and avoid using it.' —Protector MacNamara, Charter Towers, 1902.
> 'I am glad to again report that the aboriginals here do not use opium or liquor.' —Protector O'Connor, Boulia (Annual Reports, 1902)

These individual reports and others (Annual Reports 1901–1906) stated that the problem of opium use had disappeared or significantly decreased. Opium-related criminal convictions, primarily perpetrated by people of Chinese descent, were what were mostly reported in the Annual Reports under the 1897 Act. Thus, either opium was already a decreasing problem, or the 1897 Act had an immediate effect in eliminating this problem, or perhaps it was never a problem at all.

In many of her works, Rosalind Kidd (1997, 2007, 2010, 2012) suggests that labour, as a topic of parliamentary discussion and employment practices, was a key factor in the domination of Indigenous Australia in the Queensland experience. Interestingly, this pressure came from a top down approach:

> Nineteenth-Century governments in Queensland were forced to respond to local and international campaigns demanding official interventions to bring Aboriginal/European relations under orderly control. The variety of recommendations, remedial programs and administrative responses suggests that the Aboriginal plight was a target for social change. Vigorous debate and practical adjustments in the legal domain and the field of 'coloured' employment, and indeed the articulation of the Aboriginal dilemma through the prism of European reformatory rhetoric, run counter to the historical convention of a systemic racial exclusion. (Kidd, 1997, p. 35)

However, Kidd demonstrated that Indigenous Australian labour was critical to the development of Queensland from the very early stages of the colony. From the beginnings of the settlement of Queensland, Indigenous Australian peoples worked as guides, helped in the construction of huts, houses, and other structures, cleared densely vegetated areas for the construction of pathways and living spaces, supplied food such as fish and other animals, worked in domestic duties, and worked in various pastoral duties (Keen, 2004; Kidd, 2010). Kidd (2010) stated that in the early 1880s, more than 1,000 Indigenous Australian people had permanent employment in rural Queensland.

The usual payment for Indigenous Australian labour was tobacco, opium charcoal, food, liquor, clothes, and blankets (Kidd, 2010). Very few Europeans agreed to work for such 'payments' in the characteristically harsh conditions of Queensland in the late 19th century. European labour expected to receive monetary wages for the same labour that Indigenous Australian peoples would do for mercantile and consumable goods. These conditions increased the demand for Indigenous Australian labour, as well as the unaffordability of the wages that the Europeans were demanding (Kidd, 2010). It was reported that in some cases Indigenous Australian peoples preferred to work with Chinese employers because they offered better working conditions overall (Evans, Kay, & Kathryn, 1993). European Australians reportedly resented this preference, and it further nourished racism against the Chinese communities. One of the effects of the 1897 Act was that the Protectors held the monopoly over Indigenous Australian labour, largely because they were given the authority to determine whether or not an Indigenous Australian person could work with an employer. Protectors, who were police officers, favoured the European employers and the records reveal an increase in Chinese convictions, with predominantly opium-related offences. The Parliamentary Debates of the late 19th century and early 20th century on matters such as the 1897 Act, as well as the Annual Reports, demonstrated clear disapproval of the Chinese communities. The Chinese were blamed for the general problem of opium addiction and in particular for the 'degeneration' of Indigenous Australian communities (Gillett, 2011). The 1897 Act was approved in the context of this generalised resentment against the Chinese communities (Gillett, 2011). After the approval of the 1897 Act in the context of resentment of the Chinese community and the global war on opium, opium was banned in 1906 with the exception of medicinal use (Gillett, 2011), but the 1897 Act continued to be enacted for decades longer.

In the 1897 Act, opium was the rhetorical device that built the complex machinery of colonial domination not simply as an empty signifier but as a scapegoat that was specified in order to change the focus from the real function of the Act. Some historians (Evans, 2007; Gillett 2011) have suggested that opium was merely an excuse to introduce the 1897 Act as a 'Trojan horse'. However, even this history positions opium as central to the machinery of the 1897 Act. From this perspective, even if opium was the Trojan horse of the 1897 Act, it had to operate around the legal provisions of the substance in order to control Indigenous Australian peoples. Furthermore, even if this account of history denies the reality of the problem of opium addiction and simply argues that it was a lie, or at least a very selective interpretation of events that occurred throughout Queensland society, the focus remains on confirming or denying this historical account: that is, opium remains a positive (present) part of the machinery of the 1897 Act. Notably, all accounts of history have persuasive and empirically sound arguments that position opium as the pretext for the institution of the 1897 Act. However, if opium was nothing more than a scapegoat, as some of these historians suggest, then it must be accepted that it had very little to do with the function of the mechanism of the 1897 Act. However, the historical conditions that made the mechanism of the 1897 Act in Queensland, and undeniably in the Western world, followed a different pattern.

PRECEDENTS OF THE 1897 ACT

One of the first attempts that the Queensland government made to address the Indigenous 'problem' occurred in 1874, when the government appointed an 'Aboriginal Commission' to 'inquire what can be done to ameliorate the condition of aborigines and to make them useful' (Ross, 1992, quoted in Kidd, 1997, p. 25). The commission concluded that 'the aggressive conquest of aborigines in the Northern frontier districts be replaced by a policy of "conciliation" through the distribution of rations and blankets' (Kidd, 1997, p. 26). The Aboriginal Commission was dissolved shortly after that year, but the distribution of rations and blankets was adopted as a Queensland government policy: rations, tomahawks, tobacco, and blankets were distributed in different locations throughout Queensland. Blankets were used to provide early estimates of the population of Indigenous Australian peoples in Queensland (Diamond, 1997). However, blankets have also had an aggressive history in other parts of the world and other parts of Australia. Campbell (2002) discussed this history in his book *Invisible Invaders*, where he demonstrated how, in the second half of the 18th century, blankets were used to spread smallpox among the Native Americans in the United States. The use of blankets to spread diseases also occurred in Australia. Campbell states that:

> Like Curr, Butlin claimed that smallpox in Aboriginals followed an introduction at Sydney, and attributed the outbreak to the surgeon's supply of bottles of virus material. The one possibility that Butlin did not consider was that the bottles were never opened. His opinion differed from Curr's in that he proposed a second introduction in 1829 that occurred through blankets being sent ashore from a ship at Sydney. (Campbell, 2002, p. 219)

The history of the arrival of diseases like smallpox is an object of historical debate. However, there is very little doubt that one of the first ways to manage the Indigenous 'problem' was through violent conquest, and that for some these ways included the purposeful spreading of diseases (Campbell, 2002).

The next time that the Queensland Parliament actively discussed Indigenous Australian peoples was in relation to the 1881 Pearl-Shell and Beche-De-Mer Fishery Act (1881 Act). This Act aimed to regulate the very profitable practice of pearl shelling and beche-de-mer that had existed for decades before the Act. This business was primarily located in North Queensland and the Torres Strait Islands. The government was concerned about the treatment of the labourers in the industry and decided to create a law to regulate it, primarily through taxes and specific fines to the boat owner offenders. In the 1881 Act, a 'native labourer' was defined as 'any Aboriginal native of Australia or New Guinea, or of the islands adjacent there to' (Pearl-Shell and Beche-De-Mer Fishery Act 1881, p. 123). Although the Parliamentary Debates recorded many cases in which native labourers were treated cruelly, there was no single section of the 1881 Act that specifically addressed this concern. In Section 12, the Act states, 'the master is liable for expenses incurred in the maintenance of Polynesians and native labourers' (Pearl-Shell and Beche-De-Mer Fishery Act 1881). Then, in Section 13, the Act commanded that any death or desertion must be reported, and this section started with addressing the master: 'any master or employer of such Polynesian or native labourer who fails to make any such report shall be liable to a penalty not exceeding ten pounds' (Pearl-Shell and Beche-De-Mer Fishery Act 1881, p. 121). The arguments for the approval of the 1881 Act revolved around wanting to promote better working conditions, and some members of Parliament in Queensland quoted specific 'horror' stories of masters of vessels, usually Malays or non-white peoples, leaving labourers thousands of kilometres from their home ports and other stories of simply not being appropriately paid after months of (unpaid) work. Interestingly, almost all Parliamentary Debates focused on the 'native labourer' although the Act only mentioned them in Sections 13, 14, and 17 out of a total of 19 sections. It appears that this was the first time that the 'native labourer' topic of the 1881 Act functioned as a vehicle to implement a formal control in a specific area, which, in this case, was the pearl shelling and beche-de-mer industries. It was a very effective vehicle given that the entire conversation focused only on this topic, i.e., the native labourer or Indigenous Australian peoples, and not on the nature of the industry.

Three years after the 1881 Act, The Native Labourers Protection Act of 1884 (1884 Act) was passed. This law specifically intended to regulate the 'improper employment' of Indigenous Australian peoples defined by the same legal definition as 'native labourer' used in the 1881 Act. Again, this topic primed a very intense debate framed with expressed feelings such as those from the member of the Queensland Parliament, Mr. Archer: 'I see no reason why we don't protect the aborigines as we protect the Polynesians'

(*Queensland Parliamentary Debates* 1881, p. 129). From this point on, Queensland Parliament engaged in a discussion revolving around race relations:

> Mr. Archer: I am perfectly in favour of what the Hon. Premier is trying to effect by this Bill: I wish that every native labourer on board ship, or any other place, should be properly treated—have fair play and the same protection as white man . . . the bill has my complete sympathy. I do not think I ever ill-used a man on account of the colour of his skin, and I do not want to see him ill-used. (*Queensland Parliamentary Debates* 1881, p. 184)

This seemingly progressive account in 1884 of this member of Queensland Parliament evoked a proportionately opposite effect in other members, as seen in this statement:

> Mr. Morehead: I think the sentimentalism in the way of protection of the black Aboriginal race of this colony is running rampant . . . I am perfectly certain the hon. The Minister for Lands could point out how he and others assisted in sweeping the blacks out of the western portion of the colony, and very properly, too no doubt. Where the white man appears the black disappears, as was said by a very great authority, John Arthur Roebuck, in speaking with reference to the New Zealand war. There is no doubt it should be so, and it is so. We may mitigate the severity of the process, but that is all, this is merely a measure of mitigation. I am sure the junior member for North Brisbane thinks the sooner the black races are swept the better. I am sure he detests them, and I think he would support a measure that would hurry their departure to another and possibly better sphere that they now occupy. (*Queensland Parliamentary Debates*, 1881, p. 185)

In the above quote, the member of Parliament clearly states that the global discourse of blackness and indigeneity is being exerted on Indigenous peoples in Australia, while simultaneously framing Indigenous peoples as a 'dying race' for whom death must be 'mitigated', in line with what scholars like De Gobineau were stating. Mr. Morehead and Mr. Archibald Meston were part of the group who would be responsible for designing and pushing the 1897 Act (Kidd 1997; *Queensland Parliamentary Debates* 1898). In 1881, it was one of the first times that Indigenous Australian lives were formally discussed in Queensland Parliament. However, there was no discussion, or very little, about the approval or disapproval of the bill itself. The debate focused on the 'nature' of Indigenous Australian peoples. The debate revolved around the efforts needed to be undertaken to 'save' this 'dying' race, or if any effort from the government to 'save them' was an exercise in futility. For this debate around 'saving a dying race' to occur, an entire imagery of the nature of Indigenous Australian peoples was drawn from the current understandings based on preexisting colonial imagery of indigeneity and blackness, at times explicitly citing the experiences of the United States, New Zealand, and other colonised countries. The context in which this imagery was drawn was in the main topic of the bill, which was labour.

The 1884 Act intended to regulate and protect the employment conditions of native labourers through instituting a bill that exclusively addressed them. The 1884 Act was officially repealed in 1939 when the 1897 Act assumed the functions of the 1884 Act de jure (or officially), because the 1897 Act had been regulating Indigenous Australian labour since its de facto implementation. Labour appeared to be the first vehicle for the representations of Indigenous Australian peoples in Queensland Parliament. For example, one of the members of Parliament painted a picture of Indigenous Australian peoples in relation to labour in this way: 'Mr. Black: "The Aboriginal native of Queensland, or of Africa, or of the South Sea Islands, did not work in his own country: he hunted; it was the women who had to do the arduous work"' (*Queensland Parliamentary Debates*, 1884, p. 188). In relation to the nature of indigeneity, this quote summarises well the position of many Members of Parliament:

> Mr. Sim: 'Of course we know that we are dealing with a race that occupies a very low position in the scale of humanity, but at the same time we must not forget that at one period in our own history our ancestors lived under very similar conditions, and in some respects very much worse conditions, than those under which the blacks of this country live, and that our race is a product of a process of civilisation which has extended over a period of very nearly 2000 years'. (*Queensland Parliamentary Debates*, 1884, p. 192)

These conceptualisations were a product of a Social Darwinist perspective guided by the modern anthropological discourse discussed in previous chapters. However, the content appeared to be entangled with the historicity of the conceptualisations of blackness and indigeneity. Other members of Parliament expressed enigmatic arguments such as that expressed in the following quote: 'Mr. Jordan: "If those people could be civilised and taught the value of labour then the law could not operate"' (*Queensland Parliamentary Debates*, 1884, p. 197). This comment that the member made speaks to the use of law. The bill addresses a problem, but its positivity (presence) creates the space where the problem of labour lies and is therefore constituted. The irony of the expression gestures to the contradictory function of this law, which aims to regulate labour, but its very existence depends on the verbalisation of this problem. Following this line, another member expressed the following: 'Mr. Norton: "good thing that blacks are employed. This Bill, however, not only restricts their employment, but almost prohibits it, because, in order to engage them at all, they must be engaged in some seaport town"' (*Queensland Parliamentary Debates*, 1884, p. 189). The members of

Parliament knew the power that a law would have to institute the positivity of, in this case, labour.

This positivity of labour, within the conditions of the possibilities of the conceptualisations of indigeneity and blackness, was not a bad thing or a good thing, but it announced an initial 'capture' via these conceptualisations in Australia and the advent of other areas of capture that such laws implied to impose, such as education, wages control, regulation of criminality. That is, this initial positivity set the grounds for the subsequent spaces of control and 'protection'. From the regulation of labour of specific peoples, with specific conceptualising content, the grounds of 'protection' would be able to expand to all directions that arise after this capturing. However, this capture or 'protection' must always refer to the nature of indigeneity and blackness that has its roots in the Western conceptualisations of indigeneity and blackness.

Kidd (1997, 2010, 2012) is right to emphasise the role that labour had in the history of how the Australian Colonial West managed Indigenous Australian affairs. When the Australian Colonial West began discussions about labour and Indigenous Australian affairs, they found very fertile grounds to grow the complex machinery of colonial domination. The seeds of the conceptualisations of indigeneity and blackness were nurtured in the aforementioned modern grounds of colonisation. In particular, the history of the conceptualisation of blackness echoed the labour elements in slavery. The naming of the word slavery was wilfully silent in the 1881 Act, the 1884 Act, and the 1897 Act, even though many labour practices were effectively slave practices (Kidd, 2007; Lake, 1993; Reynolds, 1990). The Parliamentary Debates around these Acts and the reports of the implementation of the 1897 Act addressed slavery through evading and manoeuvring its wording in order to avoid the direct enunciation of slavery. However, this intentional tactic only caused the Act to refer to slavery at all times, which made it ever-present when talking about labour and other affairs. Nevertheless, the word slave or slavery still erupted in the form of expressions such as these: 'she apparently had no blankets, and certainly no wages—the poor thing had proved a hard-working willing slave' (*Annual Reports*, 1899, p. 18).

In other moments, the word was mentioned along the lines of 'not appearing to promote slavery', as some of the Annual Reports and letters from the protectors to the Chief Protector would not seldom state. Historians including Kidd (2010) and Lake (1993) suggest that there were existing slave conditions in Australia towards Indigenous Australian peoples. However, this research is interested in what constituted the grounds of labour and the conceptualisations of indigeneity and blackness in order for these conceptualisations to be the foundation for the machinery of colonisation in modern times, yet with its roots in a colonial history constituted by slavery, both Indigenous and African slavery. That is, all sides and aspects of this debate contributed to the formation of the 1897 Act, including the entangled foundational element of a history that was slavery inside the conceptualisations of indigeneity and blackness.

Slavery is constantly but silently addressed when discussing the 1884 Act because it explicitly discusses labour. The abolition of slavery in other parts of the world occurred decades prior to this point, and it was politically correct to condemn and avoid such actions. The topic of the 'nature' of Indigenous Australian peoples was widely discussed (the Parliamentary Debates had hundreds of pages on this topic), even though the 1884 Act had only 14 sections and was a relatively uncontroversial law. This was the first time that the Parliament of Queensland formally discussed Indigenous Australian people in the light of an Act ambiguously designed exclusively for them. However, strictly speaking, the 1884 Act was not about Indigenous Australian affairs: it was primarily directed to control the employment of 'native labourers' in ships in Queensland. It is illustrative that the 1884 Act sparked a broad debate about the Indigenous Australian 'nature' and labour. The Indigenous Australian topic found a comfortable space in the regulation of labour to exacerbate further conversations to manage the Indigenous 'problem'. These previous laws also found a comfortable space for the implementation of the 1897 Act because it continued the conversations of the Parliamentary Debates and the language of the previous laws.

In contrast, Section 18 was not consistent with the remainder of the sections of the 1897 Act. Section 18 makes the possession of a government-issued blanket by a non-Indigenous person illegal. This detailed section mentions:

> Every blanket issued by an officer of the Government to any Aboriginal or half-caste shall be and remain the property of Her Majesty, and any person, other than an Aboriginal or half-caste, who has in his possession or custody any such blanket or portion thereof which shall reasonably appear to the justices, from the marks thereupon or otherwise, to have been so issued for the use of an Aboriginal or half-caste, shall be guilty of an offence against this Act, and shall be liable, on conviction, to a penalty not exceeding ten pounds. (Aboriginals Protection and Restriction of the Sale of Opium Act, 1897, sec. 18)

Furthermore, blankets are stated in Regulation 9 of Section 31. The Annual Reports list the convicted persons in the possession of blankets for Indigenous people. It also reports the distribution of blankets in considerable detail. In the Parliamentary Debates, questions were raised about the unjustified portion of the budget for the 1897 Act dedicated for blankets and their distribution. The Queensland government spent most of the funding that accompanied the 1897 Act on these blankets: they spent between £2,000 and £9,000 per year, which typically constituted more than half of the approximately £10,000 that was allocated (*Annual Report* 1901; *Queensland Parlia-*

mentary Debates, 1899). This total is the equivalent of approximately $1 million in today's value (Ryden, 2001).

Given the context of the poor design of the 1897 Act as a policy, it can be imagined that the importance given to blankets was just another of the many shortcomings of the 1897 Act. Another approach would question who bene-fited from the large quantities of blankets purchased for the 'relief of Aborig-inals'. Certainly, there was profit to be made in supplying blankets to the Queensland government. Even if all assumptions were true, the importance of blankets was not proportional to these speculative reasons. If the impor-tance of the presence or positivity of blankets had no formal logical justifica-tion, then it had an informal relationship with the 1897 Act. These blankets are the manifestations of the 'hidden foundation' (Foucault, 1974, p. 134) of the pure function of the mechanism of power in colonisation in Queensland, in the same way that the structure of the Panopticon was the manifestation of the pure function of power in many prisons. So, what does a non-linear logical relationship between blankets and the 1897 Act look like? A tangible object is not related to the intangible 1897 Act; thus, how is the intangibility of the blanket, i.e., its function, related to the intangible function of the 1897 Act as a comprehensive law that functioned under the Western formulation of a nation-state without consultation with the peoples it governed?

TOTALISATION

The first component of the way that the 1897 Act operated is described in the elements of the specific matters that the Act regulated and therefore insti-tuted; the sum of the areas that the Act controlled such as labour and crime, and later health and education, and a more precise account of the Indigenous Australian population provided the totalisation or configuration of its ma-chinery. The 1897 Act evolved and was amended in 1899, 1901, 1928, 1934, 1939, 1946, and 1965. The 1897 Act started with nine pages, and only one page was dedicated to regulations (Section 31); in the end, it had more than 100 pages for the Act itself and more than 200 pages for the regulations. The 1897 Act functioned as a blanket or a totality in four distinct ways. First, the 1897 Act aimed to cover or control the location of Indigenous Australian peoples through removals and the institution of reservations controlled by either the Queensland government or managed by missions (Reynolds, 1990). The Western notion of location meant a capacity to move according to the will of institutions. The institutions dictated (and still dictate) ownership, town planning, definitions of communities, and where peoples were meant to be throughout the day. However, other worldview perspectives do not neces-sarily share this notion of location (Meliá, 1998; Moreton-Robinson, 2003; Watson, 2016).

Location functioned as an axis through which to institutionalise Indigenous Australian presence or visibility, which was defined by specific numbers in specific places, and to make invisible those outside the accountability
of the Act. Before the Act, the accountability of the Indigenous Australian
population depended on estimates informed by the number of distributed
blankets, employees that were accountable for the records, and those few
who lived on the periphery of the towns (Kidd, 1997). By 1910, population
control depended on the presence of Indigenous Australian peoples that were
under the authority of the 1897 Act Protectors. In Queensland, by the beginning of the 20th century, just a few years after the implementation of the
1897 Act, the total number of Indigenous Australian peoples was 12,724 in
27 locations (protectorates): these were the 'natives controlled by each Protector' (*Annual Reports*, 1910). The 'dying race' rhetoric was fuelled by the
'accuracy' of the figures of the Indigenous Australian population in the protectorates. This rhetoric was not something unseen in past experiences of
colonisation. For example, in the 16th century, it was used as a reason for the
sudden decline of Indigenous peoples in parts of the Americas. However,
historians such as Sued-Badillo (2008) argued that the Indigenous peoples
might have been hidden so that they could be used as slaves when African
slavery was imposed. Other Indigenous groups in the Americas (such as the
Aztec and other nations in what is now Mexico) were institutionally forced to
marry Europeans and their Indigenous lineage was 'erased'. This is not to say
that disease was not widely reported—records demonstrate that it was—but it
does raise the question of how many of those peoples in the history of
colonisation escaped or were hidden. This question is not meant to be answered in this research; therefore, further research is needed to help illuminate this potentially obscured area of history.

The second element of the totalisation of the 1897 Act was the creation of
the agents and institutions that would ensure that the Act was enforced. The
protagonist agent in the Act was the figure of the Protector, who was a police
officer with the exception of higher management Protectors, such as the
Northern Protector and then the Chief Protector. For example, Walter Roth
was a well-published anthropologist and he served as the Northern Protector
and Chief Protector in the first years of the Act (Ellinghaus, 2003). Other
agents were also missionaries, teachers, nurses, medical doctors, and other
relevant government and missionary employees. The Western government
institutions that were quickly included in the protectorates were the police,
labour management or human resources, schools, reformatories, and other
institutional activities such as agriculture, building, domestic chores, and
more.

The setting in which the 1897 Act made Indigenous Australian peoples
visible had various institutional dimensions. The first dimension of the institutions of the protectorates was the penal institutions. This institution was

formalised first because the Protectors were initially police officers. The penal institution deployed its power through the criminalisation of certain aspects of Indigenous Australian practices and through the restriction of what non-Indigenous peoples could do, for example, socialising with Indigenous Australian peoples, opium and liquor use, and the possession of blankets by non-Indigenous peoples were regarded as punishable offenses under the 1897 Act. All punishable offenses committed by Indigenous Australian people in the protectorates and non-Indigenous people were reported and classified as such. For example, it was recorded if the offenders were non-Indigenous and usually the race if the person was not European or white Australian. It is important to highlight that the rest of the penal laws in the colony of Queensland did not apply to Indigenous Australian peoples under the 1897 Act, primarily because they were not considered citizens under Australian law.

Another dimension of the element of institutionalisation was the restriction of employment and labour inside and outside the protectorates. A Protector was required to approve any employer who wanted to hire any Indigenous Australian person under the 1897 Act. Permits for employment were approved and administered by the Protectors under the Act, and the Protectors had the power to agree to the terms of employment. In addition, the Indigenous Australian peoples' labour wages were not paid to the worker, but rather they were sent to the protectorate. The last dimension was education, which was formalised later in the 1900s. This dimension came late, but it became one of the most influential aspects of the protectorates. The education dimension was justified in 1906 by Acting Chief Protector Richard Howard when he advised the Parliament that by associating Indigenous Australian peoples with only the 'right kind of whites', they would become more 'quickly civilised' (Kidd, 1997, p. 112).

These dimensions within the location of institutions operated as control towers to impose a specific Western worldview perspective. These institutions were prescribed by the Australian colonial West nation-state, which was enacting a state without nation. That is, these institutions formed dimensions that were characteristic of the Western notion of state, but this state did not emerge from the nation it governed as the Australian nation-state imposed it. This totalisation can appear to be pure totalitarianism or imperialism, but to state this is to overlook the process that allowed this to occur. Colonisation in the 19th and 20th centuries is distinguished in order to prescribe a state that is (often) a product of a democratic nation-state. This operation usually involves an explicit imposition, or sometimes the replacement of all important institutions and their agents, of a given nation or nations (Grosfoguel, 2003).

The third element of the totalisation component of the 1897 Act, following location and institutions and their agents, is the restriction and creation of the production modes that allowed for the capitalisation of labour. By virtue of committed historians like Kidd (2006), we know that the 1897 Act provided the conditions through which the controlled wages of Indigenous Australian peoples were stolen: under the Act, wages had to be paid to the protectorate and they were kept in trusts and not paid in full to Indigenous Australian peoples. The 1897 Act restricted the employment of Indigenous Australian peoples, as mentioned earlier, through granting or denying permission to work. The 1897 Act also commanded that the protectors controlled the wages. These wages were directed to a trust fund. Some of these wages were available to give Indigenous Australian peoples 'pocket money'. Another portion of the wages was used for the operation of the protectorates. The regulation and control of the labour and wages in any given mode of production adds an important characterisation to the 1897 Act, of which some historians have suggested is a form of slavery in practice (Kidd, 2007; Lake, 1993; Reynolds, 1990).

This capitalisation of Indigenous Australian labour shares a common ground with the capitalisation of slavery in the 16th century, and it has a close relationship with the constituting narratives of indigeneity and blackness. That is, the control of wages and labour, and the explicit intention of the 1897 Act to make protectorates sustainable and even profitable (e.g., Thursday Island, see *Annual Reports*, 1905) is the enslavement of labour (Kidd, 2006). Indigenous peoples were no longer owned, but the ownership was directed to the pure modes of production,[1] i.e., the productive forces and relations of production were considered to be the property of the Queensland government. Instead of blackness representing a direct value and labour being the use-value of slavery, the enslavement of Indigenous Australian labour was the capture of the modes of production and the resignifying of them as pure value. This relocation of value and slavery, which was hidden in the processes of control and explicit monopolisation of Indigenous Australian labour, could be possible given the previous location of value and use-value in the instauration of slavery in the conceptualisation of blackness, and more implicitly in the conceptualisation of indigeneity.

The fourth and last element of the totalisation component of the 1897 Act is the objects surrounding the Act, particularly the objects given as 'relief' and then listed as part of the 'welfare' of Indigenous Australian peoples. At first, well before the 1897 Act, certain items were provided that were interpreted by Indigenous Australian peoples as goods, such as tobacco, tomahawks, blankets, flour, fishhooks, liquor, rations, and other 'necessary items to obtain food' (*Annual Reports*, 1900) according to the Queensland government. Objects are influential to evolving social practices in any given society, and Indigenous Australian peoples are not an exception. This is not to say that objects determined the cultural practices, but that social practices occur around objects and they tend become part of everyday life. The key example recorded in the reports are the blankets because they became so important to Indigenous Australian peoples that when the distribution stopped in 1905, the reports recorded that the Indigenous Australian peoples preferred the blankets over any other relief items (*Annual Reports*, 1906). Therefore, objects that link one group of peoples with another, and then form a specific relationship between them, are influential in the way that the relationship is formed. In general, Indigenous Australian objects were not mentioned in the materials analysed, except in anthropological reports.

Blankets continue to be more consistently referred to in the Annual Reports, and even in the Parliamentary Reports, than seemingly more important topics such as crime, opium, and tobacco and alcohol consumption. The blankets were provided as an item of relief under the 1897 Act, but they had an independent section in the official documents such as the Annual Reports and in the law. The importance of blankets could be representative of the adverse conditions in Queensland because Indigenous Australian peoples were removed from their lands and relocated to unfamiliar lands. Furthermore, the government used the blankets to survey Indigenous Australian peoples, as mentioned previously. Thus, they functioned in the accountability of the Indigenous Australian population. It is the argument of this research that these reasons (and others) were not proportionate to the importance that the 1897 Act gave to the blankets, which were sometimes regarded as useless items. Even in the year after the blankets were replaced by other relief items, the Annual Report (1906) reported the following:

> Last year, on the recommendation of Dr. Roth, a change in the distribution was made so far as the Northern division of the State was concerned, in that tomahawks, knives, pipes, tobacco, print dresses, fishing lines, and fishing hooks were substituted to some extent for blankets, as it was thought then that these articles would be more acceptable than blankets to the recipients. This year, however, the substituted articles were not supplied to the same extent as last year, as the distributors reported that, in most cases, the aboriginals preferred the blankets. (*Annual Reports*, 1906, p. 9)

The reason why Indigenous Australian peoples preferred the blankets to other items is not an objective of this research: what is relevant in this research is the importance of this item (the blankets) and what it could be communicating about the 1897 Act. Why is this object found to be of such importance when unearthing the 1897 Act machinery of colonisation?

Until this point, it has been discussed that the Blanket Approach of policy analysis implies a simplistic policy that attempts to address a complex phenomenon or problem, which is a form of totalising the problem. However, the way in which a given totalisation is delivered through understanding the blankets as a form of content, which is described as the *Blanket Approach*, is very different. The state is no longer a kingdom that commands the subject by royal decree in the imperial sense of the form of government. Instead, governments serve the delegated will of the 'people' creating the nation (people)-state (government) formula. The nation-state form of governance constitutes the operation of every given state that is derived from that logic or formula. That is, the explicit[2] form of governance of the nation-state implies a conversation between the nation (people) and its representative, which is the state. The state obeys the initial command of the nation expressed in a social contract; this is the explicit and current Western formula of government. The 1897 Act functioned from Western view of a state designed by the nation-state of the colony of Queensland that commanded a nation (or a group of nations), but in a similar form to a normal state. A standard, or a totality, is designed and encrypted in law, enforced by agents and institutions, and delivered individually, just like the blankets. The totalisation operation of the Blanket Approach instituted a state without a nation with a specific set of areas of law that created legalities and illegalities (Deleuze, 1985; Dworkin, 1998) that it not only operated as an imperialistic imposition of a government (like a kingdom), which is a form of government that has been historically proven to be ineffective (Castro-Gómez, 2007), but also in the nation-state formula of production of the subject, which is a colonised subject in this case. Therefore, as a state, the 1897 Act simultaneously covers a set of nations and each individual that is under the Act: thus, how is the operation of totalisation delivered to the subjects that the Blanket Approach covers?

MULTIPLICITY

By 1899, the registered employment permits for Indigenous Australian peoples under the 1897 Act in Queensland accounted for 303 persons in Normanton, 80 in Townsville, 289 in Cooktown, 291 in Thursday Island, 54 in Charter Towers, 75 in Mackay, 151 in Coen and Cape Tribulation, and 92 in Cairns (*Annual Reports*, 1900). In 1916, the state of Queensland was divided into 64 protectorates, and the number of registered employment permits increased to 3,853 males and 823 females (*Annual Reports*, 1917). In 1937, 5,480 Indigenous people were in regular employment (3,701 full bloods and 1,779 half-castes, as was documented). The year of 1899 reported a total of 6,126 blankets issued in the three police districts of Townsville, Cairns, and Normanton. The blankets were only distributed to 'the blacks that were not in regular employment' (*Annual Reports*, 1900). The employment figures and blanket distribution assisted the state with the Indigenous Australian population estimates. The population estimates of the Queensland government in 1903 reported Queensland as having the second largest Indigenous Australian population with 25,000 people. New South Wales reported the largest population with 30,000 people and Victoria reported the smallest figure with

382 people (*Annual Reports*, 1904). For more than one hundred years before the 1897 Act, the population estimates had been being reported as problematic by members of Parliament, commission reports, and other documentation of the Queensland government. The main problem was that the numbers were 'only estimates' (Evans, 2007). From a Western perspective, it makes sense that in order to 'solve a problem', in this case the problem of Indigenous affairs, the real number of those who the problem speaks of must be produced. For the first 40 years, the 1897 Act attempted to construct a complete picture of the Indigenous Australian 'problem' primarily through using accurate population numbers.

Multiplicity, which was coined by Riemann (Derbyshire, 2004) and then used more broadly by Husserl (2009), Deleuze (1985), and other theorists, refers to the operation in between the total and the one, or its unit. Multiplicity uses numbers as a tool to consolidate the operation in which subjectivity is managed in between the spaces of totalisation and that of the subject, i.e., how the blanket of colonisation is distributed. That is, a given multiplicity is the pathway to providing a given narrative of a subject. Obviously, numbers and figures do not pose a problem and are oppressive in themselves because they served an important descriptive function for what the numbers referred to. Here, the focus is on the capacity of these numbers to simultaneously speak of each unit and of the total, because the numbers in themselves mean very little as numbers are aided by a given narrative or a total of stories. The totalisation of colonisation draws a picture of what it speaks of, the colonised subject, through elucidating a set of figures that tell a set of stories. However, these totalising stories have the capacity to reach each unit that the total speaks of. At the same time that it can speak of a total of 600 workers in a factory, this total speaks of each person through expressing that figure. The underlying story or narrative of the workers in the factory is constituted through the identification of the total number (600) and, through this, the narrative is distributed to each of the workers individually. Furthermore, it is indifferent to the problems of generalisations and individualisations given that it does not claim accuracy in deduction or in induction forms of reasoning. Discourses (are a) function to produce subjectivity. Following this line, Deleuze states: 'The subject is dialectical, it has the characteristic capacity of "being" in the first person experience, from which discourses start, but enunciative multiplicity is an anonymous primitive function that only allow the subject to live and be in the third person experience and its derived functions' (Deleuze, 1985, p. 41). Thus, multiplicity here is not only the point in which discourses and subjects meet, but it also operates as the modulator of the intentional and non-intentional experiences (Deleuze, 1985). In this dynamic state, the subjectivity and the person that meet are referred to by and through the number. That is, multiplicity is the point in which the totality enters. In the function of the administration of the colonised subject, a given story is totalised, yet a second operation is required in order to reach to the subject and that is the function of multiplicity: the operation in which a given blanket of totalisation is distributed or 'handed down'.

As the 1897 Act continued to operate, it reported more and more figures using the set of narratives from the Act; it reported figures of crime, school attendance, items of relief, labour and employment, and other topics informed by the anthropological discourse or knowledge of the nature of Indigenous Australian peoples. The set group of stories or enunciations provided a productive capacity to create more stories that are self-referential to the first stories. Multiplicity is a better method of telling the story of a number because it refers to the entry and exit points in the subject. The multiplicity of the figures of school attendance in the Protector Reports in Queensland in the early 1900s tells a different story than the multiplicity of the figures of school performance or the figures of the number of schools per population ratio. The multiplicity of the figures of removals and relocations tell a different story than that of the figures of property owners or available housing in remote and urban areas. This is not to posit that multiplicity is limited to a politics of numbers and figures; that is, multiplicity is not only the use of numerical data to support an argument. The illustrations of multiplicity tell a story that speaks to the nature of the operation of the multiplicities as a derived function of the total body of a command expressed, in this case, by a law. The productive and effective capacity of multiplicity lies in how the total picture of the story is delivered to each of the units of the whole.

One year prior to the significant amendment of the 1897 Act in 1939, opium was removed from the name of the Act, and the Annual Reports detailed the following numbers for each protectorate: hospitalisations and diseases admitted for, school attendance, figures of diseases, mortality and fertility rates, marriages (including interracial marriages), specific figures of mostly Indigenous Australian crime, vocational training figures, recreation and types of recreation, and the population of Indigenous Australian peoples divided into full bloods and half-castes (Kidd, 1997). These figures and their accompanying narratives accounted for the 18,024 Indigenous Australian peoples in the state of Queensland located in government settlements, church missions, the Torres Strait Islands, and country districts; the 1897 Act spoke of this total and therefore *of* each unit that comprised that number. At the height of the 1897 Act in 1938, it demonstrated the full deployment of the colonial narrative for the subjects it spoke of (*Annual Reports* 1939).[3]

The operation of the delivery of the totalisation of the 1897 Act was in-function of the derived function of the dispersion of subjectivity. This dispersion slowly but steadily fed back into the framework that the 1897 Act designed, which created a more complex picture and additional elements for its operation. The function or equation always presents more variables and considerations, but it is determined by the root function of a multiplicity of the 1897 Act. The 1897 Act multiplicity function of diseases operates individually through producing the question and the narrative within diseases in subjectivity *to* Indigenous Australian peoples and not *from* them. Concretely, every person could be potentially subjected by the operation of this multiplicity regardless whether the answer of the question of disease is positive or negative. The multiplicity of a report on venereal diseases imposes a specific narrative or totalisation on the reports of the numbers of people suffering from them and those who are not. The function of the operation has been already, or a priori, deployed before the numbers were provided. Multiplicity can be seen being distributed in the same way as the blankets were distributed: individually. However, the distribution of such individual blankets of multiplicity is not sufficient to have a real effect at the micro-level of people. So, how did the Blanket Approach that totalised and distributed blankets of multiplicity in the 1897 Act operate individually? What energised this operation to continue enabling the 1897 Act machine to function?

CREATION OF DESIRE

In 1900, the second year of the operation of the 1897 Act, Dr. Walter E. Roth, then the Northern Protector of Aboriginals in Queensland, stated in the Annual Report of that year:

> Personally, I might be allowed to take the opportunity of expressing the opinion that this annual gift of blankets to aboriginals is in many cases a misplaced charity, that its promiscuous grant should not be looked upon as a matter of right, but regarded rather in the light of a medical adjunct and comfort for the aged, the young, and the sick. I am accordingly impressing upon local protectors of the more outlying districts the expediency of discouraging able-bodied aboriginals not yet accustomed to them from applying 'to the Government' these articles. Of course, at the present time blankets are distributed only to such blacks as are not in regular employment; and I certainly would not recommend any stoppage of the supply to those who have thus become regularly used to them. I recognise, furthermore that the promiscuous gift of blankets in past years has tended to the utter desuetude of the native-made opossum-skin and bark-cloth rugs . . . up in the Coen and Cape, districts of the Peninsula, it is of interest to note the concurrence of view of Sub-Inspector Garraway, the local protector, with that of Sergeant Whiteford . . . 'The blacks up here would be nearly as well off without a blanket as with one; in fact, in most cases now, the blacks who do receive blankets either throw them away or get rid of them before they have had them a month'. (*Annual Reports*, 1901, p. 18)

This was the first reported argument against the distribution of blankets by the Northern Protector, Dr. Roth. His recommendation was implemented in 1905 (the year he was removed from the role) and as stated in an earlier quote: 'the distributors reported that, in most cases, the aboriginals preferred the blankets' (*Annual Reports*, 1906, p. 9).

In order to understand the form of content of the Blanket Approach, the functioning of the object it refers to must be described in the context of the historicity of the 1897 Act. Blankets were part of the relief items of the 1897 Act; yet, for decades before that, Queensland and other colonies in Australia had distributed blankets to Indigenous Australian peoples (Evans, 2007). Under the 1897 Act, blankets were the most important relief item reported. A large part of the budget of this Act was allocated for the purchase of blankets that fluctuated between 6,000 and 10,000 blankets per year. A whole section of the Annual Reports was dedicated to the distribution of blankets and the report of unlawful possession of this relief item. To think about blankets is to understand them as objects that cover the individual bodies of people and protect them from multiple effects. Blankets protect, cover, hide, enclose, and touch people. If a person does not have a blanket, they have to bear the cold; when a person has a blanket, they are *protected*. However, once a person is protected, their tolerance to the outside is reduced. In the context of the 1897 Act, blankets were objects that were present everywhere and eventually became desired as a result of the ever availability of this object.

The creation of desire for the blanket object illustrates the final mechanism of the operation of the 1897 Act. Dr. Roth was right to not see any practical reason to continue to invest a large portion of the budget (between £2,000 and £9,000 per year) on the distribution of blankets. Although the weather conditions in Queensland could have encouraged Indigenous Australian peoples to consider the use of blankets at times, this reasoning can be easily overcome when considering the long history of Indigenous Australian civilization (over 50,000 years). Occasionally, the Chief Protector and the members of Parliament reported that funding was required in order to reach certain areas to implement the 1897 Act and the cost effectiveness of the distribution of blankets was questioned (see *Queensland Parliamentary Debates*, 1899). Other than budget and policy ineptitude reasons from the Queensland government, other factors must have had a role in the importance of blankets. A modern capitalist strategy to make a product attractive is to create the desire for it, assuming that there is no apparent use for it. Sometimes, the sole presence of the item eventually naturalises it into everyday life; once that occurs, its absence will be noted. The noticing of the absence is not only activated as a result of its everyday use or due to its pure function, but it is also activated as a result of the added value of the imagined sense of need. The imagined sense of need is desire.

Leaving the psychoanalytical debate aside, desire is something that is not fully located in the realm of the real: desire can be regarded as the driving force to and for the real produced in the imaginary realm and signified by the realm of the symbolic (Lacan, 1977). That is, objects can produce an added sense of value that is not ruled by its pure function but rather is influenced by a sense of desire. The blanket distribution stopped being reported after 1917, but the instituted function illustrated by this relief item was a manifestation of the final function of the operation of the 1897 Act, i.e., the creation of desire.

The Blanket Approach operation of the 1897 Act had the final function of creating the desire for the blankets of a totalising Westernisation, delivered via multiplicity and developing a relationship with these blankets. The notion of desire in this book is conceptualised closer to the Foucauldian notion of power (Deleuze, 1985) because the psychoanalytical perspective of desire drives an individualistic focus, and we must resist the anthropological discourse dimension of colonisation. If Foucault (2007) stated that 'power produced reality' then in the same gesture, Deleuze (1985) would state, 'desire produces reality'. In that sense, Deleuze (1995) equated Foucault's notion of power with his notion of desire. In an interview, Deleuze narrates a conversation with Foucault: 'The last time we saw each other he respectfully said that he couldn't stand the word "desire" . . . He said something along the lines of, "I can't avoid it thinking it means repression or something that has been repressed, perhaps that what I call desire you would call pleasure"' (Deleuze, 1995, p. 23). However, for Deleuze, desire would mean not only the product of absence or lack of something, but the relationship between people and a given subjectivity or a given multiplicity. This understanding of desire highlights the tension, which transcends simple violence (Deleuze, 1985), between the institution of totalisation, the multiplicity, and the person. Its contact point is not in the positivity of power, but in the specificity of the imagined subject. This process operates subjectively on each person, but in a more or less copied function of a given multiplicity that refers back to an instituted totalisation. Totalisation can be regarded as the mathematical laws or their assumptions, the multiplicity the operation that performs the function of a given unit, and lastly the creation of desire is the reproductive capacity of creating a given result in a serial way, given a set of specific variables and/ or values. The creation of the desire operation speaks to the reproductive capacity of the 1897 Act in the micro-level arena of peoples to produce a serialisation of identifications or identities.

THE FUNCTION OF COLONISATION THROUGH THE BLANKET APPROACH

MacCorquodale (1987) analysed 700 pieces of legislation across Australia in which he identified 'no less than 67 identifiable classifications, descriptions, or definitions' (MacCorquodale, 1987, p. 9) of Indigenous Australian peoples. In his research, he found no clear consistency with the assumption that these definitions were based on the biological notion of race. He states, 'Australian legislation was predicated on the basis of white superiority, and white fear. Both "blood" and economic factors predicated a statutory relegation of non-Caucasoids' (MacCorquodale, 1987, p. 24). Taking aside the biological racial debate, which is not the focus of his article either, these definitions predicate the possible combinations of the understanding of Indigenous Australian peoples and it even suggests that it determines the content of the broad meaning of 'race'. One of the pieces of legislation analysed by MacCorquodale is the 1897 Act, and particularly the definition of 'Aboriginal' provided in that law, which was described in Section 4. This definition focus also framed the discussions in the Parliamentary Debates throughout the years when the 1897 Act underwent changes (for example, see *Queensland Parliamentary Debates*, 1899, 1903, and 1909).

The imposed Western definitions of Indigenous Australian peoples do not determine the identity of every single person. Rather, they are the product of the reproductive capacity of the Western conceptualisation of indigeneity and blackness. That is, the conceptualisation of indigeneity and blackness co-created the means through which Western culture drew the picture of the machine of the 1897 Act, because it was the colonial space of this discursive formation. The function of the creation of desire constituted the reproductive capacity of the Act. That is, the creation of desire is the function that serialises the individual function of the 1897 Act. It combines the serialising root content of a monstrous anthropology and blackness through the functional hierarchy of Social Darwinism.

This imposed relationship, which is instituted by a given totalisation and delivered in a given multiplicity, creates the by-product of a given imagined subject. In turn, this creates the desire that will be the void and driver of colonisation at large, which manifested in the subjugation of the colonised. As in the case of the blankets, there was no rational argument to justify the preference for them. However, eventually, the imposed object became desired because the creation of desire was instituted by the readily available blanket of Westernisation. The manifestation of the power or the process of the creation of desire is not only expressed in brute force but it is also, in the case of the 1897 Act, manifested in the disproportionate presence of the individual 'blankets' of colonisation, forcing the subject to establish a relationship with it. The function of the creation of desire is the forced relationship with a subjectivity that is manifested in a created definition of identity that modulates, either positively or negatively, the subject it speaks of.

When Foucault argued that panopticism was the way that that power functions in the operation of 'seeing without being seen', his illustration of Bentham's Panopticon could not be more precise (Foucault, 1976). Furthermore, this architectural design was (and remains) frequently present in the institutions through which power was evidently deployed in a panoptical operation. This chapter is far from claiming such ingenuity and preciseness as it cannot claim the ready availability of the physical structures in the aforementioned institutions of power like panopticism in schools, prisons, factories. The non-discursive way in which the 1897 Act functioned cannot claim that it will physically have blankets in even some of its institutions of power; therefore, a Blanket Approach operation today must be thought within a referent that does not refer to the physical but to, sometimes, the expression of a Blanket Approach. Non-discursive power, such as the Panopticon, is defined by its pure functions: panoptical power can exist without the physical structure. In turn, the Blanket Approach refers to the triple function of the 1897 Act of totalisation, of multiplicity, and of the creation of desire. That is, it refers to the pure function of a blanket as a total, as its potential productive capacity of being distributed individually and its potential reproductive capacity of being imposed. In this sense, the Blanket Approach finds its functional manifestation, at times, in the functional analysis of policy as being a totalising law that addresses a complex situation in the same way as the architectural manifestation of the Panopticon is found in the buildings of institutions that harbour and use panoptical power, such as schools, factories, and prisons.

NOTES

1. The modes of production in the Marxist sense are defined by the unity of producing necessary aspects of life, which is a step prior to the implementation of an added value system (Marx 2002).

2. It is explicit because scholars including Foucault argue that this is not the modern formula of government, but the implicit function of government is best described by biopower and biopolitics (Castro-Gómez 2007; Foucault 2005).

3. See examples of the 1939 *Annual Report*, specifically the various tables with different topics in the 23-page report and pages 3, 5, 7, 8, 10, 11, 14, and 16–20.

Chapter Seven

State of Exception in Australia

(1) The state of exception is not a dictatorship (whether constitutional or unconstitutional, commissarial or sovereign) but a space devoid of law, a zone of anomie in which all legal determinations—and above all the very distinction between private and public—are deactivated . . .

(3) The crucial problem connected to the suspension of the law is that of the acts committed during the *iustitium*, the nature of which seems to escape all legal definition. Because they are neither transgressive, executive, nor legislative, they seem to be situated in an absolute non-place with respect to the law. (Agamben, 2011, pp. 50–51)

At this point, the reader should have a sense that the pure function of colonisation is grounded on the global origins of racial markers—namely, Western aesthetic ideas of indigeneity and blackness, and their permutations—and biopolitically exerted, depending on the location's specific history. In Queensland, Australia, we found an instance of the Blanket Approach biopolitical mechanism. The pure function of colonisation operates within the root formulation of 'to make live the desired races and to let die the undesired races', focussing on the letting die of the undesired races or the 'anomies' portion of the formulation. Within this focus of the management of death, the Blanket Approach functions through totalisation, multiplicity, and the creation of desire. What follows in this chapter is a revisionist approach to Agamben's 'State of Exception' essay through the manner in which the 1897 Act operated as a Blanket Approach form of colonisation that functions in the space of a state of exception from its origins being established as anomie, and thus in the space of exception from its inception. That is, the main claim of this chapter is that the 1897 Act operation is a Blanket Approach that describes the local operation of its management of death, which occurs in a state of exception space: the 1897 Act functioned in a state of exception.

The local Australian diagnosis of the historical, political, psychological, and epistemic forms of colonisation has fertile conceptual grounds in settler colonial theory. In settler colonial theory, Patrick Wolfe used a novel approach to examine settler colonial processes as 'a conceptual structure and not a historical event' (Wolfe, 2006, p. 388), while also addressing the state of exception processes that conceptually reviewed political operations that allowed genocidal (-like) practices. However, a more grounded and authoritative diagnosis of the settler colonial processes of states of exception in Australia can be found in the work of Indigenous scholar and distinguished professor, Aileen Moreton-Robinson, particularly in her book *The White Possessive: Property, Power and Indigenous Sovereignty* (2015). This work significantly augments the implications of the relationship between the whiteness will to property and Indigenous peoples (Harris, 1993) by conceptualising white territorial possession as the irreducible substance of states built by colonisation and through race. In *The White Possessive*, Moreton-Robinson suggestively proposes that the colonisation of Australia was a privileged laboratory in which to establish the foundations of the research area of 'whiteness studies' where epistemological engagement with Indigenous, black, postcolonial feminist, queer, and poststructural thought is possible. This coalescing includes reexamining the 'post-colonising' view of contemporary subalternisations through the state of exception mechanisms, such as the 'Northern Territory National Emergency Response' 2007 intervention,[1] which Moreton-Robinson (2015) argues becomes another example of a state of exception within colonial relations; in contrast, Agamben almost completely ignores the historical and contemporary forms of states of exception and their relationship with colonisation. Referring to contemporary uses of states of exception, and suggesting a link with past policies referring to Indigenous affairs, Moreton-Robinson (2015) writes:

> While the state-of-exception thesis provides a way of explaining how sovereign states responded to terrorism through terrorism security measures, which requires disciplining detainees and citizens, the historical conditions of its possibility can be linked to colonisation. Australia, New Zealand, Canada and the USA have a long history of detaining Indigenous people, denying their rights and controlling behavior through and beyond the law. From the nineteenth century reserves, privately owned pastoral stations and missions were the places where the majority of Indigenous people in Australia lived under the control of white managers and missionaries appointed by government. Indigenous people, while living in poverty, were treated differently to white Australian citizens and were subjects to 'special' laws, regulations and policies that were racist. (Moreton-Robinson, 2015, pp. 153–154)

Beyond addressing the glaring omission of any reference to colonial history—past and present—in Agamben's *State of Exception* (2011), this chapter will contribute to understandings of the no longer exceptional nature of state of exception practices in modern nation-states in the context of colonisation using Queensland, Australia's 'special' laws for Indigenous peoples, as an example. Conversely, understanding that colonisation also occurred within the grids of state of exception juridical-political practices illuminates the governmental complexities of the former colonial nation-states (e.g., the majority of countries in Latin America), the so-called settler-colonial states (e.g., Australia), and the continuing colonial states (e.g., the Maldives, Puerto Rico), and their past and present relationships with the former empires. Similar to the colonising operations in Modernity, as exemplified in the previous chapter when discussing the Blanket Approach as a specific form of biopolitics in Queensland, the 1897 Act serves as an illustrative case study to exemplify colonisation in the state of exception space because its exceptional language is clearly codified and written into the Act. In essence, this chapter aims to provide some starting points to bridge the gap between the incomplete history of state of exception forms of governance and the history of colonisation factoring in the exceptional governance practices in colonial endeavours.

The post-Enlightenment colonisation operation of the 1897 Act focusses on the deliberate suspension or erasure of the authority of the 'people' (or nations) and replaces it with the pure function of the creation of a state from the coloniser's nation-state: a state of exception formulation constituted by a state-state. That is, a type of colonial legislated totalitarianism is represented in the case of Queensland by the 1897 Act in order to administer *every* possible element of life (as understood by Western culture) and life itself. The exceptional language excluding Indigenous Australians was imprinted in the formation of Australia as a country in its 1900 constitution, where Section 127 stated: '*In reckoning the numbers of the people of the Commonwealth, aboriginal natives shall not be counted*'; this section was repealed by referendum in 1967. To discount a racial group from the census enabled interpretations of the wide application of the law in a non-citizen space. This non-citizen space locates a specific group of peoples within the logics of pure exception, only governed not by the constitution—as they 'shall not be counted'—but governed with supra-constitutional measures or exceptional measures. This suggests that the 1897 Act, which is a legislated colonial management, then becomes a juridico-political form of governance that obeys the logics of a state of exception, the peoples in question erased from the nation-state contract, and their sovereignty superimposed by an engineered exceptional state that showcases a state without a nation where the exceptional force of law was founded as the rule.

The complex relationship between the constituted and constituting power in an imposed state and the force of law maps an interesting possible route regarding how the operation of, in this case, a colonising state's assemblage, such as the 1897 Act, could function. Agamben describes the state of exception as: 'the device that must ultimately articulate and hold together the two aspects of the juridico-political machine by instituting a threshold of undecidability between anomie and *nomos*, between life and law, between *auctoritas* and *potestas*' (Agamben, 2011, p. 86). This threshold of incommensurability is the pure function of law or the constituting power. Considering that the 1897 Act functioned in a Blanket Approach manner, seeing a state imposed on a group of people as an exceptional legal assemblage is not implausible, primarily because the Act is outside the constitutive rule of law on peoples in Australia. In colonisation, as exemplified by the 1897 Act state of exception, the incommensurable relationship between the authority of people and a form of government is suspended in order to impose a given device that stems from the Western political logics of exception, which was a device created from the nation-state of Australia.

The 1897 Act will be used once more as a colonisation case study in order to illustrate the type of colonial state of exception logics utilising a wealth of written supporting evidence (the Act, parliamentary debates, reports, etc.). In order to establish the case that colonisation provides the conditions of possibilities for a legislated state of exception, some concepts that Agamben's *State of Exception* offers will be reviewed first. A short history of some of the relevant colonial commissarial juridico-legal texts, such as the '*Requerimiento*' (Requirement), Treaties with Indigenous peoples, and legislation that provides a context of the emergence of the rule of colonial states of exception, will also be included. This will provide the pathway to target Section 31 of the 1897 Act which displays the *potestas*, or the pure function, of this colonial state of exception given its manifest functional language through guidelines that predicate the potential totalitarian power of the Act that can be directed against the peoples it speaks of. Lastly, the operation of the 1897 Act will be used to display the state of exception space in which the Blanket Approach biopolitically operated as a later form of colonisation. As a whole, it will be illustrated that the 1897 Act operates as a form of governance of colonisation as the Blanket Approach, biopolitically, and in the grounds of a state of exception.

THE STATE OF EXCEPTION'S COLONIAL CONTEXT

> But, if you do not do this, and maliciously make delay in it, I certify to you that, with the help of God, we shall powerfully enter into your country, and shall make war against you in all ways and manners that we can, and shall subject you to the yoke and obedience of the Church and of their Highnesses;

we shall take you and your wives and your children, and shall make slaves of them, and as such shall sell and dispose of them as their Highnesses may command; and we shall take away your goods, and shall do you all the mischief and damage that we can, as to vassals who do not obey, and refuse to receive their lord, and resist and contradict him; and we protest that the deaths and losses which shall accrue from this are your fault, and not that of their Highnesses, or ours, nor of these cavaliers who come with us. And that we have said this to you and made this Requisition, we request the notary here present to give us his testimony in writing, and we ask the rest who are present that they should be witnesses of this Requisition.

(Fragment of the *Requerimiento* [Requirement] from 1510 to be read by Spanish *Conquistadores* to defeat the Indigenous Peoples of the Americas)

The state of exception operation was first seen consistently as the norm and not the exception in colonisation. Similarly, colonial states of exception alone cannot explain the operation of colonisation given that they always operated within the biopolitical and geopolitical technology of a government, as well as and at the same time as operating 'on the ground' through local forms of governance (such as the Blanket Approach in Queensland) dictated by the specific history of the region.[2] The *Requerimiento* was one of the first enactments using the force of law to create a state of siege in another country, kingdom, or state that would then justify a state of exception during the 'pacification' of the given country while creating a colony. The first time this was used was in 1513 in what is today Panama, and then it was used in many places in the Americas with differing reactions, from mockery to curiosity from both Indigenous peoples and colonisers. It very quickly became part of the package of every colonising endeavour where this reading of the law was followed by pure violence that asserted the authority of the kingdom in question. This was the beginning of not only the narratives of violence that were discussed in chapters 2 and 3 of this book, but also the assemblage of a governance technology that operated within the logics of what will be understood as the state of exception. This mantra-like reading functioned as the institution of a set of normalising spheres that needed to be 'pacified' through pure violence and through the negative reaction of the force of law, which is an exceptional sphere where, once the law is instituted, it is applied through the suspension of it in order to be able to undertake the grotesque displays of colonisation. Agamben states:

the impossible task of welding norm and reality together, and thereby constituting the normal sphere, is carried out in the form of the exception, that is to say, by presupposing their nexus. *This means that in order to apply a norm it is ultimately necessary to suspend its application, to produce an exception.* In every case, the state of exception marks a threshold at which logic and praxis blur with each other and a pure violence without *logos* claims to realize an enunciation without any real reference. (Agamben, 2011, p. 40, emphasis added)

Here, Agamben almost sounds prophetic, considering the *Requirement*, or any colonisation account, is not considered in *State of Exception*. However, Agamben's suggestion that the acceleration of state of exception governance forms becomes more the norm than an exception heading into the 20th century does not consider the colonial experiences of exception that occurred in every country in the Americas from the 15th century onwards. Whilst in the 15th and 16th centuries, in the Renaissance and Classical periods, respectively, the immediate formation of exceptional governance processes was not at the heart of colonisation—as it was argued in the first part of this book—the 15th and 16th-century texts were important seeds that would grow in the context of the 18th-century formation of nation-states from former colonies, and from so-called settler colonies heading into the era of Modernity. While the focus of this part is not on the origins of these state of exception instituting texts in post-Enlightenment colonisation, it is important to consider them in order to contextualise this case study.

> The Chiefs of the Confederation of the United Tribes of New Zealand and to the separate and independent Chiefs who have not become members of the Confederation cede to Her Majesty the Queen of England absolutely and without reservation all the rights and powers of Sovereignty which the said Confederation or Individual Chiefs respectively exercise or possess, or may be supposed to exercise or to possess over their respective Territories as the sole sovereigns thereof. (Fragment from *Article the first* of the Treaty of Waitangi, 1840, the English version)

Closer to the modern period, or after the 'Enlightenment', treaties with Indigenous peoples were deployed while slavery experiences reached their highest peak in trade and its downfall with the abolition of slavery. Treaties with Indigenous peoples were one of the ways in which colonisation aimed to establish a stronghold in the life and lands, as it was illustrated in the last two chapters and will be further discussed in this chapter. In the space of treaties, the governance logic of biopower is deployed where the aesthetic marker of race determines who is 'let to die and made to live' within the discursive space of philosophical anthropology. The Treaty of Waitangi is regarded as one of the most illustrative examples of an established relationship between British colonisers and the Indigenous peoples of, mainly, the northern island of New Zealand (Aotearoa), the Maoris. As the text of the treaty suggests, the language is informed by earlier colonial experiences in the United States with Native Americans. As we have seen before, this modern period is distinguished by the incommensurable pure function of specifically governance, and the aesthetic markers of race are highlighted by anthropological discourse. In this text, the words chiefs, tribes, and so on, rather than explicate what it *means*, it maps what it is *doing*. Many treaties with Native American groups and Indigenous peoples like the Maori use anthropological language to mark an exceptional type of politics in which a dominating nation-state (i.e., the colonising nation) always preserves its ultimate sovereignty. In the aforementioned treaty, it is indicated in the racially marked words mapped into a specific type of relationship that is not prefaced by a bilateral state agreement. Rifkin states the following about analysing the dynamics of treaties in the US context:

> Failing to attend to the dialectical role biopolitics plays within the broader geopolitics of settlement can result in different but equally limiting modes of analysis. Within the forms of critique common to queer studies, the challenge to Indianization does not necessarily yield an appreciation for place-based collectivity, foregrounding the kinds of racialization performed by discourses . . . Within Native studies, the tendency either is to argue that race is being substituted for politics or to understand the circumscription of Indigenous self-determination as due to a racist imaginary. (Rifkin, 2014, p. 178)

Thus, treaties, which have their ultimate constituted power or authority lying in the function of a biopolitical view of government, might not withstand true self-determination because they are prefaced by an unusual relationship that bypasses similar political agency. Similarly, treaties based on 'racist imaginaries' or colonial aesthetics present a further normalisation of an exceptional feature in modern nation-states. Exceptional laws and constitutional measures that are only applied to Indigenous peoples are not spaces where the constituted power has the force of law, but in fact exceptional measures are reserved and frequently used against the normal positive rights of the peoples governed by the constitutive powers. Furthermore, the pure function of government when applied in an exceptional space operates not as the classical nation-state logics but, as Rifkin highlights, in biopolitical logics where the 'undesired races' are passively yet very effectively 'let to die'.

Political sovereignty, if viewed from a biopolitics logic and not a Hobbesian or post-Enlightenment one, refers to the management of life and death in direct relationship to their perceived value to the state and capitalism. It is useful to remember that sovereign meant, literally, the 'one with the right to kill' (Agamben, 2011), as discussed in previous chapters. Furthermore, as Agamben writes, it is true that: 'There are not *first* life as a natural biological given and anomie as the state of nature, and *then* their implication in law through the state of exception. On the contrary, the very possibility of distinguishing life and law, anomie and *nomos*, coincides with their articulation in the biopolitical machine' (Agamben, 2011, p. 87). Their correspondence, as he discussed earlier in the essay, is a 'fiction' that in the articulation of Western governance arises from the carefully crafted aesthetic imaginings of

Western culture, that in fact masks a type of domination that through the positivity of law, in its exceptional space, advances. One of Agamben's central arguments is that the exceptional spaces of pure violence are less and less exceptional. The virtuality of the exceptional space and its 'marriage' with biopolitical logics appears to make the Western governance view of political sovereignty an inescapable Western and colonising frame.

Colonisation in the modern period, characterised by the incommensurability of its pure function, occurs from the biopolitical logics of governance and is inaugurated in the space of exception making it a 'natural space' to occur, often hundreds of years before the 20th century European examples, for example the grotesque example of Nazi Germany. The frame for these original state of exception governances certainly belongs to Western culture (in the same way that colonisation does) from the Greek and Roman governance practices in the case of political emergencies, such as the state of siege, *iustitium*, and others rigorously explained by Agamben. However, the argument that Agamben presents on the increased frequency of exceptional measures and the effective state of exception statuses does not consider the institution of states through invasion and colonisation from the end of the 15th century onwards. From the early legal documents of the 15th century (of which the Requirement is just one example) to treaties with Indigenous peoples that still hold today, their exceptional status in relation to constitutions and current 'Crowns' of nations-states, former and current colonies operated from their very foundation in an exceptional space. A focussed example of this state of exception within a nation-state through the specific space of biopolitics is the 1897 Act. What follows is an analysis of this exceptional Act considering its local biopolitical function, the Blanket Approach, yet with a focus on mapping how the space of the 1897 Act was consistently managed in an exceptional state, effectively until the 1970s (Kidd, 1997).

EVERY-THING AND ANY-THING

In order to address the means through which the 1897 Act managed the subject it spoke of in a state of exception space where it can effectively be 'let to die', a brief review of what is usually the assertion made to describe the Act should be presented. The typical description of the 1897 Act reads more or less like the statement: the 1897 Act controlled every aspect of Indigenous Australian lives. There is much truth in this statement, and this section does not intend to contest it. However, it must be more closely analysed. In particular, a distinction is made between the words 'every-thing' and 'any-thing'. Levinas (1969) examined this distinction in his book *Totality and Infinity*. To state 'every-thing' means a defined set or a total set of 'things', whereas 'any-thing' means an infinite account of 'things'. Thus, when it is stated that the 1897 Act controlled 'every' aspect, or 'every-thing', it is very different to using the word 'any-thing'. This is not to suggest that, potentially, in practice, the 1897 Act did not control matters that were not explicitly stated by the Act. In practice, the 1897 Act, particularly through Section 31, provided for the powers to control more than what had been explicitly stated. For instance, in Section 31 Regulation 17, what appears to be open-ended power is given to the state to regulate 'all other matters and things that may be necessary to give effect to this Act'. However, this speaks to a defined set of total matters existing in Western culture's framework. This total set is not prospective, but it is defined by the presence of what constitutes the Act; what is prospective is the ways in which the Act might need to give powers 'to give effect to this Act' (1897 Act).

Levinas (1969) dedicates his book to distinguishing these two notions of totality and infinity, ethically favouring the latter. About totality and totalizers, he states:

> It is this outwardly directed but self-centred totalistic thinking that organises men and things into power systems, and gives us control over nature and other people. Hence it has dominated the course of human history. From this point of view, on the neutral and impersonal. Being, for example is important. What is it? Is the most basic question that requires an answer in terms of a context, a system. The real is something that can be brought before the senses and the mind as an object. The acts of sensing, thinking, existing, as they are lived through, are discounted as subjective. A priority is, therefore, placed on objective thinking, and the objective. The group is more powerful, more inclusive, and, therefore, more important than the individual. To be free is to sacrifice the arbitrary inner self and to fit into a rationally grounded system. (Levinas, 1969, p. 17)

In this elaboration, the word 'every-thing' suggests a set of given things, which represent a total: everything is a totality enabled through a system. In contrast, 'any-thing' is an infinite amount of possibilities or infinity: infinity enables freedom. This uncertainty does not allow the systematisation to capture an infinite amount of possibilities. Levinas states:

> To the infinitizers on the other hand, this seems like a partial and biased doctrine. Systematic thinking, no doubt, has its place. It is required for the establishment of those power structures, which satisfy men. But when absolutised in this way and applied to free men, it constitutes violence, which is not merely found in temporary and accidental displays of armed force, but in the permanent tyranny of the neutral and impersonal over the active and personal. (Levinas, 1969, p. 18)

Infinity is freedom and to affirm wording that enables this infinity is to promote this active stance against the unnecessary violence of the systems enacted through the totalizers. To state everything is to point to a totality. The 1897 Act was a law that isolated, captured, and restricted the subject that it spoke of, while referring to its specific totalistic system of law: the state of exception space was not unspecific, or it did not have categorical authoritarian force. A totality is composed by a given set of elements, but the addition (or summation) of these elements is not the totality in itself. It can be said that these elements are subordinated by their totality.

LANGUAGE OF THE 1897 ACT: A STATE WITHOUT A NATION

The power of the state lies in the language of the law. The law, or the 'force of law' as Agamben refers to it, most of the time, is used to force a 'peaceful' state on opposing forces (Dworkin, 1998)—peace maintained by pure violence (Benjamin, 1996). That is, this law is defined by stopping, voluntarily or involuntarily, the opposing force and by this opposing force being called 'illegal'. For example, legislating the social practice of drug use brings the non-use or illegality of drugs into the plane of socialisation, and through that it also results in the social practice of drug use becoming visible (positive) and administered by the regulations of the state. Previously, drug use was not an institutional concern, but in the past 100 years it has become the responsibility of the government. Therefore, what is illegal becomes as much part of the law as compliance with the law itself because it is the state's responsibility to manage it. Deleuze takes a more emphatic stance on the role of illegalities in law, as follows: 'Law administers illegalisms: some it allows, makes possible or invents as the privilege of the dominating class; others it tolerates as a compensation for the dominated classes, or even uses in the service of dominating class; others again it forbids, isolates, and takes as both its object and its means of domination' (Deleuze, 1985, p. 29). The law that takes 'both its objects and its means of domination' is where the double fold of the negation of law finds itself with the state of exception, notably in the 1897 Act through objects such as 'protection', 'opium', 'exception', 'blackness', and 'aboriginal' (*indigeneity*) that function in the space of exceptionalism. Furthermore, as Deleuze suggests, the administration of illegalisms focusses on the way or function it does this, rather than the content that the object might convey: the pure function of law is more related to form and less to content.

The 1880s and 1890s represented a threshold moment in which the Australian state gathered a language through which Indigenous Australian affairs were officially and richly spoke of, discussed, and legislated, from the grids of anthropological discourse. The language forms of Western indigeneity and blackness fed these enunciations in legal texts, and even the constitution as previously discussed. This language conversed with the language of the West and created the instituted intersections that weaved the fabric of the technology that functioned to reproduce the fictive supremacy of Western culture, in this case, in Queensland. Words such as 'protection', 'removals', and 'exceptions' pointed to the new processes that colonisation would institute. Former legislations in Queensland, such as the 1881 Act and the 1884 Act, were only vague attempts to manage the Indigenous Australian 'problem'.

> Home Secretary: The Bill proposes to deal with the subjects I have enumerated in three ways. It first repeals one section of an act now in existence in regards to the supply of liquor to blacks, and places it in this Bill so that it can be found under the heading of 'aboriginals'. It says clearly and definitely that it is the duty of everyone in the community to see that the law in this respect shall be carried out . . . Then the laws regarding the supply of opium are amended so as to overcome what has been the great difficulty in the past—to catch the offender . . . We must make of 10,000 pounds a year . . . Having dealt with these three matters, we have to make a provision for protecting these blacks and securing them in some suitable employment. The Bill makes provision, in conclusion, *for regulations dealing with the thousand and one matters which must arise, but which I could not prophesy or narrate.* The Bill is open; there is not one clause which, if argument and experience are brought before me, I shall not be prepared to modify on receiving substantial proof that the views advanced are better. (*Queensland Parliamentary Debates*, 1897, p. 1540–1541, emphasis added)

With this statement, the Queensland Home Secretary concluded his opening statement for the introduction of the Aboriginals Protection and Restriction of the Sale of Opium Act of Queensland (the 1897 Act). Even with 33 sections, the 1897 Act did not detail the broad intention of this law. That is, the 1897 Act was everything but specific or concise. For example, the definition of an 'Aboriginal' was circular. In Section 4, it addressed who was deemed as an 'Aboriginal' as 'an Aboriginal inhabitant of Queensland' or 'a half-caste who, at the commencement of this Act, is living with an Aboriginal as wife, husband, or child' or 'a half-caste who, otherwise than as wife, husband, or child, habitually lives or associates with Aboriginals, shall be deemed to be an Aboriginal within the meaning of this Act' (Aboriginals Protection and Restriction of the Sale of Opium Act, 1897). However, the words 'Aboriginal' and 'half-caste' were not clearly defined. This sparked discussions in the Parliamentary Debates and justified future amendments. Section 9 introduced the way in which 'Aboriginals' should be recruited into the designated reservations or protectorates, and removed from their current locations, without the 'Aboriginals' being properly defined. The first eight sections of the 1897 Act described the powers of the government to control and administer Indigenous Australian peoples under the 1897 Act. In Section 12, it details at first that 'any Aboriginal employed by any trustworthy person to continue to be employed by such person, in like manner, may permit any

Aboriginal or half-caste not previously employed to be employed by a like person', which made the power of employment in the 1897 Act open for interpretation to those responsible for enforcing this law.

Labour was addressed in Sections 12 to 16; Section 27 addressed liquor; Sections 19 to 25 addressed opium; and the punitive aspect of the 1897 Act was addressed from Section 26 to Section 30. This initial architecture of the 1897 Act appeared to address the main types of law in many given nation-states, such as penal law, civil law, contractual law, and labour law. These types of laws were all addressed in the 1897 Act as though the Queensland government was imposing another government or autonomous state for a specific group of peoples. The part that would function as the constitution of the 1897 Act, which gives the order and the powers of the state over the people, was Section 31. Clearly, this 'constitution' did not begin with a statement like 'We the people', because there was no consultation with the Indigenous Australian nations at the time. However, Section 31 gave the power to the Governor Council and to the 1897 Act to regulate the following:

1. Prescribing the mode of removing aboriginals to a reserve, and from one reserve to another;
2. Defining the duties of Protectors and Superintendents, and any other persons employed to carry the provisions of this Act into effect;
3. Authorising entry upon a reserve by specified persons or classes of persons for specified objects, and defining those objects, and the conditions under which such, persons may visit or remain upon a reserve, and fixing the duration of their stay thereupon, and providing for the revocation of such authority in any case;
4. Prescribing the mode of distribution and expenditure of moneys granted by Parliament for the benefit of aboriginals;
5. Apportioning amongst, or for the benefit of, aboriginals or half-castes, living on a reserve, the net produce of the labour of such aboriginals or half-castes;
6. Providing for the care, custody, and education of the children of aboriginals;
7. Providing for the transfer of any half-caste child, being an orphan, or deserted by its parents, to an orphanage;
8. Prescribing the conditions on which any aboriginal or half-caste children may be apprenticed to, or placed in service with, suitable persons;
9. Providing for the mode of supplying to any half-castes, who may be declared to be entitled thereto, any rations, blankets, or other necessaries, or any medical or other relief or assistance;
10. Prescribing the conditions on which the Minister may authorise any half-caste to reside upon any reserve, and limiting the period of such

residence, and the mode of dismissing or removing any such half-caste from such reserve;

11. Providing for the control of all aboriginals and half-castes residing upon a reserve, and for the inspection of all aboriginals and half-castes, employed under the provisions of this Act or the Regulations;

12. Maintaining discipline and good order, upon a reserve;

13. Imposing the punishment of imprisonment, for any term not exceeding three months, upon any aboriginal or half-caste who is guilty of a breach of the Regulations relating to the maintenance of discipline and good order upon a reserve;

14. Imposing, and authorising a Protector to inflict summary punishment by way of imprisonment, not exceeding fourteen days, upon aboriginals or half- castes, living upon a reserve or within the District under his charge, who, in the judgment of the Protector, are guilty of any crime, serious misconduct, neglect of duty, gross insubordination, or wilful breach of the Regulations;

15. Prohibiting any aboriginal rites or customs that, in the opinion of the Minister, are injurious to the welfare of aboriginals living upon a reserve;

16. Providing for the due carrying out of the provisions of this Act;

17. Providing for all other matters and things that may be necessary to give effect to this Act. (Aboriginals Protection and Restriction of the Sale of Opium Act, 1897, sec. 31)

These regulations covered all groups in the aforementioned sections of the 1897 Act, excluding those sections that focused on opium. One Member of Parliament in Queensland interpreted Section 31 as one that could potentially make the other sections of the *Act* inoperable because it gave too much power over Indigenous Australians to the Governor Council (*Queensland Parliamentary Debates,* 1899). Theoretically, all sections of the 1897 Act could be nullified due to the powers that had been conferred to the Governor Council. Section 31 was the section that the Home Secretary was alluding to when he discussed the '1001 matters that must arise' in relation to governing Indigenous Australian lives (*Queensland Parliamentary Debates*, 1898). In practice, Section 31 gave a 'blank cheque' to the agents responsible for enforcing the 1897 Act, who were mostly referred to as 'Protectors'. Section 31 also provided the outline for the Annual Protectorate Reports to the Home Secretary and to Queensland Parliament. It also provided the recorded narratives for Indigenous affairs that would be expressed in later debates, discussions, reports, and other manifestations of the implementation of the 1897 Act. Section 31 was the core of the 1897 Act because it functioned as the generator of the reproductive power of the *Act* to capture the subject that it spoke of in a codified state of exception space. That is, Section 31 functioned as the source of the power of the law for all other sections of the 1897 Act, in the same way that the social contract of a constitution functions as the source of the power and command of all laws created in a state, made specifically for subjects explicitly excluded from the Constitution of Australia.

Thus, it is not unconceivable that 'special measures' like the 1897 Act became long-lasting, only repealed by constitutional revisions or amendments, such as the 1967 Referendum to repeal Section 127 of the Constitution of Australia. It was inscribed in the form of a totalizing language that addresses every area of life to administer death in the form of 'smoothing the pillow of the dying [Indigenous] race' as it was repeatedly stated in the 19th and 20th centuries in Australian discourse. At this point, it should also be clear that the political language of colonisation is a Western language of politics that, whilst it is not mutually exclusive to, in the case of the 1897 Act, Indigenous governance in the Indigenous nations of Queensland, it is not the language of Indigenous forms of governance in the multiple nations in Queensland with tens of thousands of years of history and governance (Graham, 1999; Moreton-Robinson, 2015; Watson, 2016). The suspension of the authority of the Indigenous nations of Australia through exceptional laws like the 1897 Act is another chapter of the denial of Indigenous Australian ownership of the Australian lands from British settlers; the first chapter being the declaration of Australia being 'no man's land' or *Terra Nullius* that was a doctrine officially overthrown by the High Court of Australia in the *Mabo v Queensland* decision of 1992 (Watson, 2016).

STATE OF EXCEPTION IN COLONISATION

> The tradition of the *oppressed* teaches us that the 'state of emergency' (or state of exception) in which we live is not the exception but rather it is the rule. We must attain to a conception of history that accords with this insight . . . (From thesis VIII of the 'Theses of the Philosophy of History' by Walter Benjamin [1940])

The 1897 Act teaches us that, in the colonisation of Queensland, a carefully crafted state of exception was instituted as a means to govern Indigenous nations. In line with Agamben's view of a modern state of exception being 'an attempt to include exception itself within juridical order' (Agamben, 2011, p. 26)—and guided by Moreton-Robinson's provocation to reexamine 'special' laws for Indigenous peoples—colonisation as a state of exception government as exemplified by the 1897 Act is born and exerted within juridical order. Furthermore, the 1897 Act is not an exclusive case as there are various treaties and similar laws against Indigenous peoples: for example, the 1869 Aboriginal Protection Act of Victoria, Australia, the Indian Act of 1876 of Canada, and Law 89 of 1890 in Colombia. Clearly, this discussion of the specific case of the 1897 Act is not generalisable; however, the colonisation of Queensland does have explicatory power to illustrate a modern state of exception space outside of Europe yet exerted by the West. This should not be surprising in continental philosophy or critical history because, as Foucault emphasises:

> At the end of the sixteen century we have, if not the first, then at least an early example of the sort of boomerang effect colonial practice can have on the juridico-political structures of the West. It should never be forgotten that while colonisation—with its techniques and its political and juridical weapons— obviously transported European models to other continents, it also had a considerable boomerang effect on the mechanisms of power in the West, and on the apparatuses, institutions, and techniques of power. (Foucault, 2005, p. 103)

Therefore, it is unsurprising that colonisation adopts, and perhaps starts, its modern manifestation in the state of exception logics. In short, how can the incommensurable pure function of the 1897 Act for of colonisation can be described at this point? The local operation of the 1897 Act is described as a Blanket Approach showcasing the modern form of government of colonisation that functioned as an engineered Western government formulation of a nation-state, but without a nation in biopolitical form and in the space of a state of exception. The Blanket Approach description refers to the totalisation of the function of the 1897 Act, as well as to the multiplicity that distributed this totalisation individually and, essentially, tailored it subjectively. The pure colonising function of the 1897 Act was to implement a state that came from a nation-state formulation yet in a space of exception. The 1897 Act followed the same structure as the constitution of the government of a state determined by its laws of crime, family, labour, welfare. Therefore, the 1897 Act illustrates the local modern operation of the machinery of colonisation, i.e., a nation-state that produced a state-state formulation in an exceptional space. This state-state formulation was not a frivolous repetition, but rather it was a method of illustrating how the conceptualisation of a state was determined by the Western culture conceptualisation of, at least, indigeneity and blackness, and by the lack of relationship between the Indigenous Australian civilisation in Queensland and the 1897 Act. In this sense, the 1897 Act is a pure function of government because it is pure government for the colonised without conversing with the Indigenous civilisation in Queensland: it is a legislated and carefully planned state of exception. The 1897 Act can simply be described as a colonisation Act; however, the complexity of the processes operating within the force of colonisation must be named in order to describe the real effects of the government of the colonised. The settler colonial 'logics' of elimination, as coined by Patrick Wolfe (2006), do not appear to be limited to settler colonies (usually colonised by the British and thus English-speaking) but by the specific time period in which colonisation is informed by its long-standing history and also by the governance logics of the episteme of Modernity and informed by the discourse of anthropology. Further, Moreton-Robinson affirms that the illegal origin of Australia has not eliminated Indigenous Australian conceptions of land and subjectivity. Conversely, this first or 'original theft' through the legal fiction of *terra nullius* and the incommensurability (for non-Indigenous peoples) of the Indigenous subjectivity and land as constitutive or ontological is what predicates the local colonial processes in Australia. Moreton-Robinson states it better:

> The subsequent legal regimes we all live under are outcomes of post-colonising conditions. Indigenous people's circumstances are tied to non-Indigenous migration and our dislocation is the result of our land being acquired by the new immigrants. We share this common experience as Indigenous people just as all migrants share the benefits of our dispossession . . . post-coloniality exists in Australia but it too is shaped by white possession. (Moreton-Robinson, 2003, p. 37)

Aligned to settler colonial theory, yet with more depth, Moreton-Robinson endorses Wolfe's theory about the structural character of the Australian settler colonial relations, in this case predicated by race and simultaneously structured by the 'original theft' of Indigenous lands which benefits all non-Indigenous peoples. From a heterarchical perspective, the manifestation of colonial governance is specific to its local history, i.e., the Blanket Approach in Queensland, and at the same time in conversation with its global history, i.e., biopower and state of exception. In order to conceptualise the approach operating in the 1897 Act from its origins in the conceptualisation of tragedy-capture-anthropocentrism-conquest and colouring-cultural practice-social status-value or the aesthetic conceptualisation of race is to turn the gaze back onto Western culture's strategies of government and its mindset. The Blanket Approach describes the biopolitical function of the state of exception in the 1897 Act. The Blanket Approach is not a conceptualisation, but rather it is the form of content that describes the pure function of the local exemplification of the biopolitical machinery of colonisation constituted in the state of exception. Colonisation operates as a government of death with the aid of the aesthetic marks of the forms of the conceptualisation of race.

NOTES

1. The Northern Territory National Emergency Response 2007 intervention suspended the Australian Racial Discrimination Act 1975 in order to regulate and, in certain aspects, control Indigenous Australian's welfare funds, land tenure, and it militarized law enforcement, among other controversial policies through special measures dictated by the Australian federal government, given its overarching legal powers over the Northern Territory. The alleged rationale for

this 'intervention' was to address claims of Indigenous child neglect and abuse, claims that have not been fully substantiated as Moreton-Robinson (2015) and others have stated.

2. It is important to state that colonisation Australia did not happen without fierce resistance from Indigenous Australian people, despite mainstream history's insistence in erasing these wars. *Forgotten War* by Henry Reynolds (2013) is just one source that discusses this topic with more objectivity than other mainstream historical accounts.

Chapter Eight

Conclusion

Colonisation

Beyond arguing that colonisation is more than a historical moment in time that is defined in one word as invasion, this archaeology has found that it is also more than a local *or* a global logic of political, economic, and individual subjugation: colonisation is a form of governance informed by local *and* global logics and it manifests in a government of the territories of speech, of writing, of sight, and of movements. This broad description does not aim to fully answer the question, 'what, fundamentally, is colonization?', that Cesaire asked so dangerously; however, it is able to map and frame the ways in which colonisation operates from its manifest expression to its more tacit one. It is true that in conceptually moving from the biological notion of colonisation to its more sociohistorical appreciation, there is a formidable shift. This shift amplifies the view that has provided the rationale for the augmentation of the historical explanation of the past 600 years of human-kind. Moreover, a synthesis of these epistemological binaries requires a con-sideration of the reflexive balance between the individual and the social, the local and the global, and the self and the 'other'. In this fold, colonisation occupies the territories of life and freedom through the landscape transforma-tions of biopolitics and aesthetics.

While this book has been limited by the constraints of philosophical archaeology—this work is not a fully fledged genealogy of colonisation after all—the generalising character of colonisation suggests a form of 'growth' from its beginnings that focused on drawing a picture of the unknown lands and First Peoples of the Americas to its later manifestations that map an operation that constitutes nation-states and their peoples today, i.e., the way in which identity, race and racism, and inequality is constitutive of the current political and interpersonal everyday life in the past century. In this book, instead of focusing on the governance system that colonisation instituted in the beginning, part 1 highlighted the formation of race. In part 2, instead of focusing how race was formed in the heart of Social Darwinism as a tool of colonisation, the focus was on the operation of the governance of colonisation. Yet, as many early anti-colonial thinkers knew, from the beginning, colonisation could not be thought of without the formation of race and racism, and race and racism cannot be thought of without the context and operation of the 'decisive actors' (Cesaire, 1972) of colonisation. This can be also seen in the way thinkers including Cesaire, Fanon, and Glissant wrote about and against colonisation; race and racism certainly had a visual element, and thus aesthetic means, whether in prose or in creative writing, and this was used heavily here through the creation of visions of racism that directly defined the mechanisms of colonisation. Furthermore, this extension of the mechanism of colonisation to a world scale, including the West at least conceptually, is more contemporarily addressed by scholars like Mbembe with his notion of necropolitics and the notion of coloniality elaborated by scholars such as Quijano, Mignolo, Lugones, and Maldonado-Torres, among others.

In colonisation, between aesthetics and biopolitics, there is an extension of a 600-year history and a history of a nation (e.g., in Australia, almost 250 years), between visions of ugliness and domination, and between the pure violence of law and the management of death. The operationalisation of colonisation is constituted by the twofold process of racial conceptualisation and the biopolitical management of death. On one hand, the discourse of Western aesthetics provides a conceptualisation similar to the conceptual art that draws from colonial aesthetics to create the objectified other, where all the a priori discourses draw and colour the image of race using the base narratives of indigeneity and blackness. On the other hand, the biopolitical management of death uses these racial aesthetic conceptualisations as a frame and markers to kill the 'undesired races' in biopolitical code, i.e., they create the conditions of possibility where colonised peoples are 'left to die'. Exceptional instruments of biopolitical governance prime this management of death in colonisation, where local histories create specific mechanisms to facilitate colonisation, such as the case study discussed here of Queensland, Australia, that used the Blanket Approach. *Thus, race and colonisation appear to have no space between them, and they appear to be a constitutive double where one perpetually implies the other while each conserves its own distinctness.*

AESTHETIC CONCEPTUALISATION OF RACE

> Decolonization, which sets out to change the order of the world, is, obviously, a program of complete disorder. But it cannot come as a result of magical practices, nor of a natural shock, not a *friendly understanding*. (Fanon, 1963, p. 36, emphasis added)

If race is constituted by aesthetics, specifically a monstrous one within an aesthetics of ugliness, then some discourses of art can further inform the dynamics of race and by extension colonisation. Similar to what has been argued in this book regarding the aesthetic conceptualisation of race (henceforth, the conceptualisation of race), and to an extent much of the epistemological nature of representation in aesthetics, a comparison with a conceptual art shift from the fixed representation of objects to new interactions between objects, space, and temporalities can be made: a revisited conceptualisation of this art focused on form (Groys, 2011). Let us briefly reexamine this new conceptualism in light of its comparison with the reviewed history of the aesthetic conceptualisation of race.

Similar to the epistemological shift from the Classical period to the Modernity period, there is an art shift from a focus on representation and content to a focus on form or the spatial arrangement of content. That is, the epistemological shift from content to form, or from significations to syntax, is characteristic of late Modernity. Groys explains:

> We all know the substantial role that the 'linguistic turn' played in the emergence and development of conceptual art. Among other currents, the influence of Wittgenstein and French Structuralism on conceptual art practice was decisive. This influence of philosophy and later of so-called theory on conceptual art cannot be reduced to the substitution of textual material for visual content—nor to the legitimations of particular artworks by theoretical discourses. Rather that the installation space itself was reconceived by conceptual artists as a sentence conveying a certain meaning—in ways analogous to the use of sentences in language. Following a certain period of the dominance of a formalist understanding of art, with the appearance of conceptual art, artistic practice became meaningful and communicative again. (Groys, 2011, para. 3)

Thus, the form that the language of art and aesthetic discourse is informed by is an installation of narratives ordered by a syntax or in an arrangement that serves the same function of a language, which is communication. If this aesthetic logic is extended to the conceptualisation of race, then it is easy to arrive at the view that race is no longer constituted by a static description but rather by an arrangement of a set of narratives that coalesce a determined set of definitions provided by the permutations of the base colours of indigeneity and/or blackness. That is, rather than provide specific content informed by aesthetics, the arrangement of narratives paints, and thus modulates, the constitution of the object and subject in question. If this is true, then it becomes clearer why the first anti-colonial thinkers, including Fanon, Cesaire, and Glissant, attempted to make sense of the nature of colonisation outside the content of the independence movements and that communicated their anti-colonial views using aesthetics as a medium to pierce the aesthetic discourse's logic predicated mostly by form and not by focusing on disproving factual information or re-presentations. The focus on form explained the function of colonisation operating between the racial arguments and colonial arguments, and it also functioned as a way to speak back to the issues of race and colonisation at once given that these were distinct features only united through incommensurable operations.

However, the task of explaining the conceptualisation of race would not be to unveil the 'false consciousness' ideological representation to be discarded as a mask and operation as truth. In other words, this does not mean that in colonisation the aesthetic forms of race were not contemplated forms or colonisation in general was not informed by an operation using a pre-Enlightenment order. As this book emphasizes, the shift is in the *focus* from representation to pure function, from inequality defined by institutions to inequality defined by the Western conceptualisation of race, from aesthetics to biopolitics. From its beginning, colonisation has operated in the simultaneity of processes that define the nature of history. This shift in focus from content to form in race annihilates the social conventions that predicated inequality through the rules of a given ruling institution, which were considered unduly complicated, to a sober and minimalist inequality that is 'carried' in every body. As seen in De Gobineau's book, inequality is communicated using the types of coloured races and it establishes a syntax that is more concerned with prose, narratives, or rhetoric in general. Returning to mainstream Western aesthetics, Kant's *Critique of Judgement* here emerges with vigour when the spectators' experience is the focus of post-Enlightenment aesthetics, where he does not only institute the discourse of anthropology where thinking emerges and is limited by 'Western man' or Western culture in general, but its aesthetics also almost exclusively presents beauty and the sublime as the only subjects to be contemplated. Thus, ugliness, which is understood here as the parallax reflection of Western 'qualities', is no longer part of the universe predicated by the divine that included monsters, portents, demons, and so on. In Kant, ugliness is incommensurably deployed as parallax aesthetics through a projection of the negative characterisation of the Western man. In this shift in focus to a minimalistic aestheticisation of race, there is a convergence to late Modernity conceptualism. Groys explains how the creative act is not naïve: 'Every act of aestheticization has its author. We always can and should ask the questions: who aestheticizes—and to what purpose? The aesthetic field is not a space of peaceful contemplation—but a battlefield on which gazes clash and fight . . . this suggests the subjugation of life under a certain form' (Groys, 2011, para. 16). Indeed, if we follow Kant's view of how aesthetics relies heavily on spectators, or aesthetic judgement starts and ends in the viewers, then content and form here are increasingly created by them. Yet, it is important to state that Groys does depart from the 'free' and 'peaceful' depiction of Kantian contemplation, which is seen ubiquitously in the aesthetic conceptualisation of race when founded on inequality governed by a given institution or later by its very constitution of race.

In aesthetic terms, inequality is expressed in the coloniser and the colonised dialectic as the colonised being the slave artist and the coloniser the spectator that constantly creates the object though racial conceptualisation. If, in art, the artist is creative inasmuch it is self-representation, creating a Hegelian relationship in which the artist is the slave and the spectator the master, then, in colonisation, aesthetics must have a similar relationship with the Fanonian precaution of the distinctiveness of the master–slave relationship in the context of colonisation. In a footnote in his *Black Skin, White Masks*, Fanon states:

> For Hegel there is reciprocity; here the master laughs at the consciousness of the slave. What he wants from the slave is not recognition but work. In the same way, the slave here is in no way identifiable with the slave who loses himself in the object and finds in his work the source of liberation. The Negro wants to be like the master. Therefore he is less independent than the Hegelian slave. In Hegel the slave turns away from the master and turns towards the object. Here the slave turns towards the master and abandons the object. (Fanon, 2008, p. 172)

Thus, in the aesthetic coloniser–colonised relationship, the object of this conceptualisation of race is inherently a frame of objectification where the form of colonisation operates and the coloniser's volition is to be closer to where humanity lies. Colonial aesthetics forces the subject to become a slave artist as long as it satisfies the readily available frame of the a priori aesthetic conceptualisation of race. This conceptualisation unquestionably has nothing to do with the subject: the spectator only sees the conceptualisation of race as it *must* correspond to the object that frames this conceptualisation.

RACE AND THE BIOPOLITICAL MANAGEMENT OF DEATH: COLONISATION-RACE/RACE-COLONISATION

> Death here achieves the character of a transgression. But unlike crucifixion, it has no expiatory dimension. It is not related to the Hegelian paradigms of prestige of recognition. Indeed, a dead person cannot recognize his or her killer, who is also dead . . . Whether read from the perspective of slavery or of colonial occupation, death and freedom are irrevocably interwoven. As we

have seen, terror is a defining feature of both slave and late-modern colonial regimes. Both regimes are also specific instances and experiences of unfreedom. (Mbembe, 2003, pp. 38–39)

Pure conquest in the first forms of colonial endeavours manifested in the forms of wars for the purposes of 'pacification'. Sovereignty as the right to kill manifested the constituted power to create colonies through the incommensurable process of war. It is no surprise that post-Enlightenment colonisation had to abide by the logics of a 'battle to the death', as Fanon would write, as it is deeply encoded in its blueprint. However, from the written and read treaties, and Royal decrees and commands, colonisation shifts its operation to the interwoven hidden foundation of inequality through race. Race becomes the intelligible foundation of racism yet operating in its unintelligible pure function of inequality stemming from the parallax projection of Western man, i.e., the Western conceptualisation of race. What this conceptualisation communicates without words is the operation of biopolitics as it relates to the governances of the 'undesired races', which is the incommensurability of death or to simply disappear. Here, the conceptualisation of race becomes the marker or the target of nothing but the projected self-hatred of the beginning of Western man while also delusionally aspiring to become the fictional subject Western culture has created. It is illuminating how Cesaire sarcastically depicts the thinking of the coloniser: 'These Negroes can't even imagine what freedom is. They don't want it, they don't demand it. It's the white agitators who put that into their heads. And if you gave it to them, they wouldn't know what to do with it' (Cesaire, 1972, p. 60). The question that begs to be asked here is whether Cesaire was indeed depicting how the coloniser sees himself though this projection or defence mechanism. The battle to the death dictum appears to have a death drive will, which is characteristic of Western culture as Freud once diagnosed in *Civilisation and its Discontents*. This, death drive-like approach is less volitional (irrational) when exerted on the 'other' and more operationalised as a form of administration or management of death.

The mechanisms of race and colonisation inevitably appear to be mutually implicated. The incommensurable foundation of race as inequality is determined by the inequality of human races that functioned as the frame for the conceptualisation of race in the guise of human sciences through Social Darwinism to create nations through the biopolitical management of the original inhabitants of a given territory. In contrast, colonisation founded in the aestheticisation of peoples attempted to dominate through a constant state of siege in every instance of exceptionally governed peoples in a state of exception tailored for the undesired races to die out. This twofold view of the problem of colonisation produces a complex machinery that shifts focus according to context, history, situation, and activity. Furthermore, colonisation is a Western product and therefore its government logics are not outside of its worldview, which was insightfully diagnosed by Foucault not as the nation-state but as biopolitics. In this colonisation/race dialectic, many biopolitical states of exception have emerged in the guise of reservations and plantations, or more recent iterations such as economical neo-colonial oversights.[1] Thus, race and racism follow similar mechanics of those of colonisation given its analogue operation.

Race becomes the marker for managing death in colonisation. While this management to specific peoples is predicated by the local history of any given nation, i.e., in Queensland, Australia, with the Blanket Approach, with geopolitical echoes of biopolitical logics and its states of exception, this administration of peoples in general is akin to Western culture's tradition of politics. Similar to management—yet with the characteristic difference of the colonised from Western subjectivity—Agamben identifies a notion that applies to Western democracies: movement. Agamben's (2005) notion of movement is related to the administrative capacity of a government to shape the subject it governs. Agamben distinguishes between the two notions of movement previously described in Schmitt (1933). The first notion is the well-known concept of political movement: 'the decisive political concept when the democratic concept of the people, as a political body, is in demise. Democracy ends when movements emerge. Substantially there are no democratic movements' (Agamben, 2005, para. 9). The second notion relates to the 'unpolitical sphere of the administration' (Agamben, 2005, para. 9), where the unpolitical or non-political character of people becomes described as a population and its biopolitical character becomes the configuration of such movement. 'The people is now turned from constitutive political body into population: a demographical biological entity, and as such unpolitical. An entity to protect, to nurture' (Agamben, 2005, para. 7). Thus, movement is the mechanism for which the status quo administers Western subjectivity. However, the double fold of movement—in its un-political character—occurs with colonisation and it manifests in the more asymmetric view of administration which ends in management. In the same way that the colonised does not desire the recognition of the coloniser, i.e., the master–slave Hegelian relationship, but rather they desire to become like the master, the administration of Western subjectivity does not function in shaping the subject fuelled by recognition, but the management of death is fuelled by a desire to become like the manager, which is the battle to escape death. The colonised–coloniser relationship is a battle to the death not because of a Western death drive, but because of the drive to escape the management of death, to be alive, to be human. Thus, race is an aesthetic objectification that the colonised wants to escapes because it is an escape from the management of death, not to become a Western man but to become human.

The biopolitical management of death functions from a geopolitical frame that harbours the colonial conceptualisation of race and simultaneously from the frame of the local historicity of a given place which ascertains the final constitution of its expression in a heterarchical manner, i.e., not from a top-down or a bottom-up direction. Its micropolitical manifestation first considers the global and the local at the territory of subjectivity and then its geopolitical manifestation (Castro-Gómez, 2007). For example, the racial conceptualisation of indigeneity constituted by the narrative frame of tragedy, of terror, and of horror modulates the way a person may conceptualise, and therefore define, their lives. Yet their definitions are constructed from the specific historical conditions of the place and group in question—Queensland, San Juan, Bogotá, Buenos Aires, New York, African Americans, Indigenous, Mexican Americans. This does not mean that, if subjected to the racial conceptualisation focus of indigeneity, the person will be determined to live in a narrative of tragedy, but it does mean that this narrative will have significant weight in their life in conjunction with their local historical conditions. That is, their particular life will be in conversation with any given conceptualisation process, and it can be in opposition to a given conceptualisation. A classic example is the stories of overcoming adversity that can only be conceptualised as 'inspirational stories' in conversation with a given narrative that creates the genre of the story. For example, if a person is of Indigenous background and becomes a professor, it can be an 'inspirational story' only due to the underlying conceptualising racial frame that creates the place where the story departs. The power of the conceptualisation of race relies on its capacity to assemble a colonising fold in the subjectivity of the colonised that is created by the conditions of the possibilities of the local institutions and its conceptualising global reverberations. The space of biopolitical government lets the colonised die, but it is an active form of government that manages the colonised and leads to a thanatological *pathos* through imposing the readily available aesthetic conceptualisation of race as a frame and as a marker of death.

ART AS A FORM OF THINKING: THE CASE OF BLUE AND WHITE TRANSFER AS AESTHETIC CATHARSIS

How is the persistence of this reaction in the twentieth century to be explained when in other ways there is complete identification with the white man? Very often the Negro who becomes abnormal has never had any relations with whites. Has some remote experience been repressed in his unconscious? . . . If we want to answer correctly, we have to fall back on the idea of *collective catharsis*. In every society, in every collectivity, exists- must exist- a channel, an outlet through which the forces accumulated in the form of aggression can be released. (Fanon, 2008, p. 112)

Figure 8.1. *Piccaninny Paradise* **2010, Danie Mellor. Courtesy of the artist.**

Whilst it does not follow from archaeological inquiry that other forms of thinking can be explored in explaining a given concept, notion, or praxis, here we will return to the contemplation that inspired this book in the first place; thinking through art will be allowed to explore some preliminary notes of how Indigenous contemporary art, specifically Danie Mellor's art, makes sense of colonisation. In this section, the blue-and-white Spode china transfer (blue and white transfer) technique presents an aesthetic purge (catharsis) of the double movement of colonisation, and Mellor's blue and white transfer technique is used as a visualisation of the operationalisation of colonisation. It is not the aim of this part to represent the blue and white transfer technique as an argument that replaces the historicity presented in this archaeology, but to re-present or view the transfiguration of the contents of colonisation in Mellor's pieces. Mellor is a leading Indigenous Australian contemporary artist who comments on the historical, cultural, and epistemological intersections between Western culture and the many cultures of the Indigenous Australian nations. His artistic work spans photography, paintings, drawings, sculptures, and many more; the blue-and-white transfer technique is just one of his many and varied series of contemporary conceptual art. What becomes illustrative in the blue-and-white transfer technique in this work is the way in which it powerfully comments on the transformation of histories in colonisation, in this case in Australia, and how the double movement of colonisation can be mapped. In other words, the blue-and-white transfer technique illustrates how colonisation uses the global colonial history of the materials used to create blue pigments to paint the history of the specific colonised territories in question in a given specific movement.

Mellor's work paints landscapes of the places and events (imagined or real) in Australian history using the blue and white transfer technique, as seen in figure 8.1. The complicit colonial history of the colour blue was manufactured using a similar manner to that used to manufacture the conceptualisations of Western indigeneity and blackness in order to transform the landscapes of history in a detailed movement of lines that manages the 'real', in this case Indigenous peoples and animals given the non-hierarchal worldview between beings and human of Indigenous Australian philosophies. It can be said that, similar to how the blue-and-white transfer technique is used in Mellor's paintings, colonisation drew and still draws the shapes of landscapes, subjectivities, life, or death of the colonised. Yet the real is never transformed, unless it is dead in this series, commenting on the disparity between the objectification that colonisation imposes (for the purpose of inequality) and its impossibility to capture the Indigenous worldview and therefore its peoples.

In order to describe how Mellor's blue-and-white transfer technique can illustrate the operation of colonisation, this section describes the content used for conceptualising colonisation, which is the colour blue, and the movement for management in colonisation, which is depicted in the transformation of the landscapes. Blue represents a marker in colonial history that had the function to depict frames of exotic images in porcelain objects such as dinnerware. Furthermore, blue paint was a rare colour until the 18th century when it was first accidentally manufactured synthetically. The second element of the blue and white transfer technique, i.e., the transformation the landscapes, indicates a topological understanding of the conceptualisation of colonisation as a cartography of the shared history of Western culture and the original inhabitants of Australia. Mellor's blue-and-white transfer technique mimics the dinnerware porcelain that transformed the British Empire's colonial endeavours into fine dining or collectable objects to be purchased or 'consumed'. However, rather than capturing Oriental portraits and landscapes, Mellor's blue-and-white transfer technique captures Western culture's mind to be observed by the viewer. In that sense, the object to be gazed upon or to be the focus of the study is not Indigenous Australian peoples, but the worldview of Western culture.

The blue-and-white transfer technique is predicated by the colonial conceptualisation of blue as a colour that is difficult to find, and that is historically synthesized by Western culture knowledges. Blue takes a protagonist role in Western culture, whereas in other histories that was not the case. Let us remember Mellor's quote included in the beginning of this book:

> I haven't been able to find an Aboriginal language word for the colour blue. It's almost like blue was not conceptualised, it was recognised through words for sky, for instance, or water. So it's almost like the transformed landscape talks about that which was brought with Western culture—in a way talking about the symbolically manufactured, or the 'change forever'. (UQ Art Museum, 2014, p. 8)

We are reminded that blue is all too Western and a sign that can encompass the history of the West, particularly in the context of Australia. Chinese blue porcelain is regarded to be a classic representation of Chinese culture that began in the 10th century with the Yang dynasty (Zhu & Shao, 2009). In contrast, in Western culture, blue has always been manufactured. To create blue porcelain, the colour was obtained from cobalt blue. However, there are few naturally occurring materials that can provide blue pigments. The first source of blue in Western culture was lapis lazuli, which was only found in the northeastern region of Afghanistan, in Badakhshan (Kiser, 2014). It has been used since the fourth century in Mesopotamian cultures (Kiser, 2014); however, the first time that it was used in its ultramarine colour (the preferred shade of blue, which is vivid and intense) in Western culture was in paintings from the 12th century. In order to produce the ultramarine colour, lapis lazuli could not simply be crushed but had to be extracted using specific chemical ingredients. Given that there was only one source of lapis lazuli, it was very difficult to find and only a few paintings could use it. The most common material for creating this shade of blue was ultramarine ash, but it had a lower quality of lapis lazuli (Kiser, 2014). The first time that blue was synthesized in an alchemy laboratory was in 1709 when Diesbash accidentally created a blue pigment (Kiser, 2014): the chemical compound was a mixture of potassium and iron sulphides. This synthesized blue pigment, which became known as Prussian blue, was the first time a blue pigment had been manufactured in large quantities. Prior to this, because lapis lazuli had been very difficult to find, blue was an exclusive colour that symbolised wealth and beauty.

The history of blue in Western culture is very long and interesting, but other civilisations conceptualised blue, such as the Chinese civilisation in their porcelain. Given that the Chinese culture had blue-and-white porcelain that Western culture considered beautiful, particularly in the British Empire, it was targeted and acquired as a valuable exotic object. Later, blue-and-white porcelain was manufactured in other places including Britain, and it was used in teacups, decorative plates, and dinnerware sets. The images portrayed in the blue-and-white transfers communicated a global aesthetic language of colonisation. Portraits of exotic images from the Orient were embedded in the dinnerware from which meals were eaten: it can be said that the Oriental culture was 'literally eaten' (UQ Art Museum, 2014). This was an analogous way of experiencing exotic cultures, albeit from afar. Mellor states, 'blue and white talks about the idea of the exotic space' (UQ Art Museum, 2014, p. 9). In this representation of exotic spaces, blue represents the West's synthetic manufacturing of an aesthetics to present colonised cultures in a very similar way in which the aesthetic conceptualisation of race was manufactured to represent the Indigenous and then African peoples in early colonial history.

A second element of the blue and white transfer technique is the way it transforms landscapes. This refers to the use of blue to draw a map of history, in opposition to portraying factual historical events: it refers to a totality of the vignette as opposed to the 'real'. This can be seen in Mellor's paintings using the blue-and-white transfer technique, which Martin-Chew (August 10, 2014) describes as follows: 'As an artist he brings together an unusual, innovative hybridization—not unlike the way Australia has been formed. Yet unlike many artists who draw on their Aboriginality as subject, his images also echo colonial histories and European antecedents' (Martin-Chew, August 10, 2014, para. 1). The transformation of landscapes via the blue-and-white transfer technique aims to map the worldview of Western culture's history for the 'real' and for other spectators' enjoyment as it is captured by our gaze upon it, as the West 'looked' at the colonised since the beginning of the global colonial experience. The blue-and-white transfer technique that encapsulated colonial imagery for the enjoyment of the West is similar to the way that it encapsulated the image of the colonised through modern sciences and traditional history. Through colonisation, the West captured the idea of indigeneity, of blackness, and of history, as well as many other ideas, and transformed them into familiar landscapes. The landscapes that Mellor paints speak to a cultural interaction between Western culture and Indigenous culture in Australia. This interaction is not a balanced coexistence; it favours the blue-and-white transfer that surrounds the real.

The 'real' aspects in Mellor's work are painted in their distinctive colours to demonstrate that the blue and white transfer cannot 'talk about them'. The 'real' existed tens of thousands of years before the arrival of the West, and it has a different and, perhaps almost unreachable, history and worldview. The relationship between the blue and white transfer technique and the 'real' representations of the original inhabitants of Australia is shared, but with an inherent dissonance. This difference indicates the asymmetry of worldviews: one populates the surroundings of the paintings and the other exists surrounded by the blue and white transfer but is unreachable by it. In *Memento mori* (see figure 1.1), one of Mellor's more explicitly theoretical paintings, the dead body of an Indigenous Australian person is under a blanket painted using the blue-and-white transfer, while the 'real' is observed in the periphery of the painting that depicts the classic Western method of lecturing and demonstrating medical and anatomical research. Furthermore, it suggests that the rituals and the history of the knowledge, cultural customs, techniques, paradigms, and mental schemas that have not been conceptualised in the same way as the subjects of colonisation have been conceptualised.

However, agency survives precisely in the shift of the gaze and in the unreachable real in two ways. First, the real is ever present and not captured by the blue-and-white transfer or the frame at times; second, the gaze of the real and that of the spectator is being directed to look at the intricate landscape of colonisation. This mapping of colonisation seduces the spectator to closely examine the intricate web-like transformation of historical landscapes, and to be confronted by the convolution of the local and global history of colonisation given that the transformation that this map describes appears to be superimposed on the surroundings of the real. The subject of Mellor's paintings is the blue-and-white transfer technique itself; by extension, the subjects of the paintings are colonisation and Western culture. That is, the transformation of the landscapes is a cartography of the Western worldview and its colonisation, to be engaged with, to be understood, to be known, and, through that, to be captured, and perhaps its incommensurability can be *seen*.

A DECOLONIAL AESTHETIC?

The poetics of Relation (which is, therefore, part of the aesthetics of the *chaos-monde* [world-chaos]) senses, assumes, opens, gathers, scatters, continues, and transforms the thought of these elements, these forms, and this motion.
Destructure these facts, declare them void, replace them, reinvent their music: totality's imagination is inexhaustible and always, in every form, wholly legitimate—that is, free of all legitimacy. (Glissant, 1997, pp. 94–95)

It is far beyond the conceptual limitations of this archaeology to suggest any antidote to the poison of the effects of colonisation or any proposal in general for decolonisation, or decoloniality for that matter. While this book has addressed colonisation starting from aesthetics and arriving at the biopolitical management of death, which can suggest that a decolonial aesthetics—as a starting point—can function as an immunising agent, the complexity that this book inscribes to colonisation should suggest that art is not a standalone remedy to the effects of colonisation. Yet what this book establishes is that the origins of the language of colonisation do not arise from an Enlightenment rationality, but from an aesthetic discourse or logics. Thus, aesthetic

Figure 8.2.   *America can (We) Be Born Again*, 2014, Diógenes Ballester.

logics should be considered in understanding what colonisation is and how it operates in conjunction with race. Similarly, this work suggests that it can be illustrative to examine anti-colonial or decolonial resistances not only in politics, philosophy, and cultural studies, but also in the arts. The following functions as an invitation to reinstate the aesthetic quality of decolonial approaches through a re-examination of the concept in late Modernity and in previous decolonial expressions.

The coining of the phrase 'decolonial aesthetics' is rightfully attributed to Gómez and Mignolo who addressed the arts as another form to enact epistemic and aesthetic decolonial disobedience; it is an innovative phrase that has categorised art practice that is explicitly anti-colonial. However, this innovative phrase—as far as phrases can—has usefully branded an aesthetic notion that anti-colonial thinkers have been grappling with for some time, for at least Fanon, Cesaire, and Glissant. Furthermore, decolonial aesthetics works have been expressed in modern and contemporary visual art, literature, film, and other artforms. In modern and contemporary visual art, there have been political works produced by Indigenous peoples, including Danie Mellor, Tracey Moffat, Wendy Red Star, theatre plays such as Cesaire's *The Tempest*, novels such as Chinua Achebe's *No Longer at Ease*, the poetry in *Poemas del volcán de Agua* [Poems of the Water Volcano] of Mayan writer and activist Luis de Lión, and the poetry of the Puerto Rican poet and activist Juan Antonio Corretjer in *Yerba Bruja*. This 20th and 21st centuries' list of examples could continue for pages. Gómez and Mignolo describe decolonial aesthetics as:

> desobedecen a este juego (desobediencia estética y desobediencia epistémica). Esto es, desobediencia a las reglas del hacer artístico y a las reglas de la búsqueda de sentido en el mismo universo en el que tanto las obras como la filosofía responden a los mismos principios . . . las estéticas decoloniales, en los procesos del hacer y en sus productos tanto como en su entendimiento, comienzan por aquello que el arte y las estéticas occidentales implícitamente ocultan: *la herida colonial*.[2] (Gómez & Mignolo, 2012, p. 9)

This description of decolonial aesthetics focuses on aesthetic colonial disobedience in order to transform colonial subjectivity or to directly address the colonial matrix of power by targeting the coloniality of being. Furthermore, Gómez and Mignolo focus on a 'decolonised' version of the notion of aesthesis as its capacity to be pure affect or sensing to contest the rationality of Modernity, even in aesthetics. Aesthesis defined as such discounts the existence of a colonial aesthetics (effectively colonisation working through aesthetics) and assumes that colonisation or coloniality is primarily constituted by Enlightenment thinking which can be misguiding given the origins of colonisation in the 15th and 16th centuries. In this version of aesthesis, it is assumed that 'sensing' or affects are pure decolonised forms of artistic expressions, and the process in which these expressions occur are not fully delineated in Gómez and Mignolo's account. Thus, it is suggested here that the 'pure affect', even being non-rational in principle and therefore anti-modern, can carry the aesthetic seeds of the origins of colonisation and through this carry the poison of colonisation in the very core of the affects.

While the logics of aesthetic discourse rely heavily on affectations that can resist and sometimes determine rationality as understood by post-En-

lightenment thinking, this does not mean that these apparently free affectations are not still managed by colonial aesthetics, which are dominated by
colonisation and the conceptualisation of race. For example, motifs in visual
decolonial art can draw from the artist and can evoke in the viewer non-
rational cathartic affectations that are not ruled by the binary structure of the
psyche (conscious–unconscious) (Vygotsky, 1972). However, this does not
mean that in the 'chaos' of affectations there is no logics and that aesthetic
discourse does not shape or even manage its expression. In the artistic expression that communicates catharsis, we see a purge in both the artist and
the viewer, and the collective in general. The logic or order of this chaos of
colonisation corresponds to the underlying logic of destruction and death.
Communicating this aesthetic logic in itself through a transfiguration of its
mechanism becomes decolonial inasmuch it can re-present its operation and
logic, but it is not an exercise in freedom itself. Expressions of the colonial
wound disobey colonial aesthetics through mediums such as catharsis. However, they are not fully free from an aesthetic management of affectations or
from sensing with an underlying logic that pervades the very core of feelings;
colonisation is also a government of beings and its affectation as decolonial
scholars such as Maldonado-Torres have stated (see, for example, Maldonado-Torres, 2008). However, in trying to unravel the affective logic of colonial aesthetics, Glissant's *chaos-monde* provides an interesting perspective that
could best inform the complexities of a decolonial aesthetic in subjectivity:

> The *chaos-monde* is only disorder if one assumes there to be an order whose
> full force poetics is not prepared to reveal (poetics is not a science) . . . The
> aesthetics of the universe assumed preestablished norms; the aesthetics of
> *chaos-monde* is the impassioned illustration and refutation of these. Chaos is
> not devoid of norms, but these neither constitute a goal not govern a method
> there.
>   *Chaos-monde* is neither fusion nor confusion: it acknowledges neither the
> uniform blend—a ravenous integration—nor muddled nothingness. Chaos is
> not 'chaotic'. (Glissant, 1997, p. 94)

This suggests that the 'chaos' that decolonial aesthetics disobedience aims
for is not freed of a determined pre-established aesthetic. Furthermore, this
chaos or negative positioning—aesthetics of ugliness, monstrosity, disaster,
and others—obeys a set of laws or motifs that inform it. For example, the
aesthetics of the conceptualisation of race obeys the frame of indigeneity and
blackness as founding conceptualisations in the norms dictated by their monstrous anthropological narrative frame of tragedy-capture-anthropocentrism-
conquest and colouring-cultural practice-social status-value. Thus, decolonial aesthetics becomes anti-colonial when it addresses these norms that manage affectation: its disobedience is beyond rationality or the episteme of
Modernity, but it obeys another set of logics that live in the affective and

aesthetic discourse. Decolonial aesthetics becomes a transfiguration of co-lonisation that displays a contestation of the content of modern rationality, but it also focuses on the operation and frame of the logics of colonial aesthetics, at times purging its content and at other times contesting its cod-ified chaos.

BY WAY OF AN ENDING, AND A BEGINNING

Even if we accept that colonisation is over or has 'died', its operation seems to live on in the genetic makeup of racism, capitalism, nation-states, law, philosophy, and human sciences; this does not refer to the very useful con-cept of coloniality but colonisation as a constitutive process of Western cul-ture in general. Coloniality's constitution is formed in colonialism by assem-bling the logics that make Eurocentrism the invisible force that predicates Westernisation on a global scale. Thus, it operates analogously to Modernity: hence, the coloniality/Modernity phrase is used as an object of study. Here, colonisation is the parallax reflection of Western culture that is constitutive of and constituted by a form of governance using this transfiguration. There-fore, it is in opposition to Western culture, yet it preserves its constitutive dialectic. In the colonial matrix of power, its logics pervade the world as we know it through patriarchy, capitalism, and coloniality. Colonisation is fo-cused on the colonised and it unfolds in the opposite manner to how Wester-nisation operates towards its desired subjects, yet it is not less controlling as Foucault and others have unearthed. Colonisation retains the Fanonian colon-iser–colonised relationship as a constitutive macropolitical and micropoliti-cal form of governance, as opposed to coloniality in its complex global matrix of power, because the coloniser–colonised relationship is required in order to describe, if anything, racism as the major tool of coloniality that instituted the post-Enlightenment Social Darwinist inferiority–superiority bi-nary. Beyond the differences between coloniality and colonisation (as dis-cussed in the introduction), if this book can suggest anything, it is that colon-isation, and not Europeanism or Eurocentrism, becomes the conceptual space grid in which the discursive and non-discursive practices discussed in this book can be located. This becomes constitutive of the history of Western culture via its parallax view, even if colonisation has ended. In other words, in colonisation's reflection, we find the transfigured image of Western cul-ture that stems from its historical reality. This archaeology cannot fully re-flect this reality due to the abysmal difference between the real and its trans-figuration. However, this archaeology has attempted to draw a negative im-age of the reality of colonisation in the hopes that its relationships—in partic-ular, its non-linear relationships—reflect the contours of its negative sil-houette.

The feature that colonisation is heavily dependent on, i.e., the aesthetic conceptualisation of race, requires more reexamination than what this book can offer, through unearthing the logics of an aesthetic discourse that factors in ugliness. Similarly, as a second fold of the operation of colonisation, the incommensurability of the management of death requires continued critique such as that undertaken by scholars including Mbembe in his thinking about necropolitics. Furthermore, and beyond the compartmentalisation of disciplines and subdisciplines within colonisation studies in the already compartmentalised intellectual tradition, e.g., Indigenous studies, critical race or philosophy of race, Latino or Caribbean studies, colonisation is a conceptual space where Western history, philosophy, aesthetics, cultural studies, and more can aim to continue to elaborate critiques on their inquiries and thinking in general. Otherwise, glaring omissions as mentioned with Agamben's *State of Exception* or myopic foci in themes like racism in colonisation and the management of death, e.g., Foucault's examination of biopolitics and racism limited by the confines of Europe (not necessarily Eurocentrism), will continue to be a reason for not drawing a more complete picture of a given concept, notion, story, or praxis in world civilisations but specifically in Western culture. If colonisation, particularly in the conceptualisation of race and in the management of death as the twofold operation that is constitutive of this form of government, is the parallax reflection of Western culture, then what is hidden in that projection of history, thought, and aesthetics is as much part of this culture as what is visible and readily accessible is.

In addition, Western culture's apparent inability to think beyond the rational modern order is frequently contested in reexamining the history of the operation of colonisation, yet it is not fully incorporated into the thinking that addresses colonisation studies. The heuristic value of aesthetic or other types of non-rational thought can be easily demonstrated when attempting to explicate racism and contesting it, which is something that early anti-colonial thinkers including Fanon and Cesaire knew all too well. We have discussed the aesthetic logic of the conceptualisation of race predicated by the frame of certain narratives that in the last few hundred years have been used in local and global forms of inequality management in colonisation. If this view is true, then trying to contest racial inequality at the inter-subjective level cannot be from a rationality that implies a form of ignorance of the racist that can be remedied solely by acquiring more rational information: it is another type of logic that racism follows—an aesthetic logic reigned by narrative frames and, thus, lodged in the heart of affectations. Yet the realm of affectations is primed and constituted recursively by the motifs and management of an a priori operation that becomes the architecture of this 'chaos that is not chaotic', as Glissant stated. Early anti-colonial scholars such as Fanon also knew this well, and this is why in his work, particularly in *Black Skin, White Masks*, his writing takes an aesthetic form that fluctuates between the scientific and the poetic, and it attempts to capture the ephemeral logic of race and colonisation (Oto, 2003). While Fanon was a psychiatrist and much of his writing drew from a psychoanalytic tradition of writing, which facilitated the complex dynamics of colonisation and race, he was able to illustratively describe and explain the non-rational dynamics of colonisation and race through the very form or writing style, integrating poetry, creative writing, and phenomenology (Oto, 2003).

This archaeology of colonisation might well be called an archaeology of race, as stated in the beginning of this book. It can also be said that it has nothing to do with the history of colonialism or racism. I would not completely disagree with this statement, mainly because it is between these types of doubles, which appear contradictory yet are no less true, where colonisation and the colonised live, in colonisation in race and race in the colonised; in a type of perpetual 'borderlands' territory, to borrow Gloria Anzaldúa's (1999) concept. The explicit manifestation of colonisation might be over or even dead, yet its blueprint or design lives on as a result of the far-reaching global and local histories that it created. In the end, colonisation becomes more than a phantom or an amputation of a certain kind of history: it unfolds as a double bind that contracts and expands unequal sides of histories silently without its name having to be called or coined. Colonisation's complexity goes beyond words and speech, and it must be addressed in a no lesser complexity than considering its unsaid power, always returning to intricate design. To name it is not sufficient because it does not operate in that rational register. Colonisation is chaotic, schizophrenic, and obeys the nature of contradictions or double binds. Anger is turned inwards when this double bind is fully felt. The double bind of colonisation can only be understood aesthetically where catharsis or the simple purge of its poison can be an option. Again, Fanon illustrates this double bind of colonisation better with an aesthetic melancholic tone than with a rational conclusion, that should prime in us more than closure, anger, or sadness:

> The crippled veteran of the Pacific war says to my brother, 'Resign yourself to your color the way I got used to my stump; we're both victims'. Nevertheless with all my strength I refuse to accept that amputation. I feel in myself a soul as immense as the world, truly a soul as deep as the deepest of rivers, my chest has the power to expand without limit. I am a master and I advised to adopt the humility of the cripple. Yesterday, awakening to the world, I saw the sky turn upon itself utterly and wholly. I wanted to rise, but disembowelled silence fell back upon me, its wings paralyzed. Without responsibility, straddling Nothingness and Infinity, I began to weep. (Fanon, p. 108)

The disappearance of the thinking of Modernity's 'man', explicitly announced by Foucault and others decades after Fanon, leaves vacant a wager for a reconceptualisation of thought and of governance. In the end, the urgency of understanding colonisation is founded by the urgency of understanding a truer form of humanity that interprets weeping as Fanon aimed to be contemplated as; a call for newer form of thought that is truly disembowelled from anthropocentric rationality.

NOTES

1. For instance in Puerto Rico (PR) from 2015 the government has defaulted its over 72 billion national debt, and exceptional legislation from the United States Congress has created a bankruptcy process that is predicated by the assemblage of a 'fiscal oversight board' (PROME-SA) that also overrules the Puerto Rican government in all legislative matters that a budget is attached, further limiting PR's sovereignty and creating a State of Exception de facto. Significant cuts are already happening in education, wages, health, and in many other areas that are creating a volatile economic and social environment in an already weak Puerto Rican economy and augmenting its already precarious sovereign situation, given its colonial relationship with the United States since it invaded PR in 1898.

2. [D]isobeying this game (the aesthetic disobedience and epistemic disobedience). This is, to disobey the rules of artistic practice and the common sense of the same universe that philosophy and art pieces respond to the same principles . . . decolonial aesthetics, in the processes of doing and in their products, as well as in their understanding, start from that which art and Western aesthetics implicitly hide: the colonial wound.

References

Acosta, J. (1589). *Historia natural y moral de Indias*. Sevilla: *Archivo de las Indias*.

Agamben, G. (2005). Movement. (Lecture Transcription). Retrieved from: http://www.egs.edu/faculty/giorgio-agamben/articles/movement/.

Agamben, G. (2008). *El Reino y la Gloria: Una genealogía del poder* [The genealogy of power: Kingdom and power]. Buenos Aires: Adriana Hidalgo.

Agamben, G. (2009). *The Signature of All Things: On Method*. New York: Zone Books.

Agamben, G. (2011). *State of Exception*. Chicago: University of Chicago Press.

Agamben, G. (2012a). *Archaeology of Commandment*. (Podcast). Retrieved from: http://www.egs.edu/faculty/giorgio-agamben/videos/the-archaeology-of-commandment/.

Agamben, G. (2012b). *Profanaciones*. Mexico: Siglo XXI.

Alegría, R. (1947). *Cacicazgo Among the Aborigines in the Americas*. San Juan: Centro de Estudios Avanzados.

Alegría, R. (1978). *Las primeras representaciones de indígena Americano 1493–1523*. San Juan: Centro de Estudios Avanzados.

Alegría, R. (1990). *Juan Garrido: El primer negro conquistador*. San Juan: Centro de Estudios Avanzados.

Anzaldúa, G. (1999). *Borderlands/La frontera: The New Mestiza*. San Francisco: Aunt Lute Books.

Benjamin, W. (1934). 14 *Thesis for a Philosophy of History*. Boston: Vintage.

Benjamin, W. (1996). *War and Reflection: The Navy Air Corps, 1944–1946: Reflection on War Fifty Years Later*. White Bear Lake, MN: Red Oak Press.

Berridge, V. & Griffith E. (1999). *Opium and the People: Opiate Use in Nineteenth-Century England*. London: Dolphin Press.

Bhabha, H. (1994). *The Location of Culture*. London: Routledge.

Breton, A. (1929). *Surrealist Manifesto*. New York: Semiotext.

Campbell, J. (2002). *Invisible Invaders: Smallpox and Other Diseases in Aboriginal Australia 1780–1880*. Melbourne: Melbourne University Press.

Cancel, M. (2000). *Un Compendio de Historia de Puerto Rico*. San Juan: Publicaciones Puertorriqueñas.

Castro-Gómez, S. (1996). *Crítica a la Razón Latinoamericana*. Bogotá: Editorial Pontificia Javerania.

Castro-Gómez, S. (2007). Michel Foucault y la Colonialidad del Poder. *Tabula Rasa. 6*, enero-julio, 153–172.

Cesaire, A. (1972). Discourse on Colonialism. In Kelly, D. G. (Ed.), *A Poetics of Anticolonialism*. New York: Monthly Review Press.

Chalmers, G. (2014). The Con-stitutional Re-Cognition (S)Cam-Pain: The Campaign for the Hidden Recognition of First Nations Peoples' Racial Inferiority. *Law Bulletin 8 (15)*, 27–30.

Chicangana-Bayona, Y. (2008). El nacimiento del *Caníbal*: Un debate conceptual. *Historia Crítica 36*, 150–173.

Clemens, J., Heron, N., & Murray, A. (2008). (Eds). *The Work of Giorgio Agamben*. Edinburgh: Edinburgh University Press.

De Armas, J. (1884). *La fábula de los Caribes*. Boston: Harvard University Press.

De las Casas, B., & Sanderlin, G. (1552/1971). *Bartolomé de Las Casas: A Selection of His Writings*. Alfred A. Knopf.

Deleuze, G. (1985). *Foucault*. Madrid: Siglo XXI.

Deleuze, G. & Guattari, F. (1987) *A Thousand Plateaus*. Minneapolis: University of Minnesota Press.

Deleuze, G. (1995). *Deseo y placer*. Madrid: Siglo XXI.

de Las Casas. (1522/2018). *Brevísimo relación de la destrucción de las Indias*. Madrid: *Alianza Editorial*.

Derbyshire, J. (2004). *Prime Obsession: Bernhard Riemann and the Greatest Unsolved Problem in Mathematics*. New York: Plume.

Derrida, J. (1995). *Archive Fever: A Freudian Impression*. Baltimore, MD: The Johns Hopkins University Press.

Descalzi, G. (1996). *El Principe de los Mendigos*. New York: Vintage.

Diamond, J. (1997). *Guns, Germs, and Steel*. London: Random House.

Dussel, E. (1993). Europa, Modernidad y Eurocentrismo. In E. Lander (Eds), *La Colonialidad del Saber: Eurocentrismo y Ciencias Sociales, Perspectivas Latinoamericanas* (pp. 233–300). Buenos Aires: Consejo Latinoamericano de Ciencias Sociales.

Dworkin, R. (1998). *Law's Empire*. London: Hart Publishing.

Eco, U. (2007). *On Ugliness*. London: Maclehose Press.

Eco, U. (2010). *On Beauty: A History of a Western Idea*. London: MacLehose Press.

Ellinghaus, K. (2003). Absorbing the 'Aboriginal problem': Controlling Interracial Marriage in Australia in the Late 19th and Early 20th Century. *Aboriginal History 27*, 183–207.

Evans, R., Kay, S., & Kathryn, C., (1993). *Race Relations in Colonial Queensland: A History of Exclusion, Exploitation, and Extermination*. St. Lucia: The University of Queensland Press.

Evans, R. (2007). *A History of Queensland*. Cambridge: Cambridge Press.

Fanon, F. (2008). *Black Skin, White Masks*. New York: Grove Press.

Fanon, F. (1990). *The Wretched of the Earth*. London: Penguin.

Federici, S. (2010). *Calibán y la Bruja*. México: Siglo XXI.

Foucault, M. (1964). *Madness and Civilisation: A History of Insanity in the Age of Reason*. Boston: Vintage.

Foucault, M. (1965). *What Is Psychology?* California: Semiotext.

Foucault, M. (1971). *Freedom and Knowledge*. California: Semiotext.

Foucault, M. (1973). *Las Palabras y las cosas: Una arqueleogía del saber*. México: Siglo XXI

Foucault, M. (1974). *Arqueología del Saber*. México: Siglo XX1.

Foucault, M. (1976). *Vigilar y Castigar*. Siglo Madrid: XXI.

Foucault, M. (2005. *Defender la Sociedad*. México: Siglo XXI.

Foucault, M. (2007). *The Politics of Truth*. California: Semiotext.

Foucault, M. (2009). *A Brief Reading of Kant: Introduction to Anthropology in a Pragmatic Sense*. Madrid: Semiotext.

Foucault, M. (2011). *The birth of biopolitics lectures at the college de France, 1978–1979*. New York: Palgrave Macmillan.

Frankland, K. (1994). *A Brief History of Government Administration of Aboriginal and Torres Strait Islander Peoples in Queensland*. Queensland State Archives and Department of Family Services and Aboriginal and Islander Affairs.

Frankopan, P. (2015). *Silk Roads: A New History of the World*. S.l.: Bloomsbury Publishing..

Freire, P. (1970) *Pedagogia del oprimido*. New York: Herder & Herder.

Geertz, C. (1979). From the Native's Point of View: On the Nature of Anthropological Understanding. p. 225–241, in Rabinow, P. & Sullivan, W. M. (eds). *Interpretative Social Science*. Berkeley: University of California Press.

Gerhard, P. (1978). A Black Conquistador in Mexico. *Hispanic American Historical Review 58* (3), 451–459.

Gillett, A. (2011). Opium and Race Relations in Queensland, in Fiona Foley (ed.), *Black Opium*. State Library of Queensland; Brisbane. 15–25

Glissant, E. (1997). Poetics of Relation. doi:10.3998/mpub.10257.

Gobineau, A. (1852) *The Inequality of Human Races*. London: William Heinemann.

Graham, M. (1999). Some Thoughts about the Philosophical Underpinnings of Aboriginal Worldviews. *Worldviews: Global Religions, Culture, and Ecology, 3*(2), 105–118. doi:10.1163/156853599x00090.

Grosfoguel, R. (2003). *Colonial Subjects: Puerto Rican Subjects in a Global Perspective*. Berkeley: University of California Press.

Grosfoguel, R. (2008a). Towards a Decolonial Transmodern Pluriversalism. *Tabula Rasa 9* julio–diciembre 199–215.

Grosfoguel, R. (2008b). World-System Analysis and Postcolonial Studies: A Call for Dialogue from the Coloniality of Power Approach, in Revathi Krishnaswamy and John C. Hawley (eds). *The Postcolonial and the Global*. Minneapolis: University of Minnesota Press.

Grosfoguel, R. (2011). Decolonizing Post-Colonial Studies and Paradigms of Political Economy: Transmodernity, Decolonial Thinking, and Global Coloniality. *Transmodernity, 1*(1), 1–36.

Grosfoguel, R. (2012). The Concept of 'Racism' in Michel Foucault and Frantz Fanon: Theorizing from the Being or the Non-being Zone? *Tabula Rasa 16*, Enero–Junio. 1794–2489.

Groys, B. (2011). Introduction-Global Conceptualism Revisited. *e-flux. 29*. Retrieved from: http://www.e-flux.com/journal/introduction—global-conceptualism-revisited/.

Gutierrez-Usillos, A. (2011). Nuevas aportaciones al estudio de los patrones de asentamiento en el nordeste de la Península Ibérica durante la Primera Edad del Hierro. El caso del Complejo Sant Jaume. *Trabajos De Prehistoria, 68*(2), 331–352. doi:10.3989/tp.2011.11073.

Haddon, A. C., Rivers, W. H., & Wilkin, A. (2010). *Reports of the Cambridge Anthropological Expedition to Torres Straits*. Cambridge: Cambridge University Press.

Handy, G. (2018, April 27). Archaeologists Say Early Caribbeans Were Not 'Savage Cannibals', as Colonists Wrote. *The Guardian*. Retrieved from https://www.theguardian.com/world/2018/apr/24/archeology-caribbean-carib-people-cannibalism-colonial-history-wrong.

Harris, C. I. (1993). Whiteness as Property. *Harvard Law Review, 106* (8), 1707–1791.

Harvey, D. (1990). *The Condition of Postmodernity*. Cambridge: Blackwell.

Hochschild, A. (1998). *El fantasma del Rey Leopoldo*. Boston: Houghton Mifflin Books.

Gómez, P. P., & Mignolo, W. (2012). *Estéticas y opción decolonial*. Bogotá: Universidad Distrital Francisco José de Caldas.

Ianni, O. (1976). *Esclavitud y capitalismo*. Mexico: Siglo XXI.

Iglesia, R. (1942). *Cronistas e historiadores de la conquista de Mexico: El ciclo de Hernan Cortes*. Mexico: Colegio de Mexico.

Inikori, J. (1976). Measuring the Atlantic Slave Trade: An Assessment of Curtin and Ansty. *Journal of African History 17* (2) 197–223.

Kale, S. (2010). *Racism, and Legitimism: A Royalist Heretic Nineteenth-Century France in Intellectual History*. Cambridge: Cambridge University Press.

Kant, I., & Pluhar, W. S. (2010). *Critique of Judgment*. Indianapolis: Hackett.

Katz, S. T. (2003). *The Holocaust in Historical Context*. New York: Oxford University.

Keen, I. (2004). *Aboriginal Economy and Society: Australia at the Threshold of Colonisation*. Melbourne: Oxford University Press.

Keith, A. (1927). The Drift Of Modern Anthropology. *Bmj, 1*(3446), 149–150. doi:10.1136/bmj.1.3446.149.

Kellogg, S., & Restal, M. (2001). *Dead Giveaways: Indigenous Testaments of Colonial Mesoamerica and the Andes*. Salt Lake City: University of Utah Press.

Kidd, R. (1994). Regulating Bodies: Administrations and Aborigines in Queensland 1840–1988. Doctoral Thesis. Griffith University, Queensland.

Kidd, R. (1997). *The Way We Civilise: Aboriginal Affairs, the Untold Story*. St. Lucia: University of Queensland Press.

Kidd, R. (2006). *Trustees on Trial: Recovering the Stolen Wages*. Aboriginal Studies Press: Canberra.

Kidd, R. (2007). Hard Labour, Stolen Wages: National Report on Stolen Wages. Australians for Native Title and Reconciliation.

Kidd, R. (2010). Missing in Action: Industrial Relations and Aboriginal Labour. *Social Alternatives,* March, 65–91.

Kidd, R. (2012). Aboriginal Workers, Aboriginal Poverty, chapter in *Indigenous Participation in Australian Economies*. Canberra: Australian National University.

King, J. (1943). Descriptive Data on Negro Slaves in Spanish Importation Records and Bills of Sale. *The Journal of Negro History 28*, 23–48.

Kirkland, K. (2009). Bacterial Colonization: Can We Live With It? *Clinical Infectious Diseases, 48*(10), 1382–1384. doi:10.1086/598195.

Kiser, B. (2014). Science of Colour: Hue and Eye. *Nature 511* (30), 211–238.

Lacan, J. (1977). *Seminarios celebrados en el año 1959*. Mexico: Siglo XXI.

Lake, M. (1993). Colonised and Colonising: The White Australian Feminist Subject. *Women's History Review 2* (3), 223–250.

Levinas, E. (1969). *Totality and Infinity*. London: Semiotext.

Lopez-Cantos, A. (1998). *Miguel Enriquez*. Madrid: Ediciones Puerto.

Lugones, M. (2016). The Coloniality of Gender. *The Palgrave Handbook of Gender and Development,* 13–33. doi:10.1007/978-1-137-38273-3_2.

Lunn, H. (1987). *Joh: The Life and Political Adventures of Sir Johannes Bjelke-Peterson*. Brisbane: University of Queensland Press.

Lyotard, J. F. (1987). *La Condición Postmoderna*. Madrid: Editions de Minuit.

MacCorquodale, J. (1987). The Legal Clasification of Race in Australia, in *Aboriginal History*. Australian National University Press: Canberra.

Maldonado-Torres, N. (2008). La Descolonización y el Giro Des-colonial. *Tabula Rasa. 9*, julio-diciembre, 61–72.

Mann, C. (2006). *1491*. Madrid: Siglo XXI.

Martín-Baró, I. (1986). 'Hacia una Psicología de la Liberación' Boletín de Psicología. UCA. *22*, 219–231.

Martin-Chew, L. (2014, May 10). Preview: Danie Mellow. *Art Guide Australia.* Retrieved from http://artguide.com.au/articles-page/show/danie-mellor/.

Marx, K. (2002). *El Capital: Tomo I El Proceso de Producción de Capital*. Madrid: Siglo XXI.

Mbembe, A. (2003). Necropolitics. *Public Culture, 15*(1), 11–40. doi:10.1215/08992363-15-1-11.

Mbembé, J. (2017). *Critique of Black Reason*. Durham: Duke University Press.

McNeil, K. (1998). *Defining Aboriginal Title in the 90s: Has the Supreme Court Finally Got It Right?* Toronto: York University Press.

Meliá, B. (1998). *Gua'i rataypy - Fragmentos del folklore guaireño*.

Mignolo, W. D. (1995). Occidentalización, Imperialismo, Globalización: herencias coloniales y teorías poscoloniales. *Revista Iberoamericana*, 110–171.

Mignolo, W. D. (1996). Herencias coloniales y teorías postcoloniales. B. González Stephan (ed.), *Cultura y Tercer Mundo*. Tomo 1. *Cambios en el saber académico*. Caracas: Nueva Sociedad 99–136.

Mignolo, W. D. (1997) *Local Histories/Global Designs: Coloniality. Subaltern Knowledges and Border Thinking*. Madrid: Akal.

Mintz, S. (ed.) (1981). *Esclavo= Factor de producción. La economía política de la esclavitud*. Paris: Editorial Dunod.

Moreton-Robinson, A. (2003). I Still Call Australia Home: Indigenous Belonging and Place in White Postcolonizing Society. In S. Ahmet, C. Castañeda, A. M. Fortier & M. Sheller (Eds), *Urootings-Regroundings: Questions of Home and Migration* (23–41). New York: Berg.

Moreton-Robinson, A. (2015). *The White Possessive: Property, Power, and Indigenous Sovereignty*. University of Minnesota Press.

Morris, B. (1992). Frontier Colonialism as a Culture of Terror. *Journal of Australian Studies* 16 *(35)*, pp. 72–87.

Nakata, M. (2007). *Disciplining the Savages, Savaging the Disciplines*. Canberra: Aboriginal Studies Press.

Nakata, M., Nakata, V., Keech, S. & Bolt, R. (2012). Decolonial Goals and Pedagogies for Indigenous Studies. *Decolonization: Indigeneity, Education and Society 1 (1)* 120–140.

Nietzsche, F. W. (1995). *Birth of Tragedy*. Dover.

Nietzsche, F. W. (2014). *Twilight of the idols*. Lexington, KY: Publisher not identified.

Oliver, K. (2004). *Colonization of Psychic Space: A Psychoanalytic Social Theory of Oppression*. Minneapolis: University of Minnesota Press.

Ocasio, M. E. (2011). *Estados Unidos: Su Trayectoria Histórica*. San Juan: Editorial Cordillera.

Oto, A. J. (2003). *Frantz Fanon: Política y poética del sujeto poscolonial*. México: El Colegio de México, Centro de Estudios de Asia y Africa.

Pagán-Jiménez, J. R. y Rodríguez-Ramos, R. (2008). Sobre arqueologías de liberación en una 'colonia postcolonial' (Puerto Rico). *Revista de Ciencias Sociales, 19*, 8–41.

Quijano, A. (1992). Colonialidad y Modernidad/Racionalidad, in H. Bonilla (Ed.). *Los Conquistados: 1492 y la Población Indígena de las Américas*. Quito: FLACSO/Ediciones Libri Mundi.

Quijano, A. (2000). Colonialidad del Poder, Eurocentrismo y America Latina, in E. Lander (Comp.) *La Colonialidad del Saber: Eurocentrismo y Ciencias Sociales. Perspectivas Latinoamericanas*. CLACSO, Buenos Aires (p. 201–246).

Rajchman, J. (2007). *Michel Foucault: The Freedom of Philosophy*. New York: Columbia University Press.

Ramírez-Alvarado, M. D. (2015). Images for the History of Communication: The First Engravings from the Americas. *Advances in Historical Studies, 04*(01), 51–64. doi:10.4236/ahs.2015.41006.

Reynolds, H. (1990). *With the White People*. Ringwood, Vic.: Penguin Books.

Reynolds, H. (1993). *Race Relations in North Queensland*. Townsville: Department of History and Politics James Cook University.

Reynolds, H. (2013). *Forgotten War*. Sydney: NewSouth Publishing.

Rifkin, M. (2014). Making Peoples into Populations. *Theorizing Native Studies*, 149–187. doi:10.1215/9780822376613-007.

Robiou, S. (2008). *Taínos y Caribes: Las culturas aborígenes antillanas*. San Juan: Punto y coma.

Rolfe, F. (2010). *A History of the Borgias*. Chaleston: Nabu Press.

Rosenkrantz, K. (1853). *Aesthetic of Ugliness*. Munich: Publisher not available.

Rosenkranz, K., Pop, A., & Widrich, M . (2017). *Aesthetics of Ugliness: A Critical Edition*. London, UK: Bloomsbury Academic, an imprint of Bloomsbury Publishing Plc.

Rothman, J. (2014, May 12). The Origins of 'Privilege'. *The New Yorker*. Retrieved from: http://www.newyorker.com/books/page-turner/the-origins-of-privilege.

Ryden, D. B. (2001). Does Decline Make Sense? The West Indian Economy and the Abolition of the British Slave Trade. *The Journal of Interdisciplinary History 31*, (3), 347–374.

Sabine, G. (1998). *Historia de la Teoría Política*. Madrid: Fondo de la Cultura Económica.

Saco, J. A. (1879). *Historia de la esclavitud de la raza africana en el Nuevo Mundo*. 2 vols. Barcelona.

Said, E. (1978). *Orientalism*. New York: Vintage Books.

Sáez-López, S. (2011). Las primeras imágenes occdentales de los indios americanos: Entre la tradición medieval y los inicios de la anthropología. *Anales de Historia del Arte. 40*, 463–481.

Santos, B. D. (2016). *Epistemologies of the South Justice Against Epistemicide*. London: Routledge.

Schmitt, C. (1933). *Political Theology: Four Chapter on the Concept of Sovereignty*. Chicago: University of Chicago Press.

Schreffler, M. J. (2005). Vespucci Rediscovers America: The Pictorial Rhetoric Of Cannibalism In Early Modern Culture. *Art History, 28*(3), 295–310. doi:10.1111/j.0141-6790.2005.00465.x.

Sempat-Assadourian, C. (1969). El trafico de esclavos en Cordoba. *Cuadernos de Historia*, 32, pp. 1–53.

Smith, L. T. (2000) Decolonizing Methodologies: Research and Indigenous People. London: Zed Books.

Soler, C. (1997). *Lo que Decía Lacan de las Mujeres*. Medellín: No-Todo.

Solís, O. (2004). *The Aztec Empire*. New York: Guggenheim Museum Publications.

Spivak, G. (1988). Can the Subaltern Speak? *The Post-Colonial Critic: Interviews, Strategies, Dialogues*. Routledge, New York.

Spivak, G. (1999). *A Critique of Postcolonial Reason: Towards a History of the Vanishing Present*. Boston: Harvard University Press.

Sued-Badillo, J. (1975). *La Mujer Indígena y su Sociedad*. San Juan:Editorial Cultural, Inc.

Sued-Badillo, J. (2003). *General History of the Caribbean*. New York: Macmillan Publishers.

Sued-Badillo, J. (2008). *Puerto Rico Negro*. San Juan: Centro de Estudios Avanzados.

Tardieu, J. (2002). El esclavo como valor en las Americas españolas. *Iberoamericana*, 2–7, 59–71.

Uhlmann, A. (2006). *Family, Gender and Kinship in Australia: The Social and Cultural Logic Practice and Subjectivity*. London: Ashgate Publishing.

UQ Art Museum. (2014) Danie Mellor: Exotic Lies Sacred Ties. *UQ Art Museum Learning Resource*. Retrieved from http://artmuseum.uq.edu.au/filething/get/11734/Danie-Mellor-Learning-Resource-2014.pdf.

Vygotsky, L. S. (1972). The Psychology of Art. *The Journal of Aesthetics and Art Criticism, 30*(4), 564. doi:10.2307/429477.

Wallerstein, I. (1982). *World-Systems Analysis: Theory and Methodology*. London: Sage.

Watson, I. (2016). *Aboriginal Peoples, Colonialism and International Law: Raw Law*. Milton Park, Abingdon, Oxon: Routledge.

Weber, D. (2007). *Bárbaros. Los Españoles y sus Salvajes en la era de la Ilustración*. Santiago: Editorial Crítica.

West, C. (2002). *Prophesy deliverance!: An Afro-American revolutionary Christianity*. Louisville, KY: Westminster John Knox Press.

Williams, P. (1992). *Alchemy of Race and Rights: Diary of a Law Professor*. Boston: Harvard University Press.

Wolfe, P. (2006). Settler Colonialism and the Elimination of the Native. *Journal of Genocide Research, 8*(4), 387–409. doi:10.1080/14623520601056240.

Zhu, F. & Shao, J. (2009). The Origin of Blue-and-White and the Birth of Symbols. *Asian Social Sciences 5* (5) 77–101.

Zika, C. (2009). *The Appearance of Witchcraft: Print and Visual Culture in Sixteenth-Century Europe*. London: Routledge.

Index

15th and 16th centuries, 3, 4, 20, 23, 28, 32, 58n3, 61, 63, 65, 66, 69, 85, 92, 140, 167
18th and 19th centuries, 92, 100, 101, 107
1492, 23, 40–41, 44, 47, 57, 66
1967 Referendum, 148

Aboriginal Commission, 115
Aboriginal Protection and Restriction of the Sale of Opium of 1897 Act, 1897 Act, 16, 91, 109, 120, 145, 147
abstract machine, 21
administration, 111, 127, 144, 158, 159
Adrian Sánchez Galque, 16
aesthesis, 167
Aesthetics , 28
aesthetics discourse, 20, 23, 25, 27, 31, 40, 57, 82, 155, 165, 167, 168, 170;
    Aesthetic conceptualisation, 16, 62, 80, 92, 101, 102, 106, 107, 150, 154, 155, 156, 157, 160, 163, 170
aesthetics of race, 4, 79, 92, 102
Africa, 6, 51, 61, 63, 64, 65, 66, 67, 70, 74, 76, 118
African kingdoms, 64, 67
African peoples, 7, 62, 75, 80, 82, 163
Agamben, Giorgio, 4, 11, 17, 97, 101, 135–136, 136, 137, 138, 140, 141, 141–142, 144, 148, 158, 159, 170, 172n1, 177; *State of Exception* , 137, 138, 140, 170, 172n1

Americas, 8, 15, 16, 28, 32, 36, 37n6, 40, 41, 43, 44–46, 47, 50, 51, 53, 53–55, 56, 57, 58n3, 61, 62, 63, 65–68, 69, 70, 71, 72–73, 74–78, 79, 80, 81, 81–82, 84–85, 86n14, 122, 139, 140, 153;
    Abya Yala, 47
Among the Cannibals of New Guinea , 91
Annual Reports, 112, 113, 114, 119, 120, 122, 124, 124–125, 126, 128, 129–130
anthropocentric, 9, 15, 17, 20, 36, 44, 50, 51, 56, 82, 104, 171
anthropological reports, 124
anthropology, 4, 8, 9, 15, 16, 17, 20, 26, 27, 31, 47, 56, 57, 61–62, 80, 91–92, 94, 94–95, 95–96, 96, 101, 103, 104, 109, 132, 140, 149, 156
anthropomorphism, 33, 35
Anti-Christ, 36
anti-colonial, 6, 24, 25, 153, 155, 165–167, 168, 170
anything-infinity, 9, 33, 55, 56, 86n6, 95, 105, 106, 110, 111, 142–143, 143, 169, 171
Anzaldúa, Gloria, 25, 171; *Borderlands* , 25, 80, 171
apophantic and non-apophantic, 11
apparatus, 9, 13, 98–99, 149
Arawak, 47, 49
archaeology/philosophical archaeology, 4, 9–10, 153; *arché* , 4, 11; Foucauldian archaeology, 3, 4, 9, 11, 12, 21

Aristotle, 11
art, 1–2, 17, 20, 24, 25, 27, 28, 37n3, 37n7, 47, 99, 100, 154, 155, 157, 160, 161, 165, 167, 172n2
art of government, 99, 100
Asia, 61, 64–65
Australia, 3, 4, 5–6, 16, 92, 103, 107, 109, 110, 111, 112, 113, 115, 116, 117, 119, 130, 131, 135–138, 147–148, 148, 149, 150, 151n2, 154, 159, 161, 162, 163, 164; Australian Colonial West, 112, 119, 123
Aztec empire, 57, 70, 72, 104–105; Aztecs, 55, 72, 105

Basileuousa Polis , 64
beauty/aesthetics of beauty, 20, 28, 28–29, 29, 30, 32, 37n3, 156, 163
being, 1, 3, 4, 5, 6, 7, 8, 12, 13, 14, 15, 16, 19, 21, 24, 29, 33–35, 36, 40, 41, 45, 46, 49, 51, 53, 61, 62, 63, 66, 69–70, 77, 82, 83–84, 86n12, 92, 93, 95, 96, 99, 100, 105, 106, 111, 115, 116, 117, 124, 126–127, 128, 130, 132, 135, 141, 143, 144, 145, 146, 148, 150, 157, 162, 165, 167
biopolitics/biopower, 4, 16, 17, 25, 92, 97, 97–99, 98, 100, 101, 102, 107, 108n2, 133n2, 137, 140, 141, 142, 150, 153, 154, 156, 158, 170; biopolitical governance, 16, 101, 154; *To make live and to let die* , 97, 100, 135
black *conquistadores* , 69, 86n8
'black gold', 78
blackness, 3, 4, 15, 16, 25, 33, 35, 57, 59n17, 61, 62, 63, 64, 66, 68, 69, 73, 74, 76, 77, 78, 79, 80, 81, 83, 84, 85, 85n1, 91, 94, 101, 109, 110, 117, 118–119, 124, 132, 135, 144, 149, 154, 155, 162, 164, 168; western blackness, 16, 61, 62, 63, 64, 68, 83, 84, 85, 110
black-skinned, 65, 66, 67; coloured peoples, 100
Blanket Approach, 4, 16, 110, 125, 128, 130, 131, 132, 135, 137, 138, 139, 142, 149, 150, 154, 159
Boas, Franz, 104
bohío , 45
Bosch, Hieronymus, 15, 32, 33, 34

Brevísimo en relación a la destrucción de las Indias , 46
British Empire, 75, 162, 163
blue-and-white Spode China, 1, 161; blue and white transfer, 1, 3, 17, 160, 161–162, 164; blue-china, 1

caciques, 55, 80, 81, 82, 83, 84
Caliban, 31, 39, 40, 47
Cambridge Anthropological Expedition , 91
cannibal/cannibalism, 15, 39, 40–46, 47, 47–52, 53, 58n4, 58n13–58n14, 74, 80, 91
capitalism, 7, 12, 24, 25, 26, 75, 76, 77, 77–78, 97, 141, 169
capturing and enslavement, 53, 55
Caribbean, 3, 4, 8, 23, 25, 27, 40–41, 43, 47, 50, 51, 57, 66, 68, 70–71, 73, 74, 82, 84–85, 87n15, 170
Castro Gómez, Santiago, 12, 13
catharsis, 160, 160–161, 167, 171; aesthetic purge, 161
Cesaire, Aimé, 6, 39, 96, 102, 153, 158, 167, 170; *A Tempest* , 39
Catholic Church, 16, 23, 33, 66, 96, 102
chaos, 17, 24, 35, 36, 46, 167, 168, 170
chaos-monde , 167–168
Chief Protector/Northern Protector, 109, 111, 119, 122, 123, 129, 130
Chinese, 112, 113, 114, 163; Chinese culture/civilisation, 163
Christianity, 20, 66, 70, 91, 92, 106; Church, 35, 42, 66, 68, 128, 138
chronicles/*crónicas* , 31
City of God , 32
Classical period, 1, 8, 15, 16, 20, 23, 24, 25, 27, 28, 31, 32, 33–36, 36, 39, 40, 42, 43, 44, 53, 56, 57, 58n2, 61, 62, 63, 73, 74, 75, 76, 78, 79, 82, 92, 94, 95, 100, 102, 118, 140, 141, 155, 156, 157, 163, 164
Columbus, Christopher, 40, 41, 53, 55, 57, 58n10, 66, 67
colonial aesthetics, 3, 25, 31, 47, 141, 157, 167, 168; aesthetic conceptualisation of race, 16, 79, 92, 101, 102, 107, 150, 155, 156, 157, 160, 163, 170; racial markers, 16, 135

colonisation/colonization, 1, 3–5, 5–8, 9, 12, 13–14, 15–17, 18n2, 19, 20, 21, 23, 25–27, 27–28, 31, 32, 36, 37n4, 42, 44, 46, 47, 53, 53–56, 57, 59n17, 61–64, 68, 69–70, 73, 74, 77, 79–80, 81, 84–85, 86n9, 91–92, 93, 94, 96, 97, 99, 100, 101, 102, 103, 106–107, 107, 108n2, 109–110, 119, 121, 122, 123, 125, 127, 131, 132, 135–138, 139, 140, 142, 144, 148, 148–149, 150, 151n2, 153–154, 155, 155–157, 157, 158–159, 161–162, 163–165, 165, 167, 168, 169–171, 171; coloniality- decoloniality, 6; coloniality of power, of knowledge, of being, 13, 167; colonial matrix of power, 167, 169; colonisation studies, 5–6, 8, 25, 92, 170; coloniser-colonised, 9, 101; colony, 101, 110, 113, 117, 123, 125, 139; conquest, 16, 35, 36, 44, 51, 53, 57, 58n13, 61, 79–80, 86n6, 86n11, 115, 150, 158, 168

colour blue, 162, 163

colouring-cultural practice- social status- value, 79, 85, 150, 168; colouring, 16, 79, 81, 83, 85, 150, 168

command, 4, 9, 11–12, 16, 35, 36, 51, 56, 91, 102, 106, 116, 123, 125, 128, 138, 147, 158

Constantinople, 64

contemporary art, 1, 161

content, 10, 21, 25, 56, 70, 91–92, 96, 101, 102, 109–110, 118, 119, 125, 130, 131–132, 144, 150, 155–156, 162, 168

contrasting, 16, 29, 68, 81, 82, 94

conquistador, 16, 31, 37n6, 44, 46, 50–51, 54, 57, 58n13, 66, 69, 69–70, 72–73, 74, 84, 86n8, 86n9, 86n12–86n13, 139

Cortés, Hernán, 55, 70, 72, 86n12

counter-anthropocentric, 17

creole, 25

Critical Indigenous studies, 5–6, 8

Critique of Pure Reason , 20

cronistas , 40, 58n2

Cuba, 47–49, 51, 57, 69, 71–72, 86n6

culture, 2, 3, 5, 9, 12, 15, 17–18, 19, 20, 23–25, 27–28, 30, 32, 33, 36, 41–42, 43–44, 46–47, 52, 53, 53–56, 57, 62–64, 71, 74, 77–78, 82–83, 84, 92, 94, 95, 95–96, 102, 104, 105–107, 132, 137, 141, 142, 144, 149, 150, 156, 158, 159, 161, 162–164, 165, 169–170; cultural practice, 43, 56, 79, 81, 82–83, 84, 85, 109, 112, 124, 150, 168; cultural studies, 47, 165, 170

de Armas, Juan Ignacio, 50

death drive, 100, 158, 159

decolonial aesthetics, 17, 24, 165, 167, 168, 172n2; decolonial art, 167

decolonization, 155

De Gobineau, Arthur, 37n1, 64, 92, 96, 101

de las Casas, Fray Bartolomé, 46

de Oviedo, Fernando, 40

desire, 1, 17, 47, 57, 93, 97, 110, 129, 130, 131, 132, 135, 159, 169; creation of desire, 17, 110, 129, 130–131, 132, 135

diagonal relationship, 62

discourse, 4, 8, 9, 11, 12, 14, 15, 16, 17, 18, 19, 20, 23–26, 27, 31, 40, 53, 56, 57, 61, 62, 63, 82, 84–85, 91–92, 94, 95, 96, 97, 99, 101, 102–103, 103, 104, 109, 117, 118, 127–128, 131, 140–141, 144, 148, 149, 154, 155, 155–156, 165, 167, 168, 170; discursive, 3–4, 9, 11, 13, 16, 19, 21, 23, 25–27, 31, 33, 47, 50, 53–54, 57, 59n17, 62, 63, 74, 78, 79–80, 81, 84, 85, 91, 92, 98–99, 102, 103, 104, 105, 109, 132, 140, 169; discursive formation, 11, 62, 84, 91, 92, 98, 132; discursive tool, 62, 63, 79, 80

Don , 83

Dr. Roth, Walter, 109

'dying race', 117, 122

Eco, Umberto, 20, 28–29, 30–31, 32–33, 37n4, 43; *On Beauty* , 28; *On Ugliness* , 28

empire, 1, 3, 57, 64, 67, 70, 72, 74–75, 77, 91, 104–105, 137, 162, 163

employment permits, 126

engravings, 23, 40, 42, 84

Enlightenment, 4, 20, 23, 53, 55, 140, 156, 167

enslavement of labor, 124

episteme, 10, 11, 12, 16, 19, 26–27, 28, 56, 57, 91–92, 94, 95, 96, 97, 101, 149, 168; epistemological colonization, 6;

Index

epistemological period, 20, 92, 94, 101
Europe, 19, 40, 42, 43, 51, 52–53, 61–62,
    63, 64, 65–66, 66, 67–68, 71, 72, 74,
    76, 77, 80, 83, 85, 99, 103, 105, 148,
    170; Eurocentric thought, 6
everything/totality, 11, 27, 111, 121, 127,
    142–143, 164, 165

false consciousness, 156
Fanon, Franz, 3, 5, 6, 8, 25, 93, 153, 155,
    157, 158, 160, 167, 169, 170–171;
    Black Skin, White Masks , 25, 157, 170
Foucault, Michel, 19, 23, 27, 32, 131, 132,
    148, 158, 169; *Archaeology of*
    Knowledge , 4, 9, 11; *The Order of*
    Things , 4, 9–10, 23, 32
fountain of youth, 71
form, 1, 3, 4, 6, 10–11, 13, 14, 16, 19, 21,
    23, 25, 28–29, 29, 31, 32, 35, 42, 52,
    53, 55, 56, 57, 66, 69, 75, 77, 78, 80,
    82, 83, 84, 86n8, 91–92, 94–95, 97–99,
    100, 101, 102, 103, 104, 109–110, 119,
    123, 124, 125, 127–128, 130, 135–136,
    137–138, 139–140, 141, 144, 148, 149,
    150, 153, 155, 155–156, 157, 158, 160,
    160–162, 164, 165, 167, 169–170, 171;
    form of content, 21, 110, 125, 130, 150
French Revolution, 77
Frontier Wars, 109

Garrido, Juan, 16, 68–71, 72–73, 73, 81,
    84, 86n6, 86n7, 86n12
genealogy, 25, 99, 153
Genealogy of Modern Racism , 25
geopolitics, 141
Glissant, Édouard, 17, 24; *Poetics of*
    Relation , 17, 165
gold, 1, 49, 55, 58n9, 64, 65, 68, 70, 74,
    75–76, 77–83, 85n2, 87n16
governance, to govern, 4, 16, 21, 25, 31,
    92, 97, 100, 101, 107, 125, 137–138,
    139, 140, 141–142, 148, 149, 150,
    153–154, 158, 169, 171;
    governmentality, 4, 100, 148
Greek aesthetics, 25

Harlem Renaissance, 25, 85n3
head hunters, 53

heterarchy, 3, 12–14, 25, 92, 102, 104, 105,
    106, 150
hierarchy, 3, 7, 8, 23, 25, 35, 66, 80, 83, 96,
    104, 132, 160
history, 1, 3, 4, 5, 8, 9, 11, 15, 17, 19, 20,
    24, 25, 27, 28, 30, 31, 32, 39, 40, 42,
    45, 46, 47, 50, 52, 55, 57, 61–64, 66,
    69, 72, 73, 74–75, 78, 79, 81, 85, 85n3,
    87n15, 92, 94, 96, 99, 102, 104, 105,
    106, 109–110, 114, 115, 118, 119, 122,
    130, 135, 136–137, 138, 139, 143, 148,
    149, 150, 151n2, 154, 155, 156,
    158–159, 161–162, 163–165, 169–171;
    colonial history, 17, 57, 63, 81, 119,
    137, 161–162, 163; historical-
    philosophical, 3, 17; historicity, 16,
    118, 130, 160, 161
Home Secretary, 111, 145, 147
horror, 33, 46, 47, 51, 52, 53–54, 57, 69,
    80, 116, 160
human sciences, 23, 31, 94, 95, 104, 106,
    158, 169

identity(ies), 18
ideology, 7, 12, 29
imagery, 16, 23, 25–27, 31, 33, 35, 36, 42,
    46, 47, 52, 68, 85, 94, 117, 164
incommensurable, 21, 25, 92, 94, 101, 102,
    138, 140, 149, 155, 158
independence movements, 155
Indies, 40, 53, 57, 58n7, 66, 70, 86n8,
    86n14
indigeneity, 1, 3, 3–4, 9, 15–16, 16, 31, 32,
    33, 42, 43, 46–52, 53–54, 55–56, 57,
    61–63, 79–80, 82–85, 91, 94, 101, 104,
    109–110, 117–118, 118–119, 124, 132,
    135, 144, 149, 154, 155, 160, 162, 164,
    168; western indigeneity, 53, 61–62,
    63, 79, 82–83, 85, 94, 110, 144, 162
Indigenous affairs, 110, 126, 136, 147
Indigenous Australians, 104, 109, 137, 147
Indigenous Australian labour, 112, 113,
    114, 118, 124
Indigenous nations, 6, 72, 80, 148
Indigenous peoples, 1, 5, 8, 9, 15, 18n4,
    27, 40, 41, 43, 44, 45, 46, 47, 49, 50,
    51, 52, 53, 55, 58n3, 58n8, 58n13, 61,
    63, 70, 71, 72, 73, 74, 79, 80, 81, 83,
    86n10, 108n3, 109, 117, 122, 124, 136,

137, 138, 139, 140, 141, 142, 148, 162, 167; Aboriginal peoples, 47, 53, 55; First Peoples 153

Indigenous standpoint, 4, 9

Industrial Revolution, 77

inequality of human races, 16, 25, 86n4, 92, 96, 101–102, 102–103, 103, 104, 105, 106, 158; racial inequality, 8, 96, 104, 170

inferiority-superiority, 27, 53, 56, 63, 66, 80, 96, 169

institution, 4, 8, 9, 16, 17, 19, 20, 23, 55, 62, 66, 74, 86n4, 92, 96, 102, 105, 106, 110, 111, 112, 114, 121–123, 125, 131, 132, 139, 142, 144, 149, 156, 160

Invisible Invaders , 115

Kingdom of Congo, 66

Kingdom of Spain, 16, 37n6, 50, 51–52, 57, 58n12, 65, 66, 70–71, 72, 73, 74, 81, 84; Spanish Crown, 46

La Española, 70, 81

La Florida (Florida), 71

ladino slave, 68

lapis lazuli, 163

Latin America, 6, 86n8, 137

Latin American thought, 7

law, 1, 21, 92, 97, 101, 103, 110–111, 116, 118–119, 120, 121, 122, 125, 128, 131, 132, 135, 136–138, 139, 141, 143, 144, 145–146, 147–148, 148, 149, 150n1, 154, 168, 169

logics of elimination, 149

logos , 56, 139

Los tres Mulatos de Esmeralda , 16, 79, 79–80, 81, 84, 85

macro-politics/global, 12, 107

Maori, 140

Marx, Marxist, 12, 29, 133n1

master-slave relationship, 3, 157, 159; master-slave dialectic, 8

Mbemba, Nzinga, 66

Mbembe, Achille, 92, 100

means of exchange, 73, 75, 77, 78, 83

Mellor, Danie, 1, 2, 161, 167

Members of Parliament, 111, 116, 118, 126, 130

Memento Mori , 1, 2

mestizaje subjectivity , 25

metanarrative, 19, 53

metaphysics, 24

Mexico, 5, 37n6, 51, 55, 57, 70, 72, 72–73, 86n11, 122

Michelet, Jules, 40

micropolitics/local, 12, 107

modern man, 20, 104

Modernity, 4, 7, 15, 16, 19, 20, 25–26, 61, 91–93, 94, 95, 97–98, 100, 101, 102, 106, 109, 137, 140, 149, 155, 156, 165, 167, 168, 169, 171

modes of production, 124, 133n1

Mignolo, Walter, 7, 24

monsters, 31, 32, 33, 36, 41, 156

monstrous anthropology, 15, 27, 47, 57, 62, 80, 132

Montezuma Temple, 72

Moreton-Robinson, Aileen, 8, 136

movement, 7, 25, 30, 35, 37n7, 46, 57, 80, 85n1, 93, 94, 112, 153, 155, 159, 161–162

mulatos , 16, 79, 79–80, 81, 84, 85

multiplicity, 7, 8, 16, 21, 62, 107, 110, 126, 127–128, 128, 131, 132, 135, 149

Nakata, Martin, 4, 8, 9, 91, 92; *Disciplining the Savages, Savaging the Disciplines* , 8, 14, 91

narratives, 1, 14, 20, 23, 27, 31, 33, 37n5, 43, 46, 53–54, 56, 57, 63, 92, 101, 107, 124, 128, 139, 147, 154, 155, 156, 170

nation-state, 12, 63, 97–98, 106, 121, 123, 125, 137–138, 140, 141, 142, 149, 153, 158, 169

Native American, 140

Native labourer, 116–117, 118, 120

Nazi Germany, 98, 142

necropolitics, 99, 100, 101, 153, 170, 176; necropower, 92, 100, 101

neo-colonial, 158

New World, 36, 40, 47, 57, 77, 94

New Zealand/Aotearoa, 140

Nietzsche, Frederich, 24; *Birth of Tragedy* , 24; *Twilight of the Idols* , 30

non-discursive, 11, 21, 27, 94, 132, 169

non-humanity, 53

non-rational, 167, 170

non-Western cultures, 92
Northern Territory National Emergency
Response 2007, 136, 150n1

On Interpretation , 11
operationalisation, 3, 9, 92, 109, 154
opium, 16, 91, 109, 111, 112–113, 114,
120, 122, 125, 128, 144, 145–146, 147;
opium charcoal, 112, 114
Orient, 163; Oriental culture, 163
origin, 3, 4, 9, 11–12, 15, 16, 18n2, 23, 25,
26–27, 27–28, 31, 36, 37n4, 59n17, 62,
68, 80, 91, 96, 101, 106, 135, 140, 149,
150, 165, 167

pacification, 55, 57, 81, 86n6, 139, 158
panopticon, 21, 121, 132; panopticism, 21,
132
parallax, 1, 30, 32, 63, 91, 92, 102, 104,
156, 158, 169–170
pardos , 66
patriarchy, 7, 19, 20, 169
Pear-Shell and Beche-De-Mer Fishery Act
1881, 116
penal law, 21, 122, 146
phenomenology, 25, 170
philosophical anthropology, 4, 9, 16, 20,
26, 91, 94, 101, 140; discourse of
anthropology, 15, 17, 20, 26, 27, 31, 61,
62, 91–92, 95, 96, 103, 104, 109, 149,
156
Plato, 24
poetic, 17–18, 25, 165, 168, 170
Ponce de León, Juan, 70–71
postcolonial studies, 5–6, 12, 92
Post-Enlightenment, 31, 92, 101, 102, 104,
107, 137, 140, 141, 156, 158, 169
poststructural, 6, 7, 136
power relations, 12, 13, 14
praxis, 4, 9, 12, 13, 18n2, 21, 100, 139,
161, 170
Présence Africaine , 25
probanza , 70, 72, 73, 86n6, 86n7
Probanza of Juan Garrido 1538, 69, 70
projection, 42, 63, 81, 91, 104, 106, 156,
158, 170
protection, 16, 91, 109, 116–117, 117, 119,
120, 144, 145, 147, 148; protector, 107,
109, 111, 112–113, 114, 119, 122–123,

123, 128, 129, 130, 146, 147;
protectorates, 110, 111, 122–123,
123–124, 126, 128, 145, 147
psychoanalysis, 130–131, 170
Puerto Rico, 5, 47–49, 57, 68, 69, 70,
86n6, 172n1
pure function, 16, 21, 25, 31, 92–93, 98,
101, 102, 121, 130, 132, 135, 137–138,
140, 141, 142, 144, 149, 150, 156, 158

Queensland Parliament, 111, 116, 117,
117–118, 147
Queensland, Australia, 3, 4, 16, 92, 107,
109, 110, 135, 137, 154, 159

race, 3, 4, 7, 9, 12, 15–16, 17, 20, 23, 25,
27, 31, 42, 53, 55, 58n11, 62, 63,
79–80, 81, 82, 83, 84–85, 86n4, 92, 94,
96–97, 97, 99, 100–102, 102–103, 104,
105–107, 108n2, 112, 113, 116, 117,
118, 122, 131, 135, 136, 140–141, 148,
150, 153–155, 155, 155–156, 157,
158–160, 163, 165, 167, 168, 170–171;
racial, 3, 9, 15, 16, 25, 54, 57, 61–62,
63, 66, 79, 85, 91, 96, 97–98, 101, 102,
104, 106–107, 109, 113, 131, 135, 137,
140–141, 150n1, 154, 155, 157, 160,
170; racism, 3, 6, 12, 17, 25, 97, 97–99,
101, 102, 104, 108n2, 114, 153, 158,
169–171
rationality, 7, 11, 24, 165, 167, 168, 170,
171
Real, 1, 3, 17, 27, 29, 40, 46, 50, 51, 78,
85, 110, 114, 126, 128, 130, 139, 143,
149, 162, 164–165, 169
Real Cédula , 50, 51
relief items, 124–125, 130
Renaissance period, 15, 23, 25, 27, 28, 31,
45, 56, 57, 85n3, 95, 100, 140;
resemblance, 10, 15, 23, 25, 27, 28, 31,
39, 56, 57, 85n3, 95, 100, 140
Requerimiento , 138, 139
rhetorical device, 112, 114
Rosenkranz, Karl, 28–29, 37n4; *Aesthetics
of Ugliness* , 27
Royal decree, 50, 51, 62, 102, 125, 158

Satanism, 43
Saturn, 42–43, 45

savage/noble savage, 8, 14, 35, 46, 91, 96
settler colonialism, 92, 136, 149, 150; settler colonial states, 137, 140
Section 31, 120, 121, 138, 142, 146, 147
Section 127, 137, 148
similarity, 35, 53, 56
similarity and anthropocentrism, 53
skin colour, 16, 44, 66, 69, 81, 102
slavery, 16, 50, 51–52, 55, 59n17, 61–64, 65, 66–67, 68, 69, 72, 73, 74, 74–76, 76, 77–78, 79–80, 81, 83, 84–85, 86n10, 112, 119–120, 122, 123–124, 140, 157
smallpox, 115
Social Darwinism, 3, 4, 8, 15, 20, 23, 25, 56, 62, 66, 91, 96, 97, 101, 102, 104, 132, 153, 158
social hierarchies, 23
social status, 55, 66, 73, 79, 81, 83–85, 102, 150, 168
sovereign/sovereignty, 11, 16, 97, 100–101, 106, 135, 136, 137, 140, 141, 158, 172n1
state-state, 137, 149
Status quo, 159
stolen wages, 123
structuralism/structuralist, 9, 12, 155
subalternisation, 3, 6, 17, 136
subjectivity, 6, 7–8, 14, 21, 25, 109, 127, 128, 131, 132, 149, 159–160, 167
syntax, 155, 155–156

taxonomy, 23, 32, 36
technology, 20, 97–99, 100, 101, 139, 144; technology of government, 97, 99, 100, 101
Tenochtitlan , 61, 72, 86n11, 86n13
Terra Nullius, 109, 110, 148, 149
thanatology, 1, 101, 107, 160; management of death, 100, 101, 135, 154, 157, 158, 159–160, 165, 170
The Fable of the Caribes , 47, 50, 58n11
The Native Labourers Protection Act of 1884, 116
The Republic of Zambos , 81
The Tempest , 167
The Vatican, 65–66, 66–67
The White Possessive , 136
The Wretched of the Earth , 25

theology of liberation, 6–7
thingification/objectification, 96, 157, 159, 162
topology, 23, 98; topological, 9, 10, 162
Torres Strait Islanders, 8, 14, 18n4, 96
totalisation, 16, 110, 121, 122, 123, 124, 125, 127, 128, 131, 132, 135, 149
Totality and Infinity , 111, 142
tragedy, 24, 25, 36, 44, 46, 47, 51, 52, 53, 54, 57, 79, 80, 150, 160, 168; aesthetics of tragedy, 25
tragedy-capture-anthropocentrism-conquest, 57, 79
Trans-Atlantic slave trade, 63
transfiguration, 161, 167, 168, 169
Treaty of Waitangi 1840, 140
triptych *The Garden of Earthly Delights, Earthly Delights* , 32, 52
triptych *The Temptations of St. Anthony* , 15, 31, 32, 33, 34, 36, 40, 43, 49, 52
Tupinambá, 44

ugliness, 15, 20, 27, 28–31, 32, 33, 37n3, 37n4, 40, 43, 94, 105, 154, 155, 156, 168, 170; aesthetics of ugliness, 27, 31, 33, 94, 155, 168
Un-Christianised, 53
uncivilized, 40
'undesired races', 4, 107, 141, 154, 158
unearthing, 4, 9, 16, 18n2, 23, 27, 125, 170
United States, 6, 61, 115, 117, 140, 172n1

value, 10, 30, 55, 57, 74, 75–77, 77–78, 79, 81, 83, 84–85, 87n15, 112, 118, 120, 124, 130–131, 133n1, 141, 150, 168, 170; exchange value, 75–76, 77; pure value, 74, 76, 77–78, 83, 84, 124; use value, 76–77, 77, 84
Venice, 65, 67
Virgin Mary, 36

Was ist Aufkärung? , 20
Western culture, 2, 3, 9, 12, 15, 19, 20, 23, 24–25, 27–28, 30, 32, 33, 36, 40–42, 43–44, 46–47, 52–53, 53–56, 57, 62–64, 71, 74, 77–78, 82–83, 84, 92, 94, 95, 96, 102, 104, 105, 106–107, 132, 137, 141–142, 142, 144, 149, 150, 156, 158, 159, 161, 162–164, 165,

169–170; western history, 1, 24, 27, 27–28, 30, 55, 74, 105, 170; western rationality, 24; westernization, 8, 56, 131, 132, 169
white-skinned, 66
witchcraft, 42–43; witch, 28, 31, 42, 43

worldview, 3, 9, 10, 55, 94, 105, 121, 123, 158, 162, 164–165

Yoruba peoples, 82

Zambos , 80, 81, 82, 83, 84

About the Author

Carlos Rivera Santana, PhD, is a research associate at CENTRO Hunter College, City University of New York, currently researching Caribbean and Puerto Rican aesthetic expressions from a decolonial and critical cultural studies perspective. Before being a research associate, Dr. Rivera Santana was based in Australia for more than seven years where he completed his PhD and was a lecturer (assistant professor) specialising in cultural and post-colonial studies at The University of Queensland.